F Is for Phony

VISIBLE EVIDENCE

Michael Renov, Faye Ginsburg, and Jane Gaines, Series Editors

VISIBLE EVIDENCE, VOLUME 17

F Is for Phony

Fake Documentary and Truth's Undoing

Alexandra Juhasz and Jesse Lerner, Editors

University of Minnesota Press

Minneapolis

London

"Trashing *Shulie*: Remnants from Some Abandoned Feminist History," by Elisabeth Subrin, was previously published in *Lux: A Decade of Artists' Film and Video* (YYZ Books, 2000); reprinted with permission. *"Land without Bread,"* by Luis Buñuel, was previously published in the catalog for the exhibition "Buñuel: Tierra sin pan," Institut Valencia d'Art Modern, Centre Julio González, Valencia, Spain; reprinted with permission. "Surrealist Ethnography: *Las Hurdes* and the Documentary Unconscious," by Catherine Russell, was originally published as "Surrealist Ethnography" (chapter 2), in *Experimental Ethnography: The Work of Film in the Age of Video* (Durham, N.C.: Duke University Press, 1999), 26–47; copyright 1999 Duke University Press; all rights reserved; reprinted with permission of Duke University Press.

Published by the University of Minnesota Press
111 Third Avenue South, Suite 290
Minneapolis, MN 55401-2520
http://www.upress.umn.edu

Library of Congress Cataloging-in-Publication Data

F is for phony : fake documentary and truth's undoing / Alexandra Juhasz and Jesse Lerner, editors.
     p.   cm. — (Visible evidence ; v. 17)
    Includes bibliographical references and index.
    ISBN-13: 978-0-8166-4250-2 (hc : alk. paper)
    ISBN-10: 0-8166-4250-8 (hc : alk. paper)
    ISBN-13: 978-0-8166-4251-9 (pb : alk. paper)
    ISBN-10: 0-8166-4251-6 (pb : alk. paper)
    1. Documentary-style films—History and criticism. I. Juhasz, Alexandra.
II. Lerner, Jesse. III. Series.
    PN1995.9.D62F3 2006
    070.1'8—dc22

                           2006013896

Printed in the United States of America on acid-free paper

The University of Minnesota is an equal-opportunity educator and employer.

12 11 10 09 08 07 06   10 9 8 7 6 5 4 3 2 1

Contents

ALEXANDRA JUHASZ
JESSE LERNER

Introduction
Phony Definitions and Troubling Taxonomies of the Fake Documentary

●————————————————————————————————

Phony Definitions
ALEXANDRA JUHASZ

> *There's no law that says we can't start real and end fake.*
> *What are they going to do, put me in movie jail!*
> :: Albert Brooks in *Real Life: An American Comedy* (1979)

And there's no law that says we can't start fake and end real. So, there is
a movie jail: a massive, overcrowded multiplex looping this year's flops,
serving stale popcorn and overly syrupy Coke, with an antiquated sound
system, weak bulbs, and no stadium seating. Filmmakers are sent there for
infractions against movie laws: breaking codes of continuity editing, going
over budget. Viewers, too, get hard time, for crimes of self-awareness.
Films get locked up for engaging in falsehoods; breaches in labeling garner
the greatest penalties. But all this is silly—although no longer fake—and
that's the point. "The humor in these texts," write Jane Roscoe and Craig
Hight in *Faking It,* the only book-length study on what these authors call
the *mock-documentary,* "comes in part from the contrast between the
rational and the irrational, between a sober form and an absurd or comic
subject."[1] David St. Hubbins, lead guitarist of Spinal Tap, puts it this way:
"there's such a fine line between stupid and clever." This he deduces when
noting that the cover art for Tap's album, *Smell the Glove,* would not
have been censored by the label if band members, rather than a naked and
greased woman, were pictured on all fours being led by a chain. (Here,
lady film professor begins scholarly introduction with fatuous falsehood
and sexist satire. So put me in movie jail!)

A fake documentary engages disingenuousness, humor, and other

————————————————————————————————

formal devices to create critical or comic distance between itself and documentary's sobriety, truth, and rationality. Roscoe and Hight believe that it is mock-documentary's actual status as fiction, and fiction's semiotic distance from the authentic, that enables these tactics to work. "Parodic representation cannot contain a sustained indexical link to the real. Central to parody is an anti-normative convention, a built-in rejection of the referential."[2] In *A Theory of Parody,* Linda Hutcheon suggests that parody refers to "another work of art or form of coded discourse" as its primary target.[3] I suggest something more than Roscoe, Hight, and Hutcheon: that fake documentaries are a special breed of parody in that they accomplish something different, something extra; they *do* manage a "link to the real." The fake documentary is simultaneously and definitively both parody *and* satire, given that satire, according to Hutcheon, has the "moral and social in its focus."[4] Parodies look first to texts, satires toward the world. As parody, fake documentary "both is and represents" (to use Hutcheon's terms) documentary; as satire, it also is and feigns documentary's referent, the moral, social, political, and historical. The fake documentary creates a further level of engagement, on top of that already in play with a typical parody, a form that Hutcheon explains speaks doubly: first, its message, and second, the form it mimics. Fake docs—as satire *and* parody—create relations among form, content, style, representation, and the recorded world, and these relations are multiple and not additive in nature.

Fake documentaries do and undo the documentary form, the film's subject (theme, topic, storyline, characters), and the moral and social orders. They are formally rich as well as uniquely situated to reveal the certainties, as well as the lies, about history, identity, and truth that have sustained both documentary and the world it records. Although a significant subset of "real" documentaries certainly can and do self-reference their artifice, as well as the deceptions that can and do organize the moral and social, this revelatory action is the *definitive* project of the fake documentary. Its formative and visible lies mirror the necessary but usually hidden fabrications of "real" documentaries, and force all these untruths to the surface, producing knowledge about the dishonesty of all documentaries, real and fake. In so doing, the text's origins may be demystified, the spectator can be revived, and the visible world and the technologies that record it are often revealed as coded discourse. As fiction films, with all the possibilities that fiction's control and imagination can achieve, fake documentaries are also (artificially) anchored to the material world, with all the political and emotional possibilities that the body and the body politic can inspire. Fake documentaries imply, sometimes state, and often critique the crucial relations between documentary and the textual and actual authority it assumes, reflects, and constructs. This send up may be in the service of a good laugh at authority, but it as often serves as a serious critique of power.

In the critically and financially successful fake documentary oeuvre of Christopher Guest (*This Is Spinal Tap* [1984], *Waiting for Guffman* [1996], *Best in Show* [2000], *A Mighty Wind* [2003]), humor rules. *Best in Show* pokes fun at its characters' serious indulgence of the petty dictates of the competitive dog world. Meanwhile, (fake) documentary's studious eye looks upon these rather silly characters—one has two left feet, as the camera's slow tilt down from his face to the extremities in question verifies—with precisely the same authorizing glance it grants to significant subjects like rocket science, world politics, and American history. And so the silliness is doubled: how could documentary take so seriously such insignificant and inarticulate people and the stuff they say and do! Ah, reality TV . . . And then this joke is multiplied, as a (our) reality is also mocked: a reality where celebrity, or authority, is easily bestowed not for the value or quality of that which is under consideration, but for the consideration in and of itself. Gerry and Cookie Fletch win Best in Show at the Mayflower Dog Show, and return home to Fern City, Florida, to be awarded a key to the city, their picture in the paper, and three local radio interviews. This final burst of media attention convinces them that they are worthy of a full-time life in the limelight, and the couple decides to try to make it in show business by recording their terrier tunes for a national debut.

Season number one of the fake documentary BBC television series, *The Office* (Ricky Gervais, 2001), reverses Guest's logic, which itself is now familiar enough to parody. Inserting the documentary camera into this site of mediocrity does not propel its characters out of the numbing drudgery and insignificance of their lives' lot, launching them into glamorous careers in the media arts. If anything, the cameras that catch their every office move compound the workers' self-consciousness and an associated resignation about being stuck at this small-time paper company in Slough. The characters (save the boss) seem to be mostly annoyed at the crew that documents their tedious office banter and after-work karaoke. Rather than elevating their existence, the documentary evidence confirms their existential inconsequence. Quite tedious really, this real-world-plus-camera incites nothing extra: no personality transformation, no celebrity, no authority. The fake strategies of *The Office* satirize the ubiquity of the documentary camera on television and in its sister, reality.

Orson Welles's *News on the March* newsreel spoof in *Citizen Kane* (considered by Catherine Benamou in chapter 12) elevates the fake documentary's critical gaze from small-time office to big-time politics. Welles makes apparent the critical relations among the aggrandizing power of the (documentary) media and the economic, industrial, political, and personal power of a "real" individual: Charles Foster Kane (William Randolph Hearst), a "founding figure of our century. An American Kubla Khan." The newsreel's authoritative voice-over, and its linked and authenticating evidentiary footage, suggest that Kane had a hand in shaping American presidential elections and world wars. Then, through inter-title, the obituary makes an even larger claim: "1895–1943. All of these years he covered. Many of these he was." The relations among economic, celebrity, and social power are neatly punned; the film exposes the corrosive con-nections between owning the news, being news, and becoming history itself. The newsreel ends by making this explicit: "Kane's world now is history. He lived to be history." This fake documentary about Kane's life, death, and media power is of course also a real and fake documentary about William Randolph Hearst's life, death, and media power, and is also, really, about the life, death, and media power of Welles himself, and all the power the camera does and does not afford him/them. *News on the March* demonstrates the crucial relations between documentary and the textual and actual authority it assumes, reflects, and constructs.

The message is similar in *Zelig* (Woody Allen, 1983). With a nod to Welles, Allen inserts images of himself, as Zelig, and Mia Farrow, as Dr. Eudora Fletcher, Zelig's shrink and lover, into actual newsreel footage of Hearst's gatherings at San Simeon. "Hearst hosts Zelig and Fletcher and shows how the rich and famous spend their leisure," proclaims the Pathé News inter-title. The play of celebrities (real and fake) is the news, as Zelig and Fletcher tee up with celebrity golfer Bobbie Jones, and Zelig mugs at the camera with Tom Mix. In *Bob Roberts* (Tim Robbins, 1994), Gore Vidal, as Brickley Paiste, the 1960s-era democrat who loses to neo-con Bob Roberts, proclaims: "That's what politics is really about: reality not image . . . So let us be real together." Paiste's laughable sincerity, his outdated naiveté—being real? together!—is played against both Roberts's (fake) and George Bush Sr.'s (real) tactics: a politics of (fake documentary) image not reality. Roberts's winning media/musical campaign plays against the backdrop of (real) nightly news accounts of Desert Shield, Bush-pere's media/military campaign against Hussein. In this fake, Robbins/Roberts testifies that the authority of documentary images provides justification for the real-world detonation of Scud missiles: neither reality *not* image nor image *not* reality, but rather image *and* reality.

Although we enjoy a good laugh as much as anyone does, the essays collected here focus primarily upon these more serious uses of the fake documentary format, ones that most self-consciously and directly engage with history, identity, and truth in a political and formal project that links and unlinks power to the act of recording the visible world and to the documentary record produced. We understand these as productive fake documentaries, and it is their profound capacity to integrate formal, moral, and social concerns that draws Lerner, myself, and our authors to them. Our investment in the genre stems from an interest in the formal elements of documentary, the documentary's role in validating and challenging reigning interpretations of reality, and the related questions of historical and political significance that follow: how do fake docs undo and redo actual *and* textual history, identity, authority? How do fake docs redesign history and identity, rather than merely mimic and reiterate history and identity as ends? We are less interested in verisimilitude, or reality, than we are in what some artists can do by calling attention to the problematics of these as form and subject.

Thus, we are most intrigued by fake documentaries used by filmmakers—across film's history and with a variety of social aims—who engage a subversive or progressive project: to underscore that documentary can be readily linked and unlinked to other cultural and political projects that have contributed to injustice. For the most part, these films have been produced within the independent or avant-garde sectors. While almost all of the essays anthologized here refer to lesser-known films (we've provided a filmography as an appendix to help readers track them down), I've attempted to use more mainstream fare in this introduction. However, it seems crucial to remain aware—even as the more familiar films prove many of the points that I raise here—that the most salient analyses of documentary form and cultural power are found in non-industrial uses of the form. So, what may avant-garde, small-format, independent fake docs tell us about this always engaging, amusing, and vital genre, even in its most commercial and popular forms?

Certainly, fake documentary has been so routine across film history—in both mainstream and avant-garde practice, in both modern and postmodern periods—because it is easy to produce, discern, and appreciate even as it evokes extremely complex systems of signification. While *News on the March* looks authentic—because Welles expertly mimics the realist style of his time by using the all-too-recognizable structure of the newsreel—it uses this form to tell the story of a recognizably fake but almost true person. It is this known lie that brings what would otherwise be transparent form into focus. The viewer must engage in formal considerations, and more improbable still, a self-aware analysis of how this suddenly visible documentary form is linked to the questions about social power that it records. During a fictive segment of the sometimes fake documentary

The Positively True Adventures of the Alleged Texas Cheerleader-Murdering Mom (Michael Ritchie, 1993), the cheerleader-daughter, Shanna (Frankie Ingrassia), asks her alleged cheerleader-murdering mom (Holly Hunter), "When they make the movie, can I play myself?" In this made-for-HBO movie, one that contributes to and critiques the unceasing, overblown, tawdry media events based on "true stories" that increasingly dominate air time, the interplay among identity, the media, and reality becomes formally as well as thematically apparent: who does play whom, what is positively true, and does anyone know or care? By inscribing into a fake documentary its petty, morbid tale of social-climbing-through-alleged-violence and airing-through-questionably-true-media, *Cheerleader Mom* says it does care and know about acting, identity, and the media, and that so can its viewer.

The fake documentary, as a parody-with-a-difference, distinguishes itself from other parodies because the coded discourse it targets—dominant documentary, a form of popular culture with a brief and public history—does not demand a high level of cultural sophistication "to get it": to catch that there are codes and that the codes are being imitated, and that this speaks to a discourse and the effects of this discourse. Fake documentaries are so popular to watch and easy to pull off as parody because their target text is arguably the least complicated, least expensive, and least respected kind of film to make (thus the large numbers of disenfranchised producers who enter into film production via documentary, and perhaps, narrative, filmmaking through fake documentary). In *The Watermelon Woman* (Cheryl Dunye, 1995), a fake documentary that I produced, the "documentary" sequences, filmed in video with a low budget and amateurish quality, although necessary for narrative and ideological reasons, were pragmatically useful as well, in that they were significantly easier and cheaper to produce than our 16 mm narrative sequences shot following the conventions of Hollywood production and storytelling. For us micro-budget, indie filmmakers, the fake documentary portion of our film was a budget reliever as well as idea generator. Similarly, the creative team behind *Man Bites Dog: It Happened in Your Neighborhood* (Remy Belvaux and Benoit Poelvoorde, 1992) explain that they made a fake documentary about a murderous, thieving, petty gangster, and how the spotlight created by a documentary about his life moves him and the film's crew to ever more outrageous brutality and eventually their own brutal deaths, because, as broke film-school students, it was the only kind of narrative feature film they could afford.[5] In an increasingly media-sophisticated society, fake documentary allows a cheaper and easier route to a text richer than either of its fictional or documentary parts. No matter the "subject," every fake documentary is multivoiced, speaking about its subject, its target text, the moral, social, and historical, and the multiple relations among all of these. For, a fake documentary multiplies the documentary by referring parodically "to itself and that which it designates"[6] (the documentary) and at the same time satirically to the "mores, attitudes, social structures and prejudices"[7] found in the world and the documents that record it.

▶

A Phony De(f)inition

For my purpose here, fake documentaries are fiction films that make use of (copy, mock, mimic, gimmick) documentary style and therefore acquire its associated content (the moral and social) and associated feelings (belief, trust, authenticity) to create a documentary experience defined by their antithesis, self-conscious distance.

Let's break this down. I use the word "fake" because it registers both the copying and its discovery. A fake documentary is close to the real thing, but not so close as to not be found out. There is a visible brush with the real (documentary), one where form (the brushwork) stays apparent because of a close but ultimately unsuccessful and therefore legible rendering of the codes of the target text. My point is not to suggest the "truth" of the "real documentary," but rather to highlight what becomes visible through its noticeably flawed depiction: the interdependence between the copy and the real McCoy—the fake and real documentary, the documentary and real world—and the impossibility of one becoming the other. I use the word *fake* to mark a practice whose self-conscious play with form, made apparent in its very failure, effectively challenges its own integrity and that of its originary object as well. This challenge occurs without being ineffectual or illegible; it must be productive. A productive fake documentary produces uncertainty and also knowingness about documentary's codes, assumptions, and processes. The fakery of fake docs mirrors and reveals the sustaining lies of all documentary, both real and fake, producing the possibility for the contesting of history, identity, and truth.

It was suggested to me that "genre identity, like gender identity, is an effect of the performative actions that appear to be an expression of a pre-existent gender/genre but actually produce that gender/genre as an effect."[8] I use the word *fake* to identify this noticeable act of effect-making, but the words *mock* or *pseudo* are also common choices; there are many other possible terms for the distancing devices that allow a form to be copied while everyone knows what is going on—words for estrangement tactics like play, scorn, ridicule, inversion, reversal, imitation, repetition, irony, affirmation, subversion, perversion, conversion. Other authors in this collection rely upon terminologies rooted in translation, psychoanalysis, language slippage, and excess. Then, we assigned Alisa Lebow (the author of the collection's conclusion) to critique my nomenclature and definitions as well as other significant matters that comprise our intellectual scaffolding. We hope that Lebow's chapter, and other willful undoings and unsettlings permitted throughout the book, perform what I do believe to be most true, and powerful, and fun, about the fake documentary: that it cannot and will not fall back upon the authorizing function of its form, or the pedigree of its makers or subject, to make truth claims, even as it must succumb to the force of these forms in their faking.

So, back to my (fake) definition: I call fake documentaries fiction films in that they control some aspects of the profilmic with scripting, performance, direction of actors, manipulation of mise-en-scène, and the like. Bill Nichols has coined the phrases *reflexive* and *performative* for documentaries that make use of similar fictional strategies to abandon documentary's definitive presumption of objectivity and emphasize either the "assumptions and conventions" of documentary filmmaking or the "subjective or expressive" experiences of filmmakers, documentary subjects, or audience.[9] In both cases, these fabrications are shot using some conventions of fiction's opposite cinematic tradition, "nonfiction," to access realms of purpose, relationship, and expectation typically unavailable to narrative filmmakers. In *Introduction to Documentary*, Nichols explains: "Because documentaries address the world in which we live rather than a world imagined by the filmmaker, they differ from fiction. They are made with different assumptions about purpose, they involve a different quality of relationship between filmmaker and subject, and they prompt different sorts of expectations from audiences."[10] He goes on to detail these differences, arguing that documentaries rely upon an impression of authenticity that instills beliefs based upon an assumed fidelity of recording. Documentaries employ this assurance to make believed arguments about the historical world.[11]

Fake documentaries are at least in part fiction films, but we receive them as in part like a documentary. Another way to get at the specificity of the fake documentary is to say that it is a fiction film received like a documentary with a twist. And here, reception is marked as the linchpin of the definition of documentary and its fake. Dirk Eitzen in "When Is a Documentary"[12] argues that a documentary comes into being at the point of reception—that is, when the viewer recognizes within herself a feeling she associates with past documentaries, or what Vivian Sobchack terms a documentary "experience."[13] In her "Phenomenology of Nonfictional Film Experience," Sobchack describes how psychologist Jean-Pierre Meunier explains a viewer's varying subjective relations with cinematic texts, including documentaries. Meunier looks past where film theory usually gets stuck—narrative—to make sense of the multiple filmic methods with which we engage (e.g., home movies, documentaries). Sobchack writes, "Again, we must remind ourselves that a 'documentary' is not a thing, but a subjective relationship to a cinematic object."[14] She continues by noting that this relationship differs across filmic method, so that, "for Meunier, the intentional objective of documentary consciousness is comprehension, not evocation."[15]

With fake documentaries, we engage in an experience/consciousness/feeling organized by comprehension, epistephelia, communication, or rhetoric on top of the usual narrative pleasures linked to imaginary identification. "Documentary potentially sets up a dichotomy between us and them . . . a fictional character potentially allows for greater identification," writes Michelle Citron about her seminal, feminist fake-doc, *Daughter Rite* (1979).[16] Since we do know fake documentaries are at least in part not documentaries, both reception systems (the imaginary and the informational) are operational. The viewer and text are self-conscious of their lively interplay, an interplay experienced at multiple rather than additive registers. A fake documentary is received as more than a fiction film plus a documentary; the two systems refer to, critique, and alter each other's reception. In this way, *Cheerleader-Murdering Mom* can never be "just another cheap movie of the week with Barbara Eden," as Holly Hunter, as Wanda Halloway, worries may be her/their representational fate. Retelling this tale partly through a fake documentary makes central the lively reverberations between fact and fiction, image and reality, demanding a knowing viewership that self-consciously reflects upon its own role in the creation and consumption of tabloid drama. The positively true movie-of-the-week ends with this declaration: "Most Channelview exteriors were filmed at their actual Texas locations. Important interiors have been fully recreated, and some of the costumes and props—even license plates—were borrowed from the participants. This movie was based on court transcripts and exhibits in the trial of Wanda Halloway, interviews, and the public record. Some scenes, events, and characters have been created for dramatic purposes."

Elements that are created for and then marked as serving dramatic purposes locate one place where fake documentary's "twist" or "self-conscious distance" rounds off my definition. Like any successful parody, the fake documentary expertly apes the iconic conventions of another textual system, while necessarily marking within the text this doubleness.

An exact copy—the modern marvel that is mechanical reproduction, the modern marvel that is (almost) documentary film—is not the point (although it is always the subject). A fake documentary unmarked, and so unrecognized, is a documentary. While many of the contributors to this volume refer to moments in fake documentary history and reception where the audience is duped by a hoax (see Roscoe and Hight, Robert Reid-Pharr, Mitchell Block), such states of unknowing bliss must be preliminary steps toward the genre's definitive twist: when a viewer comes into a self-consciousness about documentary, authority, realism, history, and the like by recognizing the act of fakery. In some cases, recognition requires some extratextual help. Although many fake documentaries lace the text with enough clues to indicate their lies (like *Mom's* end-credit above), others rely on web pages, film critics, after-viewing dialogue, or similar framing devices to replant and shift, twist, the truths claimed. Roscoe and Hight analyze (angry) letters to the editor about (the lies of) *Forgotten Silver* (Peter Jackson and Costa Botes, 1995). For some New Zealanders, the film becomes a fake documentary not upon its viewing but after reading the outraged thoughts of their fellow citizen-viewers. Similarly, some early viewers of *The Blair Witch Project* experienced a terrifying account of witchery, but the box office magic was fueled by something richer: knowing viewers who were awed by the filmmakers' uncanny ability to look scared, and by their own capacity to feel sacred, even as they all knew better.

As with any parody, a knowing reception is key. Writes Hutcheon, "if the viewer does not recognize the text as a parody, they will neutralize both its pragmatic ethos and its double structure."[17] Successful fake docs either demand an "educated" viewer or teach their viewers to be smarter. Several of our contributors highlight fake documentary's project in smarter viewing. In his article here, Lerner argues that the many deceptive devices of *Ruins* "conspire to encourage active participation on the part of the audience, who is compelled to view the film critically, and to skeptically consider the authenticity of the images and information being presented." A self-aware viewer is primed to consider not simply the fact and influence of form, but its connections to social projects of real weight.

▶————————————————————————————

About These Truths Fake Documentaries Do Fib

Fake documentaries can invoke and challenge three linked standards of documentary: (1) the technologies of truth telling, (2) the authority granted to or stolen by those who make and receive such truth claims, and (3) the need to speak untold and partial truths that have fallen outside the registers of these very technologies and authorities. This anthology considers what particularly productive and often progressive fake docs tell us in so (un)doing. What do they contribute to conversations about the permanence and malleability of identity, nation, and location, both in and out of representation? And why is a challenge to, and application of, a representational regime of truth so useful for filmmakers with a social, as well as a formal, agenda? For, certainly, fake documentaries focus first upon the form of documentary, the technologies of truth telling. Self-referentiality and criticality is definitive of the fake documentary because "its subject is its style," according to Sobchack in her essay on *No Lies* (see Mitchell W. Block's discussion of his 1973 film in chapter 12).[18]

Perhaps not surprisingly, a majority of fake documentaries are self-reflexive films about the making of (this one) documentary. *Real Life* announces its project through an inter-title at the film's beginning: "It documents not only the life of a real family but the real people who came to film the family, and the effect they had on each other." All of the fake documentaries I have referred to thus far make documentary's machines, makers, and assumptions integral to both the mise-en-scène and the plot. *News on the March* ends with the cinematic apparatus made visible and audible when Welles pulls out from the newsreel to show us a projector and its light beams while we hear a distortion in the sound track as the machine is turned off and the celluloid abruptly stops en route to the take-up reel. Bob Reiner, as documentarian Martin Di Bergi, opens *Spinal Tap* in a sound studio, as he looks into the camera (lighting and camera equipment littering the background) and narrates why he was moved to make a movie about "one of England's loudest rock bands." In *Real Life,* the cameras are impossible to miss, given that they look like space helmets. Donning these ungainly devices, camera operators sporadically pop in and out of frame like space creatures from George Méliès' *A Trip to the Moon* ("to really heighten reality we needed new equipment"). Of course, the equipment quickly affects the reality it heightens. Albert Brooks, playing himself, a Hollywood filmmaker who is "making a film about reality," endlessly discusses the making of the film and how this affects him. We watch his "complete personality disintegration" as it dawns on him that "the culture loves fake. Reality sucks." Similarly, the film crew in *Man Bites Dog,* initially engaging in a more vérité exposé, find themselves drawn more and more into frame and the gruesome but captivating activities occurring there. They participate in an on-camera gang rape of one of their subject's (and their own) victims, and are at film's end all killed (as is the victim) as retaliation for his/their violent (cinematic and bodily) acts, as the camera rolls and catches it all, reminding us of its presence and effects.

No Lies (Mitchell W. Block, 1973)

Fake documentaries can readily educate viewers about the uncertain links among objectivity, knowledge, and power—usually the hidden, ugly secret of straight documentary. Given how fake documentaries can provide such illuminating exposés of the (true) documentary, many attempts to theorize documentary rely upon its *fake*. In Nichols' recent documentary textbook, he consistently returns to seminal fake documentaries—*This is Spinal Tap, David Holzman's Diary* (Jim McBride, 1968), *Bontoc Eulogy* (Marlon Fuentes, 1995), *Far From Poland* (Jill Godmillow, 1984), *Daughter Rite* (Michelle Citron, 1979), *No Lies, Land without Bread* (Luis Buñuel, 1932) and *Blair Witch Project* (Daniel Myrick and Eduardo Sanchez, 1999)—to explain the documentary. He writes that fake documentaries "prompt us to question the authenticity of the documentary in general: what 'truth' do documentaries reveal about the self; how is it different from a staged or scripted performance; and how can this be productively subverted?"[19] In their contribution to the present collection, an essay on *Forgotten Silver,* Roscoe and Hight stress that fake documentaries educate viewers about the uncertain links among objectivity, knowledge, and power: "the development of the mock-documentary form has arguably been both symptom and cause in the construction of an increasingly reflexive position, for the viewer, in relation to factual discourse." Fake documentaries always imply, and usually make explicit, that many documentaries lie to tell the truth, and that all documentaries are "fakes" in that they are *not* the world they so faithfully record. Lerner says about *Ruins* that "forging is employed as a metaphor for documentary." Lebow puts it this way, "the original is already a poor replica." Documentaries are not reality; fake documentaries, according to Roscoe and Hight, instruct us that documentary truth "is always relative."

And yet, authority based on a documentary lie about the truth has fathered many of the sustaining inventions of our society, race being a most obvious example. A fixed, stereotyped, recognizable documentary representation of black Americans "has come to lend a certain type of ontological stability to all American identities," according to Reid-Pharr in his chapter about *The Watermelon Woman*. Fake docs can bleed the strict binary lines that usually serve to comfort, stabilize, and segregate. Certainly, the first line so muddied is that between documentary and fiction, but other dividing lines can naturally follow: white and nonwhite, self and other, male and female, history and memory, the national citizen and the foreign outsider. Gregorio Rocha sees the early film exhibition practices of the Padilla family as a "precursor of what may be called Border Cinema—in its attempt to freely cross, back and forth, the dividing lines set between fact and fiction, Anglo and Mexican cosmogony." In his film, *Land without Bread* (discussed in detail by Katie Russell in chapter 8 and by Buñuel himself in chapter 7), Luis Buñuel challenges the distinction, so necessary for the modern nation, between primitive civilization and modern culture. He subverts such formative hierarchies by suggesting in his

Pancho Villa en Columbus (Edmundo Padilla, 1934)

film, and in his address reprinted here, that "perhaps paradoxically, *Las Hurdes* is the glory rather than the disgrace of Spain." His film marks the mean, bald distinction that documentary so naturally and greedily draws between primitive civilization and contemporary culture. By making such formative hierarchies absurd, and sick, he exposes their cruelty and absurdity. To know the unknown through a (fake) documentary camera, to participate in what the film's introductory inter-titles name "the human geography of primitives," allows this insight: the *Hurdanos* can be the glory of Spain only in that seeing how they must be seen exposes modernism's and documentary's reliance upon a pitiable and photographed other.

Many other authors in this volume consider the role that documentary has played in the construction of national pride and prejudice, and the role fake documentaries have played in challenging such identifications. Rocha and Charlie Keil note that the machine that is cinema fuels modernism's view of an available and conquerable world. The building of modern(ist) nations (and art)—the production of sites where real geography aligns with metaphoric states, where myths that build citizenship are fabricated from forceful deceptions of arbitrary and absurd (racial) classification—rests upon a domination of primitive others that is always abetted by the camera and the stereotypes it presents and cements as evidence. Our authors insist that the birth of a/the nation is uncannily linked to the birth of ethnography, the cinema, and the primitive *other* they manufacture and consume. Reid-Pharr, Fuentes, Steve Anderson, and Eve Oishi describe how the necessary untruths about the black, Asian, or *other* become memorials not to the colonialism or racism that manufactured them, but to a fake history that they confirm as true. "The medium of representation possesses a material existence that outlives its creators," writes Oishi, as she describes how Japanese-American filmmaker Ruth Ozeki Lounsbury, in her fake autobiography, *Halving the Bones* (1995), seems to take as true the racist lies built into the stereotypical images of Asians and Asian Americans that saturate the media, her private memories, and her sense of self-worth.

Like Oishi, several other authors in this collection submit that history, like documentary, is always an act of construction, more akin to the instability of memory than to what Anderson calls the "ontological status of images as historical evidence." History is always constructed from "small fictions," Robert Rosenstone suggests. Russell proposes that "memory is already colonized." "History is really an art of memory," echoes Fuentes. And "all of our attempts to recapture the past . . . are exercises in fiction," muses Reid-Pharr. By counterfeiting history, fake documentaries challenge the status of visual evidence by reminding us that much of what we may want to see or know is undocumented, unspoken, disallowed, mistranslated, misremembered, and misrepresented. And yet, several of the authors here (Roscoe and Hight, Oishi, Reid-Pharr) argue that the mere act of documenting something (fake films from early New Zealand film history, racist mass-mediated stereotypes of Asian Americans) endows a presence, authority, and permanence that transforms the lie into something awfully close to truth. From Fae (the Watermelon Woman) Richards (played by Lisa Marie Bronson) to Spinal Tap (Christopher Guest et al.), fake characters with close to true stories do end up entering history because of the naturalized link that history maintains to documentary. Spinal Tap has toured and released albums and music videos; after screening *The Watermelon Woman,* audience members have offered Dunye the names of family members who could provide more detailed information on Fae Richard's life. Filmmakers, or their viewers, substitute the authority of documentary for the authenticity of its evidence. Artists ape the forms of institutional authority and some rubs off in the process.

But the authors in this collection, and the fake documentaries they discuss, do not strive to exhume the past intact, as the perfect artifact of an alternative and pure state hitherto undocumented. To work in the multiple register of fake documentary demands a self-criticality about claiming power through history and its documents, a self-awareness about history's deceptions. The fake documentary is not an object (like the typical documentary or ethnography) made to reify difference; the productive fake will not be used in the service of what Coco Fusco calls "happy multiculturalism"[20] and Fuentes terms the "serviceable primitive." For as much as those who have been victimized—by documentary, by history, by virtue of identity—might wish to simply overturn these systems, thereby claiming their own power to define, and allowing their voice into the choir of happy multiculturalism, such adding or switching is not the fake documentary project. The goal is too singular; it is better satisfied by a documentary. Fake documentaries keep unreal their historical evidence so that they can resist incorporation into a project of nostalgia. The past needs to remain fragmented—"imperfect and improvisational," says Anderson—so that it cannot be used to affirm the "humanist mode of condescension" that is a "basic prejudice and conceit of anthropological cinema," according to Russell. Documentary lends itself to a nostalgia of authenticity, while fake documentary acts to inoculate against such easy revival and reclamation of what are, always, only images.

In her essay here, Elizabeth Subrin explains how she uses the counterintuitive distancing device of painstaking imitation to milk and also undermine nostalgia in her film *Shulie* (1997). She moves her viewer towards an active, aware relation with both the now and then: "I was amazed by the shocking sense of presence and longing the film evoked for me. The process of recontextualizing the work in 1997 was nothing short of time travel, an attempt to force the viewers to scrutinize, shot by shot, what constitutes now and then across cultural, economic, racial, generational and formal terms."

Certainly the distance created for author and viewer by a fake documentary brings a kind of freedom from the constraints, the single-mindedness, the ease of nostalgia, history, or even identity. But at what cost? Subrin's film, not really a fake documentary by my definition (Lerner takes me to task in his response that follows, as does Lebow in this volume's conclusion), is rather a shot-by-shot remake of a 1967 documentary of the same name. A litmus case for my purposes, *Shulie* reveals the many limits and limitations of what I have presented about the fake documentary thus far. For *Shulie* particularly, and the fake documentary more generally, are inextricably linked to their target texts. So, here is the first sad truth with which I must end (remember . . . start fake, end real): of course, fakery is an inherently conservative practice, even at its most explicitly political. For, as Hutcheon cautions about parody, its "transgression is always authorized"[21] because "its search for novelty is based in tradition."[22] But which tradition? The documentary has been linked to both the reifying and the deconstructing of identity, history, and truth; the tradition of the documentary has been associated with movements both reactionary and progressive.

Fake documentaries are most compelling and productive when they double back and multiply the traditional documentary object, its all too obvious counterfeit, and the moral, social, historical, and political. All of these elements shift and refocus in their reverberation, allowing the viewer, in the process of such seeing, to also become a stake holder in this lively system. This collection is organized to highlight the fake documentaries that are more productive than others, and these are the films upon which our authors will focus: films that don't just deconstruct but reconstruct; films that unmake and make reality claims; films that mark that it matters who remembers and in what context. The fake documentaries studied here are productive and also progressive in that they unlink and link their text and viewer to knowledge about many documentary truths, and an equally many documentary lies, about identity, history, authenticity, and authority. Such an awareness is necessary for personal and political action in and out of representation. Moored to the conventions of documentary and all that this apparatus produces, fake documentaries can also use fiction to unanchor from reality's constraints and freely imagine anything a person might fight for or desire in a real world that never was but may yet be.

Lying and Learning with *The Watermelon Woman*

F Is for Phony began as a film and lecture series at Pitzer College in 2001.[23] Jesse Lerner and I had both recently completed fake documentaries. He produced the film *Ruins* in 1999, and I produced and acted in *The Watermelon Woman* in 1995. We organized the series to help appease our curiosity about why we had made such films, why we so admire other films in the genre, and why, suddenly, so many films were taking up this form and doing so to critical or box office acclaim. This volume answers many of our originating questions. I'll end by delineating what I have learned about my own fake documentary practice by thinking through the phony definitions and documentary fibs anthologized in this collection.

We took up fake documentary form in *The Watermelon Woman* to make many of the related claims about history discussed above: history is untrue; true history is irretrievable; and fake histories can be real. Dunye (both as director of *The Watermelon Woman* and as doppelgänger character in the film—the African American lesbian, "Cheryl," who is making a documentary film) knows that, before she came along, African Americans, women, and lesbians did make films—in and out of Hollywood. She (Dunye and Cheryl) also knows that their presence, unrecorded and unstudied, passed quickly out of history, becoming unavailable even as she craves ancestors to authorize and situate her voice. So Dunye fakes the history of a formidable forerunner, Fae "The Watermelon Woman" Richards, so that she can tell a story that she, Cheryl, needs to know, one that is close to true yet also faked, and therefore at once beyond, but also linked to, reality and all that the real authorizes and disguises.

Dunye establishes that identity and history, the stuff of life and its images, become most authentic and empowering when mediated through technologies of preservation and display. In *The Watermelon Woman*, black lesbian (film) history and identity are simultaneously embedded in and distanced from disciplinary systems like a mainstream body of texts and textual practices that create or ignore them. Dunye/Cheryl must mimic and at the same time mine the tools, institutions, forms, and technologies of history making. She fakes and also assumes the position of one authorized to remember, represent, and have history. Unmaking (and taking up) documentary authority allows Dunye to unmask institutionally sanctioned disremembering in the form of protective archivists who disallow Cheryl access to their records, misogynist collectors uninterested in unearthing documents by women, or black community members who forget their forays with whites. And yet the result in *The Watermelon*

Woman is not a morass of misinformation, with identity and history left undone and unmade. Fuentes reminds us that the gaps and ellipses of history are "just as important as the objects we have in our hands." The intangible is not inarticulate; it speaks in an unauthorized, untranslated tongue understood by some. In *The Watermelon Woman,* Fae speaks to Cheryl in a voice both expressive and inconclusive. And Cheryl can hear her. This is enough to empower Cheryl, at film's end, to conclude, "I *am* a black lesbian filmmaker and I have a lot to say." Dunye learns a truth from the lie that she made that is Fa(k)e.

The desire to say and hear something true through words and images that are fragmentary and even false is the multiple project of the productive fake documentary, a project that can be artfully formal in its parodic riffs and intensely political in its real-world satiric referents. Dunye and Cheryl's simultaneous avowal and disavowal of the real marks *The Watermelon Woman* as a productive and progressive fake. An (unstable) identity is created, a community (of skeptics) is built, and an (unresolved) political statement about black lesbian history and identity is articulated.

It may pain some readers to see that I too will end in this place of productive instability, where definitive answers cannot be had, even after many words have been spent. This is not to let myself or this volume off the hook, but rather to highlight that skepticism, volatility, fakery, and irresolution are powerful and honest representational strategies built upon a willing and knowing dismantling and multiplying of more traditional concepts of truth, identity, and history. So I end (real) as I began (fake), once again with *Real Life,* which itself ends with this prescient inscription: "Only historians will ever know how much claim to reality this motion picture has brought us all." And here my colleague, historian and fake documentarian Jesse Lerner, will attempt to perform just that, an analysis of how much claim to reality my definitions could ever hold.

●————————————————————————————————————

Troubling Taxonomies
JESSE LERNER

There's something troubling here. Defining "fake documentaries," as Juhasz does, as "fiction films in that they control some aspects of the profilmic with scripting, performance, direction of actors, manipulation of mise-en-scène," while using documentary styles, does not help us understand or classify many of the troublesome hybrids that have long lurked around the edges of documentary film. I will trouble Juhasz's definition by raising some of the issues (and by discussing briefly some of the films) that we must consider as part of the fake documentary subgenre but which fall outside this definition. I will then offer a taxonomy that may guide us as we explore these edges where documentary comes into contact with fiction film, and that suggest some of what is at stake with all of this faking.

Throughout film history there are numerous instances of these sorts of hybrids. Silent cinema, to begin with, is full of anarchic, seat-of-your-pants mixtures of actuality and acting, like the lost reels described by Gregorio Rocha, rescued from an El Paso basement. With the documentary not yet defined, and the demands of ethics less pressing than those of the market, early filmmakers found numerous ways to fake it, sometimes while using nonfiction footage. Francis Doublier, an itinerant Lumière exhibitor eager to capitalize on the public's interest in Alfred Dreyfus's plight on Devil's Island, for example, pieced together "newsreels" from stock footage of a military parade, a French naval vessel, and a shot of a remote atoll.[24] This material was in fact documentary footage, though it was not footage of what it purported to represent. In the first decades of sound film, the so-called "semi-documentary" saved studios money by beefing up low-cost narratives shot on a studio sound stage (most typically noirs or tabloid crime dramas) with stock B-roll filmed on location and an authoritative, documentary-style voice-over; *The House on 92nd Street* (Henry Hathaway, 1945) is an example. A significant part of mainstream documentary production made before the advent of portable sync sound recording equipment controlled the profilmic in order to approximate an observational narrative style. *Louisiana Story* (1948), for example, directed by documentary's patriarch, Robert Flaherty, is at the heart of a documentary canon, though there is little of the profilmic that was not scripted and controlled (other than perhaps the celebrated spider web, apparently shot spontaneously.)[25] The same could be said about *The Quiet One* (Sidney Loeb, 1948) and any number of other realist films made without any intention of "faking it."[26]

We need to consider fake documentary in a way that lays out criteria for discriminating between, and reaching a better understanding of, the varieties of fictional narratives that incorporate documentary tropes: films that perpetuate hoaxes, those that duplicate preexisting documentaries as latter-day postmodern twins, those that attempt to deceive the audience with sensationalistic pseudodocumentary tales of the uncanny, to name a few of the host of strategies practiced in the murky borderlands of documentary, fiction, and fake. There is a small but intriguing set of documentaries that follow the lead of Pierre Menard, like *Shulie* (or what the filmmaker, Elisabeth Subrin, in this anthology calls *Shulie #2*), in duplicating a rather banal observational-style documentary. Jill Godmillow's *What Farocki Taught* (1997) works its honorific doubling of Harun Farocki's earlier (real, albeit scripted and highly performative, even Brechtian) documentary *Inextinguishable Fire* (*Nicht Löschbares Feuer*, 1969). Neither is satiric or parodic; these films are as faithfully devoted to their originals as Gus Van Sant's *Psycho* (1998) is to Hitchcock. The films of both Godmillow and Farocki address the inexpressible horror of napalm, but what in the original was a mix of documentary material (testimonials of napalm victims at the Stockholm tribunals, etc.) and performance becomes the basis for a script to be acted out by Godmillow's doppelgängers. Subrin and Godmillow have not made fakes so much as replicas, differing from each other in their attraction to the respective originals, differing from the originals in their documentary status. The filmmakers lose the presumed authenticity of documentary by repeating faithfully, but gain that new, rarer quality (not unrelated to fakeness) that led Borges to proclaim Menard's Quixote superior to Cervantes'.[27]

Another distinct subset—complicit, innocent, or noncommittal—centers upon hoaxes and frauds. *The Couple in the Cage* (Coco Fusco and Paula Heredia, 1993) is a "real" and relatively traditional documentary (in its use of talking heads, narration over archival stills and moving images, and observational footage) about an exhibition in which two Latino performance artists put themselves on display as previously undiscovered aborigines from an out-of-the-way Caribbean island. How this performance was framed in either museums of art or museums of natural history (two significantly different kinds of sites), and how much the viewers knew or picked up on, shaped the reception and reaction of the public, ranging from indignation to curiosity to knowing recognition. In the documentary, viewers are made aware of the deceit, unlike some of the more gullible audience members present at the events documented. Fusco and Heredia's documentation of the performance/hoax is not a work of fiction, yet it is certainly at the very least a close cousin, if not a member, of our "fake documentary" family.

Other film hoaxes approach deception very differently. In the case of *A Message from the Stone Age* (John Nance, 1983), the filmmaker was himself taken in by a ruse, and so the film unsuspectingly perpetuates the hoax of the Tasaday, the isolated Philippine people sold to the world by *National Geographic* (through their magazine and their film, *Last Tribes of Mindanao*, 1971), NBC (*Cave People of the Philippines*), Ferdinand Marcos's dictatorship, Charles Lindberg, and others as "the last Stone Age tribe."[28] Nance has no satiric end in mind as he preaches earnestly to the camera about the virtues of the Tasaday's simple, tranquil lifestyle devoid of conflict, and the moral lessons (the "message" of the title) we might learn from them. Quite the contrary, he is painfully sincere.

These instances and many others complicate the most earnest efforts to define "fake documentary" in a satisfactory way. Perhaps *A Message from the Stone Age* is a variation on the case of an unmarked fake documentary, received, at least for a time, as simply a documentary, and now read, in light of the revelations about the Tasaday deception, as a documentary about a fake. For those, like Nance, who maintain that there was no deception involved, the film remains a documentary. Were we to do this, however, must we then be prepared to grant documentary status to the credulous reception of *The Helstom Chronicles* (Lawrence Pressman/Walon Green, 1971), *In Search of Ancient Astronauts* (Erick van Daniken, 1975), and the host of other sensationalist and tabloid films liberally borrowing documentary devices for the dissemination of untruths?[29] That, to borrow Lebow's expression, would *really* make a mockery of documentary.

The troubles of definition can be clarified, if not resolved, by partitioning this book's terrain into parcels, each considered in turn. This segmentation can serve to identify and analyze the subversive functions not of all fake documentaries, but certainly of the most productive ones. The structuring device we shall use is to organize this collection by exploring, in turn, three of the corrosive actions that the best and most stimulating fake documentaries perform: on history, on identity and difference, and on the truth claims of documentary itself. Given these concerns, it is perhaps not surprising that, among the films we consider, there is a significant representation of experimental documentary made by graduates of art schools or university-based film or visual anthropology programs, artists who make fakes in service of a theoretically savvy poststructuralist or postcolonial critique. If, in the end, this collection then neglects more mainstream film (the *Blair Witch Project* and *Spinal Tap*) in favor of more independent or underground fare, this is a loss we are willing to accept, as the latter films are more likely to ask and get the most from documentary and its phony kin. Finally, it should be made clear that this taxonomy does not employ exclusive categories, and the points of overlap and convergence are multiple. To highlight these relations and to contrast diverse perspectives, we have paired scholars and filmmakers who write on the same movie (Buñuel and Russell, Anderson and myself), and at times we have placed the critical essays, statements by filmmakers, interviews, and archival documents here anthologized into a section that pushes our immediate categorization of a film.

The oft-repeated stories, perhaps apocryphal, of audiences fleeing the theater in fear as the train arrives at the station are richly suggestive of just how different the reception for silent film, especially early film, must have been. The implications for the understanding of nonfiction film in its historical context are multiple and significant.[30] The conflation of the projected film with the reality it purports to represent is, as Charles Keil points out later, a recurring theme in the early cinema, functioning as the narrative premise of "rube" films including *The Countryman's First Sight of the Animated Pictures* (sometimes called *The Countryman and the Cinematograph,* Robert W. Paul, 1901) and *Uncle Josh Goes to the Motion Pictures* (Thomas Edison, 1902), and subsequently reconstructed in Godard's *Les Carabiniers* (1963). These films show an unsophisticated member of the early cinema audience who attempts to grope the projected image of a woman, flees the arriving train in terror, or engages in other such comic misinterpretations of what it is to watch a film on the screen. That the early audiences found these scenarios funny implies that they possessed sufficient visual literacy to recognize the behavior of "Uncle Josh" (or the "rube") as foolish, though they may have been close enough to the character's experience of misunderstanding to laugh in an embarrassed, knowing recognition. A couple of decades after Uncle Josh's hasty exit from the theater, the scenario repeats, this time at the birthplace of documentary. As Flaherty projected *Nanook* rushes for Nanook: "The projector light shone out. There was complete silence in the hut. They saw Nanook. But Nanook was there in the hut with them, and they couldn't understand. Then they saw the walrus, and then, said Bob, pandemonium broke loose. 'Hold him!' They screamed. 'Hold him!' And they scrambled over the chairs and each other to get to the screen and help Nanook hold that walrus."[31]

These experiences of reception are at the heart of any discussion of the fiction/nonfiction divide in early film, as in that of other periods. Reception is only one of a number of reasons—relating to context, audience, and filmic text—why questions of "fake documentary" in the silent era must be addressed as a separate area of inquiry. Before *Nanook* (1922), and even earlier, before *In the Land of the War Canoes* (1914), there could be no generic parody, as the conventions of the genre had yet to be established (thus, nothing for "mockumentary" to mock). Instead we find, in early cinema, practices of filmmaking that, in David Levi's words, "allow for a lot of two-way traffic across a weak ontological frontier."[32] The norm for presentation in early cinema was a heterogeneous film program in which fiction and nonfiction shorts were mixed, even blended, into found footage jumbles that recklessly defied categorization. This practice highlights the creative role played by exhibitors, as in the case of Felix and Edmundo Padilla, described by Rocha in his contribution to our anthology. Like today's experimental collagists, the Padillas took on a role not only involving the recycling of found footage from diverse sources into the heady montages that became their own films, but also the shooting of additional materials to be added to the mix.

Two essays in this collection address the question of the "fake" in nonfiction film preceding the documentary. Charles Keil analyzes the boundary between nonfiction and fiction in early film, finding that Lumière's train and Méliès' rocket "were following a more similar trajectory than is usually acknowledged." Keil's analysis yields its own taxonomy: three different blends of fiction and nonfiction common before narrative established its dominance over the new medium. Rocha looks closely at the work of one team of practitioners particularly relevant to this discussion, a father-and-son operation whose regionally specific career Rocha salvages from oblivion. The Padillas were itinerant projectionists and, in an idiosyncratic sense, filmmakers, active in the United States–Mexico border region in the first part of the twentieth century. Rocha makes the provocative claim that the Padillas are the first Mexican American filmmakers, thereby placing the fake documentary at the origins of this diasporic border cinema. The Padillas' films, *La venganza del General Villa*, 1937 *(The Vengeance of General Villa)*, *El reinado del terror*, 1932 *(The Reign of Terror)*, and *Pancho Villa en Columbus*, 1934 *(Pancho Villa in Columbus)* are promiscuous pastiches that blend fragments of newsreels, fiction films, and the Padillas' materials, footage they staged and filmed in their reconstructions using friends and relatives. The essays of both Rocha and Keil suggest the variety of approaches to "fake documentary" that preceded the official birth of documentary, and dissuade us of the notion that fake documentary is a specifically postmodern film practice.

For contemporary filmmakers interested in addressing topics from history, the options available do not differ significantly from those available to and used by the Padillas: recycling and recreating. Some redeploy period materials, uncovered (and sometimes licensed) in their search through archives, private collections, or trash heaps. Others recreate what was never filmed or, in the case of a film like *Shulie* (#2 again), what was filmed but not seen. Some, like Luis Escartín's documentary *Ivan Istochnikov* (1997), on a tragic mishap censored from the official history of the Soviet space program (based on Joan Fontcuberta's research about the cosmonaut of the video's title), mix and match these options. Filmmakers may mislead the audience about which of these strategies is being pursued. José Luis Guerín's *Tren de sombras* (*Train of Shadows*, 1997) purports to be a compilation created from the partially decayed home movies of one Monsieur de Fleury, an aristocrat on holiday with his family and team of servants. On the one hand, the film announces itself to be an optically printed reworking of archetypical orphan film footage, the small-gauge documentation of domestic rituals and leisure activities shot for private consumption, yet simultaneously it provides multiple clues—footage from another camera position of Le Fleury himself in the act of filming, color footage shot in the same location and clearly years later—that this is not home movie material, but rather a series of performances created specifically for Guerín's film. It is these sorts of moments of revelation, of pulling back the curtains to expose the device and inner workings of the artifice, that are Subrin's particular focus in her text, for it is here that imitation and mimicry give way to something much more radical.

How have contemporary notions of historiography informed the production of documentary films about the past? If historians have begun recently to take film seriously as something more than a (generally) hopelessly inaccurate and much abused popularizer, how have filmmakers, especially those from experimental circles, reciprocated with a renewed interest in history, its theories and methods? How might approaches to

Shulie (Elisabeth Subrin, 1997)

history reject the model of the objective transcription of facts in favor of one acknowledging what Steve Anderson calls "an ongoing process of discursive and cultural struggle" that inform documentary film, fake or otherwise? Anderson tackles these questions, taking on a subcategory within fake documentary, the fake historical documentary. His essay and mine both address *Ruins* (1999), my compilation documentary of real and fabricated archival footage about the history of collections and exhibitions of pre-Columbian objects, the archaeological site as one of multiple erasures and reconstructions, and the transformation of ancient Mesoamerican objects from scientific artifact to art object. Meeting and getting to know the protagonist of the film, Brígido Lara, marked the start of my own engagement with issues of forgery and faking. As I explain in my piece, the probable mistatements in Lara's own account of his career, the deceptions I utilize in the documentary, and the misrepresentations propagated within the archival footage I recycle, all conspire to create a sustained assault on conventional tropes of documentary truth.

▶━━

Double-Cross Cultural Filmmaking

Distant places, like the (not yet so) distant past, make for fertile ground for all kinds of hoaxes, ruses, and misrepresentations, deliberate or otherwise. Visual anthropology and ethnographic film, the use of the camera as a tool for social scientific inscription, can very convincingly persuade viewers of all sorts of half- or untruths about other cultures that the audience is all too ready to believe. These untruths, the postmodernists tell us, reveal less about the "other" than they do about the "self," the culture of the anthropologist(s). If we are to believe Derek Freeman's provocative interpretation of Margaret Mead's fieldwork, the work of the most respected ethnographers exposes more of the anthropologist's prejudices and ideological needs than it does of the culture being studied.[33] Recent accusations leveled at Napoleon Chagnon's fieldwork among the Yanomamo (extensively documented in Timoth Asch's seminal ethnographic films) are considerably more troubling.[34] The spectacles of the "primitive" at the center of the collaboration of Fusco and Guillermo Gómez-Peña (as recorded in *The Couple in the Cage*) and in Marlon Fuentes' *Bontoc Eulogy* (1995), a found footage investigation of the "Philippine Village" at the 1902 World's Fair in St. Louis, may both be phony ethnographies, but are very real sounding boards for the study of deeply felt Western racial hierarchies, fantasies of the tropics, and imperial ambitions. Intercultural shams of one sort or another have functioned as a mechanism to examine and critique one's own culture ever since Montesquieu penned the *Persian Letters* (1721), if not earlier. Similarly, the phony ethnography of the Tasadays presented in *A Message from the Stone Age* is a very real document of a Vietnam War era longing for an Edenic antidote to so many "bad savages," a heartening relief after the spectacle of perpetual violence in *Dead Birds* (Robert Gardner, 1963), the brutality of *The Ax Fight* (Tim Asch, 1975), or, worse yet, the histrionic anthrophagic display of the trashy Italian fake, *Cannibal Holocaust* (Rugero Deodato, 1979), and its subsequent spin-offs (should we call them bogus docs?) like *Cannibal Ferox* (a.k.a. *Make Them Die Slowly,* Umberto Lenzi, 1981). What is real about the Tasaday "documentary" is the longing for an ancestry more inclined toward peace and love than war and human sacrifice.

James Clifford, taking cues from Georges Bataille, has famously characterized surrealism as ethnography's "secret sharer,"[35] and it is from this productive convergence that Buñuel's deeply disturbing short *Land without Bread* (*Tierra sin pan* or *Las Hurdes,* 1932) was made. Two texts in this collection examine this exceptional work, the director's only nonfiction film, characterized as "simultaneously a documentary and a dismantling of the documentary form."[36] One is Buñuel's own statement about *Land without Bread,* which provides background on the making of the documentary, unequivocally taking an objectivist position: "When I made this film my intention was to give the bare facts, not to interpret them or to invent new ones."[37] This statement can be read as further deception in the smokescreen of "surprising duplicity [that] serves to undermine the film's claims to objectivity and, more importantly, our own certainty about where the film stands morally and politically."[38] Catherine Russell offers a close reading of how Buñuel's film uses the sound track, unreliable visible evidence, the discourse of modernist primitivism, and the omnipresence of death to undo what were then still barely formed documentary conventions.

Marlon Fuentes' *Bontoc Eulogy* (1995) places the ethnographic spectacle of the human zoo in the context of an early cinema where the staged actuality and bogus newsreel were commonplace. The "naval engagements" of the Spanish-American War choreographed with toy boats in Siegmund Lubin's Philadelphia studio, in Edward Amet's bathtub in Waukegan, Illinois, or on the American Vitagraph Company's Manhattan rooftop studio, and the "Battle of Manila" acted out for the film camera in rural New Jersey with African Americans playing the "Pilipino insurgents" are just the sort of deceptions that led filmmakers and exhibitors to become ever more insistent about the authenticity of their often spurious newsreel footage. Exhibitors, retailers of stock shots, all sorts of early film industry purveyors of reconstructed newsworthy events—from military clashes replicated with miniatures or actors, or boxing matches remade (perhaps with doubles)—issued warnings about their competition, like Lubin's advisory "BEWARE OF IMITATIONS."[39] Long before Flaherty stated "sometimes you have to lie. One often has to distort a thing to catch its true spirit,"[40] nonfiction filmmakers often took a more disingenuous tack and enticed the audiences with the rhetorical (and unorthodoxly spelled) question "Why fool with a fony when you can get the original?"[41] Fuentes uses an interview with himself as a forum to explore the fiction/nonfiction divide, the construction of a serviceable primitive other, and the display of the authentic ethnographic or cinematic artifact, both in his own film and more generally in early cinema.

These manipulations make us rethink the impulse to identify the fake documentary as inherently allied with the subversion of authorities; in some cases the fake ethnographic cinema has justified repressive causes more horrific than the misguided primitivist search for the noble savage. The American Museum of Natural History's anthropological documentary melodrama *The Silent Enemy* (1930) is a film predicated on the fated extinction of the Native American. The film, a hybrid text that links a silent narrative with an introductory segment with sync sound, opens with Chauncey Yellow-Robe's address to the camera: "Soon we will be gone. Your civilization will have destroyed us. By your magic we will live forever. We thank the white man who helped us to make this picture. Look not upon us as actors." The central fraudulent impersonation of this counterfeit ethnography is the performance of the film's star, Chief Buffalo Child Long Lance. Born Sylvester Long in Winston-Salem's "colored" section, his was a lifelong performance as Indian that began at Indian schools and Wild West shows. In time he transformed himself into a professional spokesperson for "the Indian," lecturing and publishing widely on Native American lore. Abandoning blackness for a fictitious identity as Indian, Long Lance escaped the South of Jim Crow and the Klan only to find himself imprisoned in another restrictive racial masquerade.[42] The film that showcases his performance of Indian reinforces multiple North American myths about Native Americans and their imminent extermination. Long Lance's intercultural impersonation echoes the indigenous masquerade of African Americans performed by the Mardi Gras Indians of New Orleans, survival tactics of escaped slaves who integrated into Indian communities, as well as, more generally, other attempts to subvert or confuse North American racial taxonomy that were perpetrated by its victims. The only film document of this racial makeover, (made, needless to say, by filmmakers oblivious to Long Lance's deception), calls attention once again to the fake documentary's kinship with the work of con artists, impersonators, forgers, and myriad other practitioners of deceit.

A different racial masquerade comes into focus when Robert Reid-Pharr unravels the intertwined narratives of (falsified) archival images and of a personal quest in *The Watermelon Woman* (Cheryl Dunye, 1995), delineating the threads binding the present to the past. His contribution places the film in the interconnected contexts of Black American cinema and Black American film criticism, of the Black liberation movement of the Sixties and the racial politics of the generations that proceeded it, and of black (in)visibility on and off the screen.

▶

Would I Lie to You?

Fake documentaries don't simply play with the real world, its cultural diversity, and its past—they also undo documentary form and its traditional tropes of truth telling. At different moments in history, documentary has relied on distinct strategies to establish this claim to the real. The advent of lightweight, portable synchronous sound recording technologies in the late 1950s precipitated the development of cinema vérité and direct cinema. The enthusiasm of the documentarians was nearly boundless, and the promise of an unmediated, faithful transcription of real life seemed on the verge of fulfillment. One of these practitioners, D. A. Pennebaker, proscribed the approach characteristic of observational cinema:

> The cameraman (myself) can only film what happens. There are no retakes. I have never attempted to direct or control the action. People said whatever they wanted and did whatever. The choice of action lay always with the person being filmed. Naturally, I edited the material as I believed it should appear, but with the absolute conviction that any attempt to distort events or remarks would somehow reveal itself and subject the whole to suspicion. The order of the film is almost entirely chronological and nothing was staged or arranged for the purpose of the film. This is only a kind of record of what happened.[43]

The impact of these new rules was considerable, allowing documentary to break from the expository mode (characterized by narration and music recorded in postproduction) that had dominated the genre since the advent of sound. The "new" documentary's champions made grand claims for the technology's ability to provide an unmediated, objective, and truthful transcription of the real.[44] What filmmakers chose to do with these new possibilities varied greatly, most notably in the distinction between the presumed invisibility of the Anglophone fly-on-the-wall approach and the more interactive and engaged tactics of the Francophones.

Particularly relevant to this discussion of the documentary/fiction boundary are some of the films of Jean Rouch, who in his pre-vérité film *Moi, un Noir* (1957) played with a new form of spontaneous dramatic documentary in which his subjects might be thought of as acting out the roles of movie stars performing in a documentary. The narration added in postproduction by the film's protagonist, a laborer calling himself "Edward G. Robinson," the mobile, kinetic camera, and the film's narrative structure all contributed to a film that was not simply a documentary, or fiction, or fake documentary, but rather used "fiction," in Rouch's words, as "the only way to penetrate reality."[45] Subsequent Rouch films continue to experiment with performance, ritual, dramatization, and stagecraft as tools for representing a documentary reality.

Almost simultaneously with the development of the observational, vérité, and autobiographic/diary modes, these same styles were the target of numerous parodies, critiques, and appropriations, all questioning their assumptions of truthfulness: films such as *The Connection* (Shirley Clarke, 1961), *No Lies* (Mitch Block, 1973), *David Holzman's Diary* (Jim McBride, 1967), *Cascabel* (Raúl Araiza, 1976), and, more recently, *Man Bites Dog* and *Close Up* (Abbas Kiarostami, 1990). All of these fakes, despite significant differences, consciously deploy the tropes of the observational or vérité documentary styles to present a scripted and acted drama. Certain culturally and historically specific usages are attacked as well, as in *Agarrando pueblo* (Luis Ospina and Carlos Mayolo, 1978), in which the film crew berates the "wretched of the earth" for looking insufficiently miserable. Here the target is Third Cinema, the revolutionary filmmaking of the so-called developing world, first defined by Octavio Getino and Fernando Solanas in 1969, and that school's use of this film technology to create a testimonial cinema of liberation.[46]

Mitchell W. Block makes clear in his contribution to this volume how often the films that questioned and subverted documentary's assumptions of referentiality came not from outside but from deep within the community of filmmakers most engaged in developing the paradigm. His text situates the making of *No Lies* (1973), his critique of the ethics of cinema vérité, in the context of the moment in documentary history. As Orson Welles points out in *F for Fake* (1974), the film that also inspired this anthology's (appropriately counterfactual) title, his career is one marked by a succession of deceptions and illusions. Catherine Benamou surveys Welles's conflicted relationship to reality and to modernism in her essay that explores the contradictions of Welles's self-presentation as illusionist

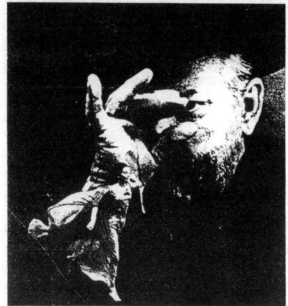

F for Fake (Orson Welles, 1973). Reproduction courtesy of Gary Graver.

and the critical embrace (especially by André Bazin) of his work as realist, focusing on his first feature film, *Citizen Kane* (1941), his notorious radio hoax with the Mercury Theater, *The War of the Worlds* (1938), and of course *F for Fake*.

Jane Roscoe and Craig Hight address the context of production of, the use of documentary tropes in, and especially the public reception of the New Zealand broadcast of the film *Forgotten Silver* (Peter Jackson and Costa Botes, 1996), a fake documentary about the "rediscovery" of a major figure of silent film, Colin McKenzie. This character embodies Kiwi national mythologies even as it stands them on their head. Roscoe and Hight's attention to the reception of the film's first television broadcast is particularly useful, given that a film is, at the moment of viewing, classified as documentary, fiction, or fake. Eve Oishi investigates the strategies of authenticity and realness in three recent Asian American videos and films that likewise address personal, family, public, and underground histories—Ruth Ozeki Lounsbury's *Halving the Bones* (1995), Nguyen Tan Hoang's *Pirated!* (2000) and Ernesto Forondo's *Cherrybomb!!!* (2000). Oishi argues that the strategies of fake documentary have

> a particular power and relevance for Asian American artists because of the particular ways in which Asian American history has been marked by silences, gaps, mistranslations, and caricatures. Examples of lost or nonexistent evidence of the past are myriad: the documents of early Asian immigrants, fraught with untruths and misinformation from deliberate lies or careless translation; the endless stereotypes of Asians on film and television played by white actors in yellowface; or simply the guarded silence within families, as one generation holds on to its knowledge and secrets about its experiences.

Expanding on my own sense of trouble, the volume concludes with Alisa Lebow's questions about the usefulness of our guiding term, "fake documentary," and what exactly those uses might be. Finally, Juhasz and I put in our last words, conjuring up one last film to bring to a puzzling end these explorations of documentary fakery.

A few last words of warning may be in order. Most readers will realize early on that our collection includes not only exemplary models of academic writing by premier cinema scholars—as one would certainly expect in an anthology edited by two reputable academics and published by a respected university press—but also, less predictably, some less characteristic contributions: the transcription of a filmmaker who conducts an "imaginary interview" with himself, writings that draw on the traditions and methodologies of American studies or communications, nonacademic writings, and even, perhaps, a text by a fake contributor or the discussion of a made-up film. Like documentary, academic writing is one of those sober discourses whose forms and conventions we hope to question, trouble, tweak, and perhaps take out for a drink or two. Like the fake documentaries that we highlight, our collection has a serious purpose, and the questions we (and our contributors) are asking are significant ones. But this does not obligate us to humorlessness, nor does it prescribe a single methodology or disciplinary perspective. On the contrary, our contributing authors invite us to address these concerns with a variety of approaches, from a variety of academic traditions, and sometimes with a sense of humor or a bit of deception. Having warned the readers of these deviations from the norms of academic writing, we shall leave it up to them to find their way through the collection with the appropriate intellectual care and some cautious skepticism.

Nearly any film, be it fiction, animation, experimental, or documentary (fake or otherwise) asks the viewer to begin at the beginning and follow through to the end. We do not make the same demand here. As with Julio Cortazar's novel *Rayuela (Hopscotch)*, which opens with a number of suggested sequences in which to read the chapters that follow, and that also invites the reader to construct others, we imagine any number of pathways one might take through this book. A reader particularly interested in questions of racial masquerade might find a path that leads directly to Fuentes, Reid-Pharr, and Oishi. Another might construct a chronological sequence that begins with Keil's contribution and follows a timeline toward the present day. Similarly, given that the fake documentary remains very much an area of considerable activity both for filmmakers and for scholars, we would encourage readers to add their own additional readings and to supplement the films discussed with additional titles. This further reading and film viewing might well begin with some recommended materials that we were forced to exclude because of space constraints. Mitchell Block's statement on his *No Lies* might be paired with Vivian Sobchack's widely anthologized essay on this film, "No Lies: Direct Cinema as Rape."[47] Similarly, one might add Walid Raad's *Hostage: The Bachar Tapes* (2001) or Igor Vamos's *Le Petomane: Fin-de-Siècle Fartiste* (2001) to the screening list for the section on history. Both reanimate archival documents of dubious authenticity. Raad's video purports to be the testimony of the only Arab taken hostage in Lebanon with a group of Westerners in 1985 and held for ten years. *Le Petomane* uses the biography of a flatulent turn-of-the-century Parisian cabaret performer to explore the relations between an emergent modernity and the human body. "Double-Cross Cultural Filmmaking" might be supplemented with faux ethnographies such as David Lamelas's *The Desert People* (1974), a record of an unsuccessful road trip in search of an elusive Southern Californian Indian tribe, or Ken Feingold's

Un Chien Delicieux (1991), yet another encounter of the surrealists with ethnography. And those searching for other additional materials to complement the final section might seek out Peter Adair's *Some of these Stories Are True* (1981) or the sexploitation cinema of mysterious low-rent auteur J. X. Williams. The latter's heady *Peep Show* (supposedly from 1965) leaves the viewer unsure which is less believable: the conspiratorial counterhistory of President Kennedy, the mob, Castro, and Sinatra offered in the film, or the existence of the filmmaker himself.

Alexandra Juhasz and I would like to acknowledge and thank a number of individuals and institutions that helped us at different junctures as our original screening series and panel evolved into a book proposal, a manuscript, and finally this volume. Pitzer College's award for "The Forum" provided initial support for the events on campus in Claremont, California. In curating this film and video program, Steve Seid, Elaine Charnov, and Andrea Ferreyre suggested titles and provided video copies of several works previously unknown to us. We were able to further explore these ideas at the Tenth Visible Evidence Conference at the University of Provence in Marseille, where Dina Iordanova, Michael Zryd, and Alisa Lebow joined me on a panel that brought these ideas better into focus. A number of scholars whose work does not appear in this volume contributed in multiple ways; recognitions go to fake documentary theorists Michelle Citron, Coco Fusco, Kathleen McHugh, Carl Plantinga, Lauren Rabinovitz, Steve Seid, and Vivian Sobchack. The manuscript benefited from the careful copyediting of Hillary Baker and Nizan Shaked, who also provided indispensable assistance with the book's images and filmography. The staff at the University of Minnesota Press were consistently encouraging, and their readers—some anonymous, as well as those named: Carolyn Anderson, John Katz, and Matthew Tinkcom—made many suggestions that we have heeded. Finally, to our contributors, who bore with us during this long process, go our thanks, both for their support and for their wonderful contributions.

NOTES

Alexandra Juhasz's introduction was workshopped in the Los Angeles Women's Group for the Collaborative Study of Race and Gender in Culture. The group, whose members include Gabrielle Foreman, Alexandra Juhasz, Laura Hyun Yi Kang, Rachael Lee, Eye Oishi, and Cynthia Young, theorizes, writes, and produces new scholarship within a collective progressive feminist framework.

1. Jane Roscoe and Craig Hight, *Faking It: Mock-Documentary and the Subversion of Factuality* (Manchester: University of Manchester Press, 2001), 68.
2. Ibid., 33.
3. Linda Hutcheon, *A Theory of Parody* (New York: Methuen, 1985), 16.
4. Ibid.
5. Interview with the filmmakers, in Criterion Collection DVD.

6. Hutcheon, *Theory of Parody*, 114.
7. Ibid., 69.
8. From an unidentified reader's report on this manuscript. Thanks to its author for this and several other ideas that contributed to our critical reconceptualization of the topic.
9. Bill Nichols, *Introduction to Documentary* (Bloomington: University of Indiana Press, 2001), 34.
10. Ibid., xi.
11. Ibid., xiii–3.
12. Dirk Eitzen, "When Is a Documentary: Documentary as a Mode of Reception," *Cinema Journal* 35, no. 1 (1995): 81–102.
13. Vivian Sobchack, "Toward a Phenomenology of Nonfictional Film Experience," in *Collecting Visible Evidence*, ed. Jane Gaines and Michael Renov (Minneapolis: University of Minnesota Press, 1999), 241.
14. Ibid., 251.
15. Ibid., 249.
16. Michelle Citron, "Fleeing from Documentary: Autobiographical Film/Video and the 'Ethics of Responsibility,'" in *Feminism and Documentary* (Minneapolis: University of Minnesota Press, 1999), 283.
17. Hutcheon, *Theory of Parody*, 27.
18. Vivian Sobchack, "No Lies: Direct Cinema as Rape," in *New Challenges for Documentary*, ed. Alan Rosenthal (Oxford: Oxford University Press, 1988), 332–41.
19. Nichols, *Introduction to Documentary*, 127.
20. Coco Fusco, "The Other History of Intercultural Performance," in *The Feminism and Visual Culture Reader*, ed. Amelia Jones (New York: Routledge, 2003), 206.
21. Hutcheon, *Theory of Parody*, 26.
22. Ibid., 29.
23. This collection's contributions by Marlon Fuentes, Eve Oishi, and Robert Reid-Pharr were originally presented as talks at a forum on fake documentary at Pitzer College.
24. Stephen Bottomore, "Dreyfus and Documentary," *Sight and Sound* (Autumn 1984): 290.
25. Ricky Leacock comments on this in the sound track of the *Louisiana Story Study Film* (Museum of Modern Art, New York City).
26. Changing patterns of reception have also altered the boundaries of documentary. When released in the United States, the Italian neorealist films (as well as French and other European films in a similar mode, e.g., *Bataille du Rail/Railway Battle* [René Clément, 1945] or *Die Mörder Sind Unter Uns/The Murderers are among Us* [Wolfgang Straudte, 1946]), tended to be understood as documentaries, though today they are of course categorized as fiction films. Their use of location shooting and their gritty feel, so distant from Hollywood norms, both contributed to this reception.
27. Jorge Luis Borges, *Labyrinths: Selected Stories and Other Writings*, ed. Donald A. Yates and James E. Irby (New York: New Directions, 1964), 36–44.
28. For more on the Tasaday hoax, see Kenneth MacLeish and John Launois, "Stone Age Men of the Philippines," *National Geographic* 142, no. 2 (August 1972), 219–50; Joan Foancuberta, "El tribu que nunca existió," in *El beso de Judas: Fotografía y verdad* (Madrid: Gustavo Gili, 1997), 113–38. Nance and others to this day insist the only hoax was the accusation that the Tasaday were a hoax.
29. There is little scholarship on this kind of film; the rare exception is Jane Gaines's (unpublished) "'Believe It Or Not Land': Robert Ripley's International Oddities and Documentary's Spectacle of Actuality." This scholarly neglect seems to confirm the subgenre's status as one of documentary's shameful idiot stepchildren, better left hidden in some deep archival nether region.
30. See Tom Gunning, "An Aesthetic of Astonishment: Early Film and the (In)credulous Spectator," *Art & Text* 34 (Spring 1989): 31–45; Rachel O. Moore, *Savage Theory* (Durham, N.C.: Duke University Press, 2000).
31. Frances Hubbard Flaherty, *The Odyssey of a Film-Maker* (Putney, Vt.: Threshold Books, 1984), 18.
32. "Reconstructed Newsreels, Reenactments, and the American Narrative Film," in *Cinema, 1900/1906: An Analytical Study*, ed. Roger Homan (Brussels: International Federation of Film Archives (FIAF), 1982), 249.
33. *Margaret Mead and Samoa: The Making and Unmaking of an Anthropological Myth* (Cambridge, Mass.: Harvard University Press, 1983).
34. Patrick Tierney, *Darkness in El Dorado: How Scientists and Journalists Devastated the Amazons* (New York: W. W. Norton, 2000).
35. "On Ethnographic Surrealism," in *The Predicament of Culture* (Cambridge, Mass.: Harvard University Press, 1988), 121–22.
36. James Lastra, "Why Is This Absurd Picture Here? Ethnology/Equivocation/Buñuel," *October* 89 (Summer 1999), 53.
37. Luis Buñuel, in the typewritten statement reprinted later in this volume.
38. Lastra, "This Absurd Picture," 52.
39. See Dan Steible, "A History of the Boxing Film, 1894–1915: Social Control and Social Reform in the Progressive Era," *Film History* 3, no. 3 (1989), 235–58. Also Hillel Schwartz, *The Culture of the Copy: Striking Likenesses, Unreasonable Facsimiles* (New York: Zone Books, 1996), 286.
40. Quoted in Arthur Calder-Marshall, *The Innocent Eye: The Life of Robert Flaherty* (London: W. H. Allen, 1963), 97.
41. From a newspaper advertisement reproduced in the outstanding analysis of "greaser films," newsreels (staged and

otherwise) on the Mexican Revolution, Margarita de Orellana, *La Mirada circular: El cine norteamericano de la Revolución mexicana, 1911–1917* (Mexico City: Joaquín Moritz, 1991), 25. This text provides a useful context for Rocha's essay, and is now available in English translation as *Filming Pancho Villa: How Hollywood Shaped the Mexican Revolution*, trans. John King (London: Verso, 2003).

42. For more on Chief Buffalo Child Long Lance, see his autobiography, *Long Lance* (New York: Cosmopolitan, 1928); Laura Browder, *Slippery Characters: Ethnic Impersonators and American Identities* (Chapel Hill: University of North Carolina, 2000), 121–31.

43. Quoted in Louis Marcorelles, *Living Cinema: New Directions in Contemporary Documentary*, trans. Isabel Quigley (New York: Praeger, 1970), 25.

44. See, for example, the claims made by the Maysles in G. Roy Levin, *Documentary Explorations* (Garden City, N.Y.: Anchor, 1971), 276.

45. Quoted in Brian Winston, *Claiming the Real* (London: British Film Institute, 1995), 182.

46. Octavio Getino and Fernanco Solanas, "Towards a Third Cinema: Notes and Experiences for the Development of a Cinema of Liberation in the Third World," in *New Latin American Cinema*, ed. Michael T. Martin, vol. 1 (Detroit: Wayne State University Press, 1997), 33–58.

47. This text is reprinted in *New Challenges for Documentary*, ed. Rosenthal, 332–41.

I   History as Bunk

CHARLIE KEIL

[1] *Steel Engines and Cardboard Rockets: The Status of Fiction and Nonfiction in Early Cinema*

It was once a commonplace of film histories to root the opposed tendencies of cinema toward documentary or fiction in the respective achievements of early film pioneers Louis Lumière and Georges Méliès.[1] The obvious differences between the engine of steam and steel pulling into Ciotat station and the cardboard rocket hurtling toward a papier-mâché moon were cited as incontestable textual evidence of this split heritage. Although such a schema offered the comforting historical coherence that binary oppositions often provide, it also implied that these tendencies were clear from the outset—that the categories of fact and fiction were demarcated and easily observed in cinema's origins. Production trends from the first decade of film's existence appear to confirm this, as the documentary form (usually termed "the actuality") significantly dominated until the early 1900s. But this assumes that all actualities were made and understood as undiluted fact, and that fiction was always presented as a distinct entity. Pitting the documentary impulse within the Lumière films against the predilection for storytelling in Méliès' work only reinforces the view of film documentary that fully divorces it from fiction, a view that still informs debate on films like *Roger and Me* (Michael Moore, 1989) and *The Thin Blue Line* (Errol Morris, 1988). Instead, we need to reinvestigate the status of fact and fiction in cinema's early years. If, indeed, as David Levy has concluded, we are dealing with "a lot of two-way traffic across a weak ontological frontier,"[2] it may well turn out that Méliès' rocket and the Lumière train were following more similar trajectories than is usually acknowledged.

As an alternative to the strict dichotomy represented by the Lumière versus Méliès model, I prefer the more fluid relationship between document and fiction embodied within early self-reflexive comedies like *The Story the Biograph Told* (Biograph, 1903) and *Uncle Josh at the Moving-Picture*

Show (Edison, 1902). Such films introduce how actualities may be read in humorous terms. In *Uncle Josh,* the title character is unable to distinguish between the two levels of reality represented by the film auditorium and the images on the screen; in *Biograph,* a philandering husband finds his office indiscretions, filmed without his knowledge, projected in the neighborhood theater. In both instances, the reception of actualities is viewed as a joke within a fictional context, but, just as important, the fragment of documented reality shown serves as the catalyst for narrative action. In their comedic form, then, the films serve as testimony both to the power of cinematically recorded fact and to the ease with which fact comes to be bound up with fiction. Depicted in these movies as projected images, the actualities retain an indisputable (and for the diegetic viewers involved, even shocking) separateness, all the while fueling the narratives in which they appear. Although fact is what the viewers within the films come to see, the stories these actualities tell resonate beyond their status as mere records of reality. It is this quality of being *part* of the fiction, while also existing *apart* from it, that I wish to explore.

From the outset, audiences and filmmakers alike certainly distinguished between actuality and fiction filmmaking; otherwise the public would not have demonstrated a marked preference for the former in the first years of filmgoing. But whatever hesitation attended discriminating between the two modes only increased with the ascendancy of narrative in the period around 1905. And, just as early cinema scholarship has endeavored to establish that the transition from a noncontinuous to a classical style was a halting and uneven one, so we can propose that the movement toward narrative filmmaking as the dominant practice occasioned a no less remarkable blending of factual and fictional elements during the same early period. For this reason, even though instability marks the distinctions between fact and fiction throughout the first twenty years of cinema's existence, I will concentrate on the period 1905–1906, when this instability manifests itself with a concerted force born out of the transitional moment.

Consideration of the status of fiction and nonfiction during this period opens onto larger questions of what constitutes narrative within film, and whether the actuality itself contains elements deemed essential for narrative—questions I will consider briefly. One can begin by stating that most films, fictional or not, possess a narrative structure, and that we can distinguish fiction films from nonfiction by the means of presentation rather than by content. If we employ Gérard Genette's terminology, we can say that whatever their story (i.e., narrative content), many films share a similar type of narrative discourse. This notion underlies much of the scholarship on the relationship between fiction and nonfiction filmmaking

Train Arriving at the Station (Louis Lumière, 1895). Courtesy Anthology Film Archives.

in early cinema.[3] Marshall Deutelbaum has noted that the Lumière films, though often characterized as formless documents, do in fact possess a structure and patterning which indicate premeditated shaping designed to foreground process or closure. Certainly, some of the best known Lumière films, such as *L'Arroseur arrosé* (1895), operate as protonarratives, with both the profilmic event and its staging belying any claim to the films' status as documents. Moreover, Deutelbaum goes on to argue that, due to their presentational strategies (such as the manipulation of the mise-en-scène, and acknowledgment of the camera's capacity to alter the image captured through choice of angle and distance), the Lumière films approach their material with a different narrative sense than do contemporaneous Edison films.[4] The latter, though records of performances themselves a kind of fiction, otherwise demonstrate no attempt to render the material depicted as a story.

If the key is in the rendering, then David Levy's remarks regarding the influence of newsreels assume special significance. Levy has pointed out how certain stylistic features that we now consider constitutive of psychological realism in cinema derive such power from their use in early actualities.[5] In other words, through their adoption within fictive contexts, newsreel devices became associated with continuity practices. While such arguments look to purely filmic techniques for indications of how actualities might constitute a form of narrative discourse, Charles Musser has advocated increased attention to exhibition practices. Musser has shown how commentators supplied interpretations of the films they accompanied, thereby introducing narrative elements; this is one example of how an extratextual feature could produce stories.[6] Moreover, the central role of exhibitor-created montage meant that fictional material could be interpolated into a straightforward travelogue, further demonstrating how the exhibition practice of the day facilitated the exchange between fictional and actuality elements.

Musser's and Levy's work has focused on the years up to 1904 in order to demonstrate how the transition from actuality to story film was played out through the interaction of the two modes of filmmaking. I will concentrate instead on the years 1905–1906, to demonstrate how the lingering influence of the actuality continued to inform what was becoming a medium primarily invested in narrative. To organize the large body of relevant work from this period, I have grouped the films into three categories, each representing a distinct use of fiction and nonfiction. I do not think that these are the only types of blended films during the period, though they are probably paradigmatic. During the process of watching dozens of 1905-era films, I discovered three types in greater quantities than any other. The three categories are motion films with interpolated fictional material,[7] travel films, and fiction films employing scenes of an actuality nature. As all three occur during roughly the same period, it may be somewhat misleading to say that one type gives way to the next; however, I have intentionally listed the categories in this order (i.e., with the ratio of fictional to nonfictional material increasing with each type) because eventually fictional film would more or less absorb the actuality elements, until the latter ceased to have an appreciably distinct status. Phil Rosen has aptly described this process of absorption as the "sublimation of actuality into narrative."[8] As Rosen has demonstrated in his analysis of *A Policeman's Tour of the World* (Pathé, 1906), and as I will demonstrate further, this process was not without its contradictions, both formal and ideological.

That two of the three categories I have devised involve travel is no accident, for, as Charles Musser has pointed out, the travel genre was the ideal format to allow for the combination of story and documentary elements.[9] Moreover, a conflation of motion and travel, via the capacities of the motion picture camera, occurs within the spectatorial experience itself. Any viewer becomes a traveler when caught up in the moving images presented to her. Early motion pictures, cognizant of their power to provide a view, emphasized the mobility of this view through extensive pans, and more spectacularly through the mounting of the camera onto a moving object. The sensations attributed by Wolfgang Schivelbusch to the train passenger are figuratively appropriate for the motion picture spectator, an idea to which Lynne Kirby and others have drawn attention.[10] Schivelbusch notes that annihilation of conventional notions of space and time occurred during the railway journey, producing within the traveler a sense of dislocation, compounded by the presence of train technology. "[The] machine ensemble," Schivelbusch writes, "interjected itself between the traveler and the landscape. The traveler perceived the landscape as it was filtered through the machine ensemble."[11] Nonetheless, this mode of perception became accepted within the industrial age, and, according to Stephen Kern, "evolution of the means of locomotion has affected the way people see and the art they like . . . The view through the door of a moving railroad car . . . is fragmented, although at high speeds it becomes continuous the way continuity is created out of a series of stills by the cinema."[12] One of the more compelling demonstrations of Kern's thesis is the Hale's Tours phenomenon of 1905–1912, wherein the analogy between rail travel and cinematic spectatorship was rendered literal.[13]

If the context of the Hale's Tour exhibition encouraged the viewer to position himself as a traveler on a cinematically rendered voyage, various contemporaneous motion films (often shown as Hale's Tours attractions) compounded the conceit via their own operations. Numerous examples of films photographed with the camera mounted on a moving locomotive emerge during this period.[14] In this way, films consolidate the power of the apparatus by foregrounding through motion the means by which the spectators' view is shaped and directed throughout the viewing experience. Quite simply, these films adopt the train's point of view. The locomotive is both the engine of the film, driving it forward to new sights, and, simultaneously, the focal point of interest—the originating site of the new scenes. The engine/camera, then, both moves the film and sees it. By increasing the proximity of the camera to the engine, the films merely highlight in spatial terms the functional similarities of the two pieces of technology; both provide a view while also propelling that view forward. However, the similarities go even further, for, just as the camera is always unseen, so, in these films, is the train. With the train functioning literally as the look, the absence at the center of cinema itself is doubly inscribed.

What distinguishes the 1906-era motion films of this variety from earlier types is not the conceptual matching of train and camera, however. In the later films, the long, unbroken shots of landscape, seen from the vantage point of the engine, are sites of more than visual wonders—they also hold figures who represent an impulse toward a more conventional form of narrative. For frequently, out of the landscape will emerge a character—a hobo sleeping in front of the train, an old man who is fishing and blocks its path, or a robber who tries to halt its progress. These are not characters in any developed sense, but they are narrative functions, interchangeable personifications of a narrative will to interrupt, and thereby heighten, the pleasure narrative flow can provide.

Eventually, the purity of the conceit of the motion film will be disrupted altogether, as the unbroken shots of landscapes are deliberately suspended, and staged scenes of action set within constructed train interiors become the structural center of these films. The latent (but emblematic) narrativity of the train engine gives way to the more obviously fictionalized setting of the passenger car, peopled with stock figures and a site for low comedy. On a formal level, the seductive flow of camera movement is stopped short by a cut to the static framing of the train interior set. But is the latter more inherently narrative than the former? Certainly the emphatic fictionality of the comic hijinks in the train car encourages us to enfold the entire film within a fictional framework, but one could argue that the shots of rolling hills and small towns possess their own narrative pull, driven forward by the trains which propel these films. The promise of narrative fulfillment lies within these engines, which Peter Brooks has argued are the most apt metaphor for "the dynamics of the narrative text, connecting beginning and end across the middle and making of that middle—what we read *through*—a field of force."[15] What these motion films further suggest is the existence of different orders of narrative, the impact of which again hinges on a presentational difference.

The same questions inform the travel film, which by 1906 typically features a couple's honeymoon or some other narrative situation as a frame for location shots of a famous site. Typical of this strategy is *Honeymoon at Niagara Falls*, an Edison film from 1906. The film, with a beginning announced via the arrival of a train, the initiating gesture toward narrative propulsion, soon becomes a series of travelogue shots, with the featured couple prominent in each one. The identity of this couple, despite their elaborate entry on the train, is irrelevant. The couple serves merely as a set of surrogate tourists—these films are the home movies that viewers are not yet able to make on their own. But the strategy of transforming actuality shots through their visual association with previously identified characters distinguishes travel films from those of the third category, wherein documentary footage will become actively integrated into the fiction. In *Honeymoon at Niagara Falls,* each location shot is a document of the site, but one that is relentlessly narrativized by the presence of the recurring couple, figures who either sit in the foreground, their outward glances defining what is to be seen, or enter the shot at some point, reminding us that their "honeymoon" has occasioned the sights on view. The film goes so far as to end as it began, with the train delivering the couple back to the point of narrative origin, further confirming that, although the Falls may be the film's point of visual interest, the narrative begins and ends with the couple.

In this way, the film renders the documentary as a personalized narrative. The operative logic is that the characters' presence renders each view more interesting. Certainly this is the case with tourists' photographs and home movies, which usually feature a strategically positioned family member or friend to designate the site viewed as personally memorable, and part of a larger narrative to be commemorated as "our trip."[16] The problem, at this stage in cinema's development, is that the characters on screen cannot compare with the viewers' own acquaintances, lacking as they do any individuation. Hence the film's reliance on the framing device of arrival and departure, that invites the audience members to compare the depicted trip to their own (real or projected) experience. Later, when cinema would perfect this strategy, the visited site would serve as the photogenic backdrop for more established narratives.

If the travel films indicate how the real world could be pressed into service as a site for the fictional, my third category, those early films that feature actuality footage integrated into a fully constituted narrative, operate both more and less like films of the classical era: more, because narrative concerns dominate and render the claims of the documented footage secondary, but less, because the process of integration is as yet not fully accomplished. In terms of both form and content, the actuality sections announce their difference, as diegetic prohibition against such infringement has not yet emerged. Accordingly, the documentary footage operates as a disruptive force and, rather than supplementing or supporting the story, can even serve as a form of unintentional commentary upon the fiction. Nonetheless, such films cobble filmed fiction and documented reality together, and so obvious was the realization of this, that separate paragraphs are devoted to each mode in the Biograph Bulletins for such prototypical productions as *The Tunnel Workers* (1906) and *Skyscrapers of New York* (1906).

In these films, actuality sections may serve to bolster the appeal of the central story, but rarely supply any additional narrative information. Occasionally, the situation arises wherein characters from the fiction appear in the documentary sections. One such case is *The Tunnel Workers,* three shots of which involve actuality footage. In the final moments of the last of these shots (after a noticeable splice) the fictional characters enter the frame and integrate themselves into the action by going down into the mine like the real workers. But this is a telling instance of how aspects of recorded fact oppose the constructed nature of fiction. Clearly visible in the shot are numerous black miners, whose labor in the tunnels points to a racially based social reality of the workplace never alluded to in the course of the drama. Although the narrative of *The Tunnel Workers* concerns standard romantic misunderstandings, the documentary elements speak to a far more pertinent social question. But because the world of filmed fiction was almost exclusively white, the sphere of the documentary stays as separate from that of the drama as the black men do from the domestic interiors.

If the dichotomy of fiction versus fact exists at all in early cinema, it manifests itself most clearly in the representations of people of color, particularly blacks and Native Americans, who can be themselves within an actuality format, but are translated into blackfaced or warpainted white actors at the point of dramatic representation. An example from a later film, *Davy Jones in the South Seas* (Vitagraph, 1911), shows how the terms of representation are shifting by 1911, though not necessarily for the better. In this film, real Native American people are used within the context of the narrative itself, but either as exotica or comic counterpoint, or for reaffirmation of the white's inherently civilized nature. The actuality-styled depiction of nonwhites inadvertently reaffirms their status as "other" by relegating them to the margins of fictional discourse, a situation that would scarcely change, well into the studio era. But the more independent existence of nonwhites within the documentary mode also points to its less controllable aspects (at least on the profilmic level) and indicates the potential for shock or even political effectivity that nonfiction film possessed. It is little wonder that, as filmmaking moved toward greater emphasis on narrative, attempts were made to exert increasing control over nonfictional elements.

Within this period of early cinema, then, documentary elements operate in a variety of ways—to support the narrative, to stand in contradistinction to it, or to become narrative themselves. An emblematic example of the oscillating "value" of the nonfictive in early cinema is a single shot from a 1909 Lubin comedy, *Sporting Blood*. The twelfth shot of the film is a pan of a large crowd at the races. Obviously unstaged, the shot is the actual record of a crowd attending a horse race. But as the camera pans, it eventually reveals within the crowd the faces of the film's two protagonists. Does the revelation of characters within a "real" crowd (one recorded for the purposes of the film, no doubt, but not assembled for that

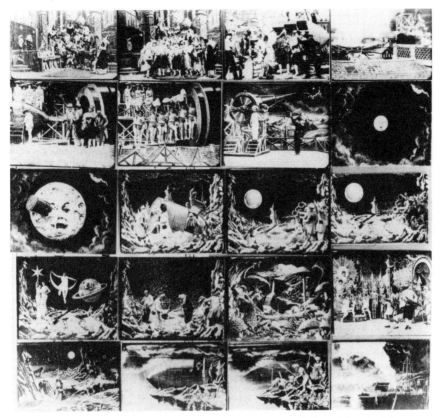

Trip to the Moon (Georges Méliès, 1902). Courtesy Anthology Film Archives.

reason) render those surrounding them a fiction as well? Do the various faces in the crowd suddenly belong to characters, just as the two more familiar ones do? The answer would seem to be yes and no. Obviously composed primarily of documentary elements, but still offered up within the context of fiction, the crowd can lay claim to being both.[17] And the camera movement that begins by emulating the familiar panoramic function of earlier actualities transforms itself into a narrational device to reveal the characters at the races. Both the crowd figures and the technical device resist easy classification, much like early cinema itself. Not yet availing themselves of the smooth technique used by classical cinema to suspend valid questions concerning the relationship of fact to fiction, films of the early period occupy a halting middle ground, where fact and fiction, narrative and documentary, coexist—but in odd and often unexpected interrelationships. Continued consideration of this period not only will aid us in achieving a sensitivity to the fluidity of modes whose functions respond to historical change, but will also force a reevaluation of the way we currently understand the categories of fact and fiction.[18] Perhaps the eventual destinations of Lumiere's train and Mélies' rocket are not what we once supposed.

◆————————————————————————————————————

NOTES

I wrote the original version of this essay fifteen years ago, when my ideas concerning early film, fiction, and documentary were still very much in development. I would like to think that the process of development continues to this day; certainly if I were to write this essay now it would differ substantially from the version presented here. I have decided to refrain from overhauling the original; instead, I have modified and expanded the text only slightly in an effort to preserve the intent of the original while still incorporating editorial suggestions to improve clarity.

1. By employing the term *documentary* to describe tendencies evident in early film actualities, I do not mean to imply that such films were conceived of as documentaries in the contemporary sense. My point, rather, is that such films have been subsumed into a documentary tradition retroactively, as a perusal of any number of overviews of the documentary that begin with the work of the Lumières reveals. When I use *documentary* to convey the nonfictional facets of early film, I recognize that filmmakers of the day would not have availed themselves of the same conceptual framework as later practitioners.

2. David Levy, "Reconstituted Newsreels, Re-enactments, and the American Narrative Film," in *Cinema 1900/1906: An Analytical Study,* ed. Roger Holman (Brussels: FIAF, 1982), 249.

3. Both André Gaudreault and Tom Gunning have employed the narrational concepts of Gérard Genette in their writings on early cinema. For a representative sample of their work, which directly applies to the issues discussed here, see André Gaudreault, "Film, récit, narration: Le cinéma des frères Lumière," *Iris* 2 (1984): 61–70.

4. Marshall Deutelbaum, "Structural Patterning in the Lumière Films," *Wide Angle* 3 (1979). Reprinted in *Film before Griffith,* ed. John L. Fell (Berkeley and Los Angeles: University of California Press, 1983), 299–310.

5. Levy, "Newsreels," 249.

6. Charles Musser, "The Travel Genre in 1903–1904: Moving toward Fictional Narrative," *Iris* 2 (1984): 47–59.

7. The term *motion film* is applicable to a large number of early films whose chief aim was to exploit the visual capacities of distinct camera movements (such as pans or tracks), thereby promoting cinema's ability to provide a view, extend space, follow movement, etc. For an extended discussion of such films, see Tom Gunning, "An Unseen Energy Swallows Space: The Space in Early Film and Its Relation to American Avant-Garde Film," in *Film before Griffith,* ed. Fell, 361–65.

8. Phil Rosen, "Disjunction and Ideology in a Preclassical Film: *A Policeman's Tour of the World,*" *Wide Angle* 12 (1990): 21.

9. Musser, "Travel Genre," 47–59.

10. For a representative sampling, see Lynne Kirby, "Male Hysteria and Early Cinema," *camera obscura* 17 (1988); Musser, "Travel Genre," 52; and Tom Gunning, "An Aesthetic of Astonishment: Early Film and the (In)Credulous Spectator," *Art & Text* 34 (1989): 40.

11. Wolfgang Schivelbusch, *The Railway Journey: The Industrialization of Time and Space in the Nineteenth Century* (Berkeley and Los Angeles: University of California Press, 1986), 24.

12. Stephen Kern, *The Culture of Time and Space, 1880–1918* (Cambridge: Harvard University Press, 1983), 118.

13. For a description of Hale's Tours, see Raymond Fielding, "Hale's Tours: Ultrarealism in the Pre-1910 Picture," in *Film before Griffith,* ed. Fell.

14. A Biograph Bulletin from June 30, 1906, lists over forty such railroad films, many of which may have been reissues of earlier scenic actualities. Most of those that I have seen appear to have been shot near the time of their release, and usually incorporate some aspect of fictionalized material, be it obstruction of the tracks by a character (*A Trip to Berkeley, California* [Biograph, 1906], *In the Haunts of Rip Van Winkle* [Biograph, 1906], *In the Valley of Esopus* [Biograph, 1906]), or actual scenes of comedy within train interiors (*Grand Hotel to Big Indian* [Biograph, 1906], *Holdup of the Rocky Mountain Express* [Biograph, 1906]).

15. Peter Brooks, *Reading for the Plot: Design and Intention in Narrative* (New York: Vintage, 1985), 47. Thanks to Shelley Stamp for reminding me of this reference.

16. Fred Camper's comments regarding home movies provide some context here: "One result common to many home-movie forms is a sense in which the movie itself, rather than the event depicted, is the real event. Thus, it can seem from some travel movies that the sole purpose of visiting Paris, Mount Rushmore, or whatever is to have oneself photographed there. The resulting film then has little to do with the places visited and everything to do with the way in which the participants see themselves, each other, and the external world, which becomes a terrain into which one continually inserts one's own image." See Fred Camper, "Some Notes on the Home Movie," *Journal of Film and Video* 38, no. 3/4 (Summer/Fall, 1986): 12.

17. In his *Acting in the Cinema* (Berkeley and Los Angeles: University of California Press, 1988), 15, James Naremore points to a similar situation in a 1914 Chaplin film, *Kid Auto Races at Venice,* and suggests that even photographed bystanders are filmic performers, insofar as they "provide evidence of role-playing in everyday life." What concerns me more, however, is how the historical moment affects the conception and use of these photographed bystanders within the filmic text, which is already different again (e.g., more self-conscious and deliberately integrative) by the time of *Kid Auto Races at Venice.* Thanks to Tom Gunning for pointing out the similarity between the two examples.

18. More recent attempts at blurring the boundaries between fact and fiction, or, perhaps more specifically, the modes of documentary and fiction filmmaking, can be grouped as "fake documentaries," a label that incorporates titles as diverse as *Daughter Rite* (Michelle Citron, 1978), *Man Bites Dog* (Benoit Poelvoorde, Remy Belvaux, and André Bonzel, 1991), and Christopher Guest's films. Where these later films differ from their early cinema predecessors is in their conscious play with spectatorial expectations deriving from the deployment of documentary conventions, conventions not yet established in cinema's early years.

GREGORIO C. ROCHA

[2] La Venganza de Pancho Villa:
A Lost and Found Border Film

On January 5, 1914, Frank N. Thayer, representing Mutual Film
Corporation, and General Pancho Villa, head of the Constitutionalist
Army in the Mexican revolution, gathered in the office of attorney
Gunther Lessing in El Paso, Texas, to sign a contract. In it, Pancho Villa
agreed to give exclusive rights to Mutual to film the triumphant campaign of his army on its way to Mexico City. As a result of this contract,
the film, *The Life of General Villa* (William C. Cabanné, 1914),[1] was
made, becoming one of the first biographical films ever made and "one
of the oddest episodes in film history," according to film historian Kevin
Brownlow.[2] *The Life of General Villa* opened its commercial run in the
Lyric Theater of New York in May 1914. Then, when World War I started, the film was apparently junked by the company that produced it, and
it became another lost film, though a legendary one.

   After an exhaustive two-year search, digging in the film archives in
Amsterdam, London, Paris, New York, and Mexico City looking for film
materials for my documentary *The Lost Reels of Pancho Villa* (2003),[3]
I stumbled onto one of the most precious treasures a film researcher
can find: dozens of nitrate film reels from the 1920s, lobby cards, photographs, film artifacts, glass slides, and memorabilia, all sitting in the
basement of the house of the Padilla family in El Paso, Texas, since the
late 1930s. This amazing find followed a previous one. While I was visiting the Special Collections of the library of the University of Texas at El
Paso (UTEP), the librarian put in front of me a set of photographs. To
my surprise, the photographs showed many unknown scenes from *The
Life of General Villa,* with the characters portrayed by Raoul Walsh,
Teddy Sampson, and other players hired by Mutual Film Corporation.
As this film was the ultimate goal of my quest, I was excited to believe I
was getting close to a surviving print, if there was one. Along with the

photographs, there were copies of exhibition leaflets announcing the film *La Venganza de Pancho Villa (The Vengeance of Pancho Villa)*, a title that I had never heard of.[4] Since the leaflet was dated from 1937, my first thought was that it was announcing a "talkie" film, but small letters at the bottom of the page read "We will soon have sound equipment!" I was then positive that the leaflet must refer to a silent film—but surely there was only one film made about Pancho Villa in the silent era, *The Life of General Villa*. Where and what was this new "lost" film? It happened to be very near, in the vault of the library, nested in a metal container, where it had been since 1985 when it was donated to UTEP.

La Venganza de Pancho Villa had been slowly decaying in its container. When we opened the lid, a strong smell of nitrocellulose filled the air. We pulled seven reels out. While examining the positive print, multiple glue splices showed that the film had been cut from different sources—both fictional and documentary—and used different brands of film: Eastman Kodak, Pathé, and Agfa. Even at first glance, it was possible to date most of the strips of film as 1916 nitrate film stock. All seven reels showed a melting of the emulsion in the section closest to the core, and it was clear that at least one-third of the film was irremediably lost. At first glance, too, it was possible to see in some frames the image of Raoul Walsh playing

Lobby poster for *La Venganza de Pancho Villa* (Edmundo Padilla, 1936)

the young Pancho Villa, and fascinating bilingual English-Spanish inter-titles telling a somewhat obscure story about Pancho Villa. My conclusion was that I had found not *the* lost film, but rather *another* lost film, about Pancho Villa. Subsequently, with the help of the Institute of Oral History at UTEP, I came to meet the Padilla family, former owners of *La Venganza de Pancho Villa,* who welcomed me, allowed me in their basement to open those rusty cans filled with film treasures and to carry on my investigations in their documents, and who shared with me the story of their ancestors.

Between 1920 and 1936, Félix Padilla, an impresario from Cd. Juarez, Chihuahua, traveled extensively with his son Edmundo throughout north-ern Mexico and the southwestern United States, exhibiting silent films that he rented or purchased from film distributors based in Mexico City and Los Angeles. Félix and Edmundo Padilla toured in a pickup truck, carrying with them 35 mm films, a portable film projector, a manual phonograph, lobby posters, and several 78 rpm records, which they used to add music to the projections. In the afternoons, Félix Padilla would traverse the center of each town, announcing the day's program through a voice amplifier. Screenings usually took place in the local theater, where he shared the profits on a 50-50 basis with the owner. Occasionally, when no movie theaters were available, Padilla would set a huge white canvas in the main plaza and the screening would take place in open air, the audi-ence bringing their own chairs. For five cents per child and ten cents per adult, the people of places like Ciudad Juárez, Chihuahua, Gómez Palacio, Durango, Coyote, and Deming could enjoy an exhibition of American short comedies followed by silent Mexican melodramas such as *En la Hacienda* (Ernesto Volrath, 1922).[5]

In the early 1930s, when the family had already moved to El Paso, Texas, Félix and Edmundo decided to create their own film version of the life of Pancho Villa, cutting and reediting fragments from films they had in their collection. By doing this, they unknowingly became the first Mexican American filmmakers. Edmundo Padilla's fascination with Pancho Villa probably began, it should be noted, when, as a child, he witnessed the Mexican revolution.

> At midnight you could listen [to] the gunfire. The shout of "Viva Villa!" would unleash yelling and thundering all around. Sometimes the revolution-aries would take the town, but at other times they would be defeated. I also became aware of the executions that took place in the municipal cemetery, where federal soldiers would fire their rifles at the revolutionaries who were standing in front of a wall. I also got to see Pancho Villa in person when one time he arrived in his own car pulling a wagon loaded with corn and beans. He personally distributed the goods to the poor people, who arrived carry-ing baskets.[6]

Frame from *The Life of General Villa* (William Christy Cabanné, 1914)

The Padillas' fascination with Pancho Villa rivaled their fascination with the moving image. Out of the first assemblage of appropriated footage, they came up with a compilation film—exhibited under titles that varied with the version. *El Reinado del Terror* (*The Reign of Terror* [1932]) was the title of the first release of the film. It is possible that Félix and Edmundo Padilla began their project using the remaining few reels of the legendary *The Life of General Villa.*

The hypothesis that *The Life of General Villa* was the basis for the Padilla film may be proven by the stills used for the lobby cards advertising their film. These are, in fact, images from *The Life of General Villa*. By carefully examining these photographs, it is possible to see the "Eastman Kodak Nitrate Film" brand printed in the borders, which suggests that these are frame enlargements rather than "stills" taken during production. In the interview recorded by Magdalena Padilla in 1976, Edmundo Padilla remembered:

> The film of Pancho Villa was about the Mexican Revolution. There were many scenes shot in real battlefields. My father brought that film to the U[nited] S[tates] and exhibited it in many places here, Arizona, New Mexico, California, and Texas, always in small towns. He would bring his projector,

rented the theaters, and went for a percentage, including schools. The film of Villa was about when Villa was young, how he was pushed into the revolution, his first accomplishments after he was a bandit, and then when he became a general. People loved this film, especially Mexican people.

This statement from Padilla clearly references the story line of *The Life of General Villa*. Although Félix Padilla claimed it as his film and never mentioned the sources from which he gathered the scenes for *El Reinado del Terror,* it seems clear that, besides drawing from *The Life of General Villa,* the Padillas also drew from other sources, mainly from the 20-episode serial *Liberty, A Daughter of the U.S.A.,* directed by Jacques Jaccard and produced by Universal Film Manufacturing Co. in 1916.[7] Most likely, Félix had purchased several episodes from *Liberty* at a very low price after the film had lost its commercial value. This episodic film, released in August 1916, showed a "patriotic" response to the attack of Villista forces on the town of Columbus, New Mexico, on March 8 of that same year. This attack, which resulted in the complete destruction of the center of the town, caused several American civilian and military casualties, and marked a downturn in Pancho Villa's image in North American public opinion. The response of the American government, led by President Woodrow Wilson, was the immediate invasion of Mexican territory with an army of fifteen thousand soldiers, under the command of General John Pershing, in pursuit of Pancho Villa. The attack on Columbus and the resulting "punitive expedition" set the two countries on the brink of war and exacerbated nationalist feelings on both sides of the border.

For Mexicans, Pancho Villa's dimension as a hero grew; he was seen as the sole man able to defy the imperialist power by attacking U.S. continental territory. On the North American screen, however, Pancho Villa's image, once compared to that of Napoleon or Robin Hood in *The Life of Villa*, shifted to that of the worst of villains, becoming a sort of Public Enemy Number One.[8] In an advertisement published in August 1916 by *Moving Picture World, Liberty* was announced as "A great love story; scenes laid along the Mexican border; with enough of the military atmosphere in each episode to stampede your audiences into bursts of patriotic feeling and appreciation."

In *Liberty,* the actress Mary Walcamp plays the young heroine Liberty, who is kidnapped by an evil character named Pancho López, a Mexican bandit who demands ransom to finance his revolution. While engaged in this action, Pancho López invades Discovery, destroys the town, and kills most of the inhabitants. Major Rutledge, played by Jack Holt, heads an army of Texas Rangers into Mexico to rescue Liberty and destroy Pancho López and his band.

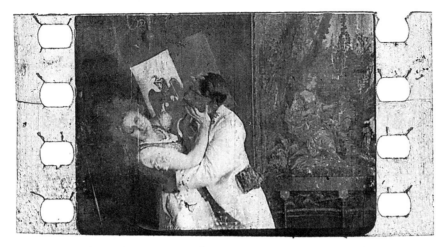

Frame from *Liberty* (Jacques Jaccord, 1916)

Liberty offers ground for the study of the symbolic representations of gender, race, and politics in early American melodramas. On the one hand, it provides an excellent example of where female protagonists could find a utopian space to develop as the "New Woman,"[9] yet *Liberty* may also be considered the ultimate *greaser* film, given its profound and furious anti-Mexican content, perhaps unsurpassed by any other American film of the period. This same kind of analysis can be applied to *Patria* (Jacques Jaccard, 1917),[10] a "war readiness" serial, also related to the American paranoia regarding Mexico (as well as Japan), produced a year later by William R. Hearst.[11]

Padilla's strategy, in including scenes from this episodic film in his project, was to eliminate most of the scenes where Liberty appeared, bringing instead Pancho López to the front as protagonist of the story. When creating new inter-titles in Spanish and English to convey his meaning, Padilla renamed the characters and places invented by Universal's screenwriters. To avoid any direct offense to a Mexican sensibility, Padilla used the real names instead: Pancho López became Pancho Villa, and Discovery became Columbus. But, in the few scenes where Liberty appears, she became "La güera Amalia" (the "blonde Amalia"). With nationalist fervor—a form of cultural resistance common in the Mexican borderlands—Padilla transformed the original anti-Mexican intent of *Liberty* into a (dubious) glorification of Pancho Villa.

Subsequently, in 1934, Padilla released another version (or, more exactly, another episode) of the film—*Pancho Villa en Columbus*—which he probably exhibited to the same audiences. Mariano de la Torre, grandson of Félix Padilla, witnessed some of the screenings when as a child he was hired as phonograph operator: "I was cranking the phonograph and when the attack to Columbus appeared on the screen, my grandfather would cue me to crank it with more impetus, making the crowd go wild. They would yell '*Viva Villa! Mueran los gringos!*'"[12] During the Depression, when the Padillas were screening their films, intolerance toward Mexican immigrants was high and racial segregation was the norm in the border area. However, the Padillas edited their films to be appreciated by both Anglo and Mexican audiences. With bilingual inter-titles and sufficient space for interpretive ambiguity, the films could satisfy audiences from both cultures.

When Félix Padilla passed away in 1936, Edmundo took up the family tradition and came up with the definitive installment of the film, *La Venganza de Pancho Villa*. Edmundo added historical value to the film by incorporating documentary scenes borrowed from *Historia de la Revolución Mexicana*,[13] a Mexican compilation documentary made by Julio Lamadrid in 1928.[14] From it, Edmundo drew sequences showing the "real" Pancho Villa, as well as different events of the Mexican revolution. This is an example of his method: he would start the sequence showing a Mexican newsreel of the actual event, suddenly would cut to an action-packed fake battle filled with hundreds of extras from one of the episodes of *Liberty,* and call the whole "The Battle of Celaya." While trying to arrive at a coherent cinematic discourse on the life of Pancho Villa from such contradictory materials, Edmundo found it necessary to film additional sequences to later inter-cut within his assemblage of appropriated footage. These include the opening sequence, now lost, where the mother makes a fateful confession to the young Pancho Villa; the abduction and subjugation of his father by federal soldiers, which sparks Pancho's rage; and his assassination, recreated with friends and relatives of the Padillas in the outskirts of El Paso in 1930.

Edmundo did not modify other sequences, and we see for the first time in *La Venganza de Pancho Villa* early cinematic representations of some of the historical events that shaped the United States and Mexico's hazardous border in that era: the attack on Columbus, New Mexico; the Santa Isabel incident in which sixteen American engineers were slaughtered; and a little-known event, called the Battle of Ojos Azules, when Pershing's troops unsuccessfully confronted Villista soldiers. But perhaps the best example of Padilla's method is an amazing cutting-room denunciation of the 1914 American invasion of Veracruz, where he inter-cuts scenes from *Birth of a Nation* (D. W. Griffith, 1915),[15] World War I naval battle newsreels, *Liberty* (1916), and *The Life of Villa* (1914), to contest American representations of the Other and of the *enemy,* in this case Mexicans. Acting not only as a metaphor, the title *The Vengeance of Pancho Villa* suggests Padilla's unstated intention: *La Venganza de Pancho Villa* is vengeance against the cultural stereotypes propagated by early North American cinema.

La Venganza de Pancho Villa now exists as a film *maudit*, precursor of what may be called Border Cinema—not only for the geographical location of its practitioners, but for its attempt to freely cross, back and forth, the dividing lines set between fact and fiction, Anglo and Mexican cosmogony, *gringo* and *greaser* stereotypes, and, most of all, original and transformed meanings.

It is stated in Padilla´s logbook that *La Venganza de Pancho Villa* made \$1,280.00 pesos from September 1936 to May 1937. This figure represents the paid admission of at least twelve thousand spectators, given the 10-cent (adult) admission fee. The Padillas' leaflets for *La Venganza de Pancho Villa* suggest that it had its last run in October 1937. As I have noted, small letters at the bottom of one leaflet read "We will soon have sound equipment and films!" but *Empresas Padilla* never made the leap to the sound era.

If, in this book, "F" stands for phony, "H," in the Padilla film, stands for hoax. The hoax in *La Venganza de Pancho Villa* works on multiple levels: on the level of authorship, as the Padillas neither claimed nor denied their interventions, though they did misleadingly announce the film as having been "shot entirely on the outskirts of Torreón"; on the level of historicity, by recontextualizing facts and characters who were already fictionalized; and on the level of veracity, by deconstructing the meanings intended by other filmmakers. In the end, the hoax of *La Venganza de Pancho Villa* was intended to mislead not audiences but, rather, film historians. *La Venganza de Pancho Villa* is one of the oddest and most complex compilation experiments in the history of the silent cinema.[16]

NOTES

This research was made possible by grants from the Fulbright–García Robles Research and Lecturing Program and the Fondo Nacional para la Cultura y las Artes, Mexico. I would like to thank Claudia Rivers, head of the Library Special Collections Department of the University of Texas at El Paso; Kenneth Weissman, head of the Film Preservation Center of the Library of Congress; Ivan Trujillo, director of the Filmoteca U.N.A.M; and, above all, the Padilla family for their generous support in the development of this research.

1. *Life of General Villa* (William C. Cabanné, 1914). This film was produced by the U.S. company Mutual Film Corporation; surviving fragments were restored by the American Film Institute/Cinema Ritrovato. In the Padilla Collection, Library of Congress.

2. Kevin Brownlow investigated the participation of camera operator Charles Roser and his relationship with Pancho Villa in *The War, the West, and the Wilderness* (New York: Alfred Knopf, 1978), 87–105.

3. *Lost Reels of Pancho Villa* (Gregorio C. Rocha, 2003). This 49-minute video was

produced at the Universidad de Guadalajara and Banff Center for the Arts.

4. *Venganza de Pancho Villa* (Félix and Edmundo Padilla, 1935); produced by Empresas Padilla, Mexico/United States, the film was restored by the American Film Institute/Cinema Retrovato. In the Padilla Collection, Library of Congress.

5. *En la hacienda* (Ernesto Volrath, 1922, Mexico); a lost film.

6. From an interview with Edmundo Padilla, recorded by Magdalena Arias, Institute of Oral History, UTEP, El Paso, Texas, 1976.

7. *Liberty: A Daughter of the U.S.A.* (Jacques Jaccard, 1916). Surviving fragments of this 20-episode serial produced by the U.S. company Universal Film Manufacturing were restored by the American Film Institute/Cinema Ritovato. In the Padilla Collection, Library of Congress.

8. According to *Moving Picture World*, it is possible to establish the following figures. In 1914, four feature films with Mexican villains were released; the figure rises to nine in 1915 and twenty in 1916, after the Columbus, New Mexico, incident. Between 1914 and 1920, at least seventy-nine *greaser* feature films were released.

9. These ideas about feminine roles in early American films are developed in Benjamin Singer, *Melodrama and Modernity* (Bloomington: Indiana University Press, 2001).

10. *Patria* (Jacques Jaccard, 1917, United States). The 15-episode film is held, incomplete, in the Museum of Modern Art, New York.

11. William Randolph Hearst owned enormous extensions of land and large numbers of cattle in the state of Chihuahua. By 1917, when *Patria* was produced and released, Pancho Villa had seized Hearst's cattle and distributed them among the peons. The contents of *Patria* were so offensive to Mexico that President Woodrow Wilson ordered film production companies to remove all signs that referred directly to Mexico or to other Latin American countries. From 1914 on, Hearst continuously demanded of the American government an armed intervention in Mexico.

12. From an interview of Mariano Alatorre, recorded by Gregorio Rocha in El Paso, Texas, June 2001.

13. *Historia de la Revolución Mexicana* (Julio Lamadrid, 1928, Mexico); a lost film.

14. Julio Lamadrid and Salvador Toscano were prominent filmmakers and exhibitors in the silent era. Both assembled compilations on the Mexican Revolution.

15. *Birth of a Nation*, David W. Griffith (Triangle Corporation, 1915); various versions available.

16. Perhaps the other compilation film experiment comparable to *La Venganza de Pancho Villa* is the epic *Fall of the Romanov Dynasty*, created by Esther Schub in the Soviet Union in 1927, approximately the same time that Félix Padilla was beginning his appropriation project.

ELISABETH SUBRIN

[3] *Trashing Shulie: Remnants from Some Abandoned Feminist History*

Shulie uses conventions of direct cinema to explore the residual impact of the 1960s, and to challenge the parameters of historical evidence or material. The project was initiated upon my seeing an obscure 16 mm documentary portrait of a young Chicago art student, shot in 1967 by four male graduate film students. Their subject was a young Shulamith Firestone, months before she moved to New York and tried to start a revolution. Other than a few screenings in 1968, the film has sat on a shelf for thirty years.

My *Shulie* (let's call it #2) is a scene-by-scene recreation of the original *Shulie (#1)*, reproduced with actors in many of the original Chicago locations. In it, a 22-year-old woman, looking strangely contemporary, argues confidently and cynically for a life on the margins. She willingly performs for the young directors, allowing them to film her waiting for the train, photographing trash and workers at a dump yard, painting a young man's portrait in her studio, working at the U.S. Post Office, and enduring an excruciating painting critique with her professors at the School of the Art Institute of Chicago (SAIC). In shadowy medium shots, she discusses her views on religion, language, art, relationships with men, institutional power structures, motherhood, and race. Because the original filmmakers had a mandate to document the so-called Now Generation, questions about time, generations, and what constitutes the "now" recur throughout the text.

Watching it and subsequently remaking it, I was amazed by the shocking sense of prescience and longing the film evoked in me. In the ironic nature of style cycles and the repetitive rituals of postadolescent malaise, Shulie's fashion and attitudes were uncomfortably familiar. But I yearned to inhabit *her* reality, to feel this moment of pre-1968, before the haunting political and social revelations of her era, to say nothing of my own.

Beyond this nostalgic impulse lay a more troubling observation. Having attended the Art Institute as an undergrad in the late 1980s, and having taught there in the mid-1990s, I recognized her experience as if it were my own, literally. Her lack of belief in meaningful experiences other than creative achievement; her cynicism about men ever truly tolerating her as an equal; her hilarious observations about the limitations of motherhood; the classically patronizing thesis review in which her own desires and impulses are repeatedly dismissed; her sublimated depression: these were experiences most of my female students, classmates, or colleagues could have shared.

Why, if we had reaped the benefits of second-wave feminism, should Shulie's life seem so contemporary? Similar to accounts of 1990s-style racism in its insidious and subtle forms, contemporary experiences of sexism and misogyny often result in eye-rolling, get-over-it responses that imply that such concerns are paranoid, unresolvable, and, frankly, dated. In representing history so that audiences would have an ambivalent relationship to its status as "past," I found a stronger method of argument.

I was two years old when the original film was shot. Resurrecting it thirty years later triggered complex questions about how one generation inherits and processes the residual representations of its predecessors, particularly of a generation whose legacy is so critical and mythic. The process of remaking the work in 1997 became an act of conceptual time travel. In both its production and dissemination, I hoped to compel viewers to scrutinize, shot by shot, what constitutes the historical present versus the securely located *past,* and to do so across cultural, economic, racial, sexual, generational, and formal lines. *It looks like 1967, but was that a Starbucks cup?* In turn, both the audience's knowledge of (and inexplicable resistance to) the work's status as a remake pushed the interpretive stakes: why would one reproduce with such obsessive precision such a minor document? Why should I care about this girl? Why represent a key figure of Women's Lib without telling us anything *meaningful* about her life? Both the production and reception of *Shulie (#2)* has been shaped by these issues of legibility and value, in turn triggering other questions about translation, biographical practices, and the representation of history and heroes.

To explain how these issues played out in the film, I offer as example a particular scene that takes place early on. Shulie is photographed waiting for the subway on her way to work at the U.S. Post Office. In voice-over, she confesses that even though her salary is decent, getting up so early in the morning and waiting alone on the tracks makes her feel like a derelict. There follows a sequence of vérité shots inside the post office, where we observe Shulie sorting mail, surrounded by white male supervisors and black coworkers. The scene ends with Shulie taking a coffee break with two young, female, black coworkers. Over the interior shots, we hear her voice-over:

> The percentage of Negroes there is very high, which would automatically make you wonder about the kind of job it is . . . uh, well, first of all, Negroes can't get anything except for a federal job; that would account for the high rate of Negroes. If you meet a Negro and you want a subject of conversation, the first thing you ask them is: how long have you worked at the post office? and then you have something to talk about! You know it's like this giant fraternity of people who work at the post office at sometime or another and once you've worked with them it's like having gone to jail with them; you know, it's a kind of a brotherhood.

Sitting with audiences, one feels this scene as a turning point. Up to this moment, Shulie (as a character) is perceived as a benign, alternately interesting, precocious, understandably naïve, but passionate post-adolescent "droning on" about her life. Some viewers may have empathy for her self-reflexive and gendered discussion of language, or may experience some vague confusion about what the film *is about*. Some others are still simply trying to determine if what is onscreen is past or present. But suddenly we get very specifically dated racial and social signifiers, through the use of the word "Negro." A viewing tension is stressed, relieved, and then restressed. At first there is tension because Shulie no longer is an uncomplicated documentary subject. She said the "N" word, and we hate her (ourselves) for it. But we also feel relief because we can now locate the scene clearly as the "past," right?—because we don't use "that word" anymore, and (I suspect) because suddenly the film may have a "purpose" in its exposure of racism.

But then for feminist viewers there is another discomfort in hearing Shulie discuss race, as we are reminded of the problem of exclusion within the history of American (white) women's liberation movements. It's embarrassing and disturbing. And whether Shulie's voice-over was originally taken out of a larger context that might render a different meaning or not—whether she is being ironic or not—does not eliminate the hauntingly familiar representation we witness. A similarly symptomatic fact is that I, as a white filmmaker, initially planned to cut this scene from the project. The scene felt so problematic, and yet ultimately speaks most powerfully to the fundamental bind in this film. How do we locate something as the past? Are we secure in its status as an outdated discourse simply because we don't *say* the word Negro anymore? In both formal and discursive terms, Shulie's well-intentioned efforts at an analysis of race relations will reek of white privilege to some viewers, and not only as history. To others it will painfully evoke the preconsciousness of the early sixties.

And to others it will simply be another example of a boring scene, where time moves slowly: Shulie's observations aren't groundbreaking and nothing happens. Many viewers will still wonder why we should be watching these banal, daily routines of a twenty-two-year-old woman. Why should we care?

By reshooting this scene thirty years later, even with the coded vintage discourse, I am forced to ask myself, what has really changed other than discourse? Obviously eliminating racist discourse hasn't solved the problem. As Firestone later would write about the problem of sexism, no matter how deep you go, the problem only goes deeper. Questioning what has actually changed exposes me as prototypical "Gen X," cynical about my inheritance and ignorant about the complexity of historical cycles. I have neither the knowledge nor the perspective to truly interrogate the legacy of the sixties. Further, as a fake documentarian who was barely conscious in 1967, aren't I an unreliable participant observer? What do I gain by producing a fake document, rather than just resurrecting the original? On what grounds can I offer this remake as *evidence*?

Throughout the shooting process, I found myself constantly negotiating all sorts of historical and biographically specific signifiers. The most subtle deviation from the "original" text triggered self-reflexive shifts in meaning, reflecting back on the thirty years of history that have passed, whether after noting a subtly placed contemporary prop, observing an

Shulie (Elisabeth Subrin, 1997)

historically implausible notice on sexual harassment, or registering the substitution of a beatnik gathering with a post-grunge scene of counter-convention activists during the 1996 Democratic Convention. In the 1990s version, 1960s politics endure mostly through style: on the t-shirts of the twenty-something activists, in the performance of alterna-cultural activities in Chicago's ultra-hip Wicker Park, or, contrastingly, in the out-dated modes of political protest. The tedious and sometimes insensitive critique panel that Shulie endures from her (all male) painting instructors, and the problematic analysis of race relations I described above, are other moments that reverberate between past and present, refusing to lie still. While we can understand the film as a "fake," a copy of an original, and therefore clearly located in the past, nonetheless, each scene resonates today. Watching the "fake," recognized as performed from an "original," creates the effect of viewing two films and two time periods at once: a doubling, a haunting, a generational negotiation. *Shulie (#2)*, filtered through thirty years of history, performs as a repetition of a quiet emotional trauma that has yet to be healed. Like any compulsive act, it resurfaces from a lack of resolution.

Much of the most confusing generational slippage comes from actress Kim Soss's impossible task of rendering a vérité 1960s identity in a 1990s body. Often I am asked if I see her stellar performance as acting or simulation. Was she mimicking Shulie through repeated viewings of the original,

Kim Soss in *Shulie* (Elisabeth Subrin, 1997)

or did she inhabit the character as an actor would? Like any performer, Soss knew the purpose of her character's role and where her actions would lead. On the other hand, Kim Soss was performing as a documentary subject (Shulamith Firestone) herself performing her own "authenticity" for the camera. Yet Soss's performance was significantly altered by her undeniable awareness of her character's future life: as groundbreaking activist, successful writer, poet, and, later, feminist missing in action. As Jonathan Rosenbaum wrote in a 1998 review in *The Chicago Reader*:

> It's not a commentary on Soss's skill as an actress that her manner of speaking is colorless and more guarded than Firestone's and that she conveys a certain emotional vacancy. But it's difficult to pinpoint how much this is a matter of the differences in everyday speech and body language now and 30 years ago and how much this is a matter of existential authenticity. (Subrin describes Soss's performance as an "interpretation" rather than an attempt at duplication, but this in no way prevents Soss's behavioral tics from reeking of the '90s.)

While I can't speak for Soss, my motivation for casting her and my experience directing her were informed by my sense of her deep connection with Firestone (Soss also attended the Art Institute, is an assertive, verbal, Jewish woman artist, etc.). This identification was filtered through thirty years of history by an actress who had inherited both the gains produced by feminist activism and the psychic trauma that in part defines our generation: of change promised but not yet delivered. It wasn't mimicry, but empathy and identification, that shaped the performance. In order to actually channel such emotions, undeniably Soss's own "behavioral tics" would surface and, as subtle as they were, perhaps contribute to the strange dual time frame the film evokes. As Rosenbaum adds:

> The paradox is that even historical hindsight isn't enough to give an actress playing Firestone 30 years later the kind of emotional urgency Firestone conveyed in the original film through her own shyness and confusion; Soss projects the kind of contemporary coolness we tend to identify as normal. Yet it's only through this juxtaposition that we begin to see the petrifying fear that describes our present moment—the kind of fear that makes the very notion of a remake seem like a logical response.

As a film, *Shulie* communicates in strikingly different ways for different viewers. For some, depending on their relations to feminism, female subjectivity, concepts of difference, Firestone, and film form, the film generates the vertical and lateral layers of meaning I have suggested. For others, it is completely opaque. We often forget that experimental form is as susceptible to conventions and canons as is dominant cinema. That people get fascinated with the formal issues of *Shulie* is only interesting to me if its feminist purpose is considered. I want the audience members to ask themselves: why does the film concern this moment in her life? Why this moment before the Moment—i.e., the period when Shulie became actualized as a feminist, activist, revolutionary, best-selling writer? Why this woman? She's certainly no sexy downtown Edie Sedgwick or Nico icon, certainly no Left Bank Marguerite Duras. For some viewers, hints of Firestone's emerging conceptual and intellectual work press to the surface. For other viewers, watching Shulie talk on about her life is frustrating. I've been accused of "ripping off" viewers by not giving the "true" story. One filmmaker commented that she "couldn't understand why anyone would ever want to copy such a bad film with such an uninteresting portrayal." Another dismissed the subject on the grounds that she "sees students like this every day" and that the discussion of Shulie's work is interesting but not "in the film." My sense from these viewers is that, although the subject is to be celebrated, this is not the right representation. In other words, if I am to honor the life and struggles of a dedicated feminist writer and activist, I should represent her in recognizable cinematic forms.

My compulsion to repeat is certainly not groundbreaking. Yet I relate this impulse to an increased, perhaps even perverse, need within my generation to recreate struggles we did not physically experience. Or did we? Why would one repeat, fetishize, or desire a historical moment if there was not an intimate connection, if one was not somehow a product of (or participant in) that time period? The year 1967 can only exist as myth to me. I have no material access to it, yet its meanings have created me. Questioning who and what merits historical preservation, and why we crave this history, is what provoked the particular repetitive strategies of this project.

If we are to create histories that recognize difference, we also need to preserve moments that don't look like history with a capital H. We need to record and analyze minor, awkward, multiply coded, and irreducible representations. Why should the life of a groundbreaking intellectual who sought to transform consciousness be presented with the mind-numbingly reductive and repetitive format of the Biography Channel (or other overly familiar hagiographic strategies)? *Shulie (#2)* is not a traditional portrait or a PBS documentary or a lyrical collage, but an experimental film masquerading as a case study and submitting itself as evidence: of daily, unremarkable, but excruciatingly familiar female negotiations with language, performativity, subjectivity, framing, and power relations. I would propose that the phony *Shulie* is not necessarily *about* the young Firestone, but about the conditions of a woman's cinematic representation, with the privileged recognition that she, and many other women of her generation, survived, or even conquered that representation, often at enormous risk and sacrifice. My generation is utterly indebted to these women, even if we identify with them from radically different vantage points. In the compulsion to remake, to produce a fake document, to repeat a specific experience I never actually had, what I have offered up is the performance of a resonant, repetitive, emotional trauma that has yet to be healed.

Had I simply screened the original, Firestone's experience would be understood as the antiquated past, with all its romance, flaws, and faded logic. As a fake that blurs its own location in time, Shulie may also speak to the present. The amateur, sexist, and self-aggrandizing strategies of the original four male filmmakers and their positioning of Firestone in the documentary; how she is treated by her painting teachers; how she articulates her subjectivity as a white, middle-class Jewish woman: these moments represent critical and problematic evidence of a time that has not necessarily passed. Resurrecting *Shulie* (1967) is a stubborn (yet illusory) historiographical act, an attempt to insist that this trash (this minor, flawed, and nonheroic experience) be seen and heard, and to throw its identity as the past into question.

JESSE LERNER

[4] *No Lies about* Ruins

When the cops busted the *Veracruzanos*, they thought they had some major league looters of pre-Columbian artifacts on their hands. Although such objects have long been protected as national patrimony in Mexico, the high prices they fetch in the auction houses and galleries of New York and Europe, the relatively unmonitored and isolated condition of many of the country's archaeological sites, and the country's relative poverty all conspire to perpetuate the contraband traffic in antiquities.[1] The destructiveness of those engaged in gathering objects for this illegal trade—sawing, chopping, and prying objects off pyramids and out of tombs—deprives researchers of a good portion of the archaeological record the world over. The fact that these objects are infinitely more useful to the scientist in context makes this practice the equivalent of ripping unique pages of irreplaceable information out of archives. At the 1974 trial of the accused looters from Veracruz, archaeologists from the National Institute of Anthropology and History (the Instituto Nacional de Antropología e Historia, or INAH) testified that the ceramics had been taken from ancient sites in the Cempoala region, in the central part of the state of Veracruz, an area very rich in archaeological sites. Convicted largely on the basis of this testimony, the traffickers were sent to prison for their role in this illegal commerce.

From prison, one of the convicted individuals, Brigído Lara, made an unusual demand. He asked his lawyer to bring clay to his cell. Then, within the jail, Lara proceeded to sculpt indisputable proof of his innocence— identical reproductions of the pieces that had sent him to jail. He was not a looter at all, it seemed, but rather a wrongfully accused forger, an accomplished mimic of ancient styles. For the past twenty years he had been fabricating contemporary imitations of ancient ceramics. Although he worked in many styles, including Aztec and Maya, his specialty was the ceramic wares of the ancient Totonac, a population that inhabited Veracruz and flourished between the seventh and twelfth centuries A.D. Lara's prison-made replicas were taken to those same experts from the INAH whose testimony had led to the convictions. Once again the verdict was rendered: these too were judged by the INAH specialists to be ancient objects from Cempoala. Cleared of the charges of looting, Lara was released from jail in January 1975. He was subsequently employed by the state's Anthropology Museum of Xalapa, second in Mexico only to the National Museum in Mexico City, to restore damaged pieces and to review the collection for fakes. Certified by the INAH as a licensed maker of reproductions, Lara continues to sculpt what look like ancient objects, pieces that he likes to call "original interpretations."

It was not until about a decade after Lara's release from jail that he began to learn something of the fate of the approximately forty thousand pieces he (claimed to have) made prior to his arrest and reform. Agustín Acosta Lagunes, then governor of Veracruz, spent considerable sums of state funds overseas to purchase and repatriate numerous ancient objects for his pet project, the Anthropology Museum of Xalapa. After the governor returned with a number of purchases made at Sotheby's in New York, Lara came forward with a dramatic announcement. He had made these ceramic pieces during his earlier career outside the law. Further investigation revealed more and more of Lara's objects all over the world, some in the most prestigious international collections. The Dallas Museum of Art, New York's Metropolitan Museum, the Morton May collection at the Saint Louis Art Museum, and important collections in France, Australia, Spain, and Belgium all contained pieces that Lara maintained he had made. In fact, Lara may have been so prolific that he had a hand in shaping what is today understood as the classic Totonac style. In 1971, the Los Angeles County Museum of Natural History presented a large exhibition entitled "Ancient Art of Veracruz," accompanied by a catalogue with the same title.[2] Lara appears to have made at least a dozen of the objects exhibited there. Although cautious about any expression of pride in his accomplishments, Lara is uncomfortable when his works are designated "forgeries." He prefers to think of them as "my own originals."[3]

Brigído Lara is the central character of *Ruins* (1999), my documentary on the history of collections and exhibitions of pre-Columbian objects. Given the scale of the topic, the film cannot pretend to offer a comprehensive survey of this history, but offers instead five vignettes, or short chapters, on key moments or themes within that history. The final chapter, the one that provides the conceptual foundation of the entire film, is about the forging of pre-Columbian objects and features Brigído Lara. Elsewhere the film discusses the restoration of pre-Columbian sites (with scenes of

Sylvanus G. Morley, dean of Mayanists, painting murals on the walls of Chichén Itzá),[4] the manufacture and sale of replicas for tourism, and other practices distinct from, yet reminiscent of, the work of the forger. But more than simply representing these kindred practices, throughout the film forging is employed as metaphor for documentary filmmaking, making the movie a metadocumentary.

Many forgers, Lara among them, find it necessary to add a (false) patina of age to their creations, thus making objects from the twentieth century look like they were from, say, the eleventh. As pieces that are intact can raise the suspicions of collectors, traffickers and forgers often break an object intentionally. Breaking an object into pieces also facilitates transport.[5] All sorts of other techniques are used to give new objects the weathered sheen of antiquity and to put to rest doubts about the piece's authenticity. In another film of mine, *Frontierland/Fronterilandia* (1995, with Rubén Ortiz Torres), a forger from Tabasco, Carlos Venegas, tells of burying forged objects and then photographing the process by which the objects, now caked in dirt, are once again dug up in order to provide a "proof" of their authenticity.

These and other techniques for artificially "aging" the forged object are the inspiration for my approach to the film's emulsion and sound track.

Ruins (Jesse Lerner, 1999)

Much of the film is constructed from archival audio and images, which, like objects on display at the archaeological museum, have been taken from their original context and used to create a new narrative. About half of the images and audio are mine. Like the forger, I have attempted to artificially induce the illusion of age onto the surface of some of these original materials to match the visual quality of the archival materials. Hand-processing produces the desired effect for film images. Rather than sending the exposed film stock to the lab, one can easily process black-and-white negative in any light-tight bathroom. The film does not travel through the chemistry on runners without scratching or rubbing against other pieces of film, as is the case in a professional lab. Instead the film is tangled and bunched up during processing, and the result is covered with scratches and splotches, frames that came in contact with less chemistry and other frames that contacted more, a damaged appearance that replicates the look of much-used, partially deteriorated, archival footage. Similarly, reticulation, selective flashing and flaring, scratching, and a host of other techniques can be deployed as calculatingly as Lara's "100 percent original finishes." The emulsion itself is in ruins.

Analogous results can be achieved with greater precision on the sound track using digital, rather than kitchen sink, technologies. While many of the audio elements in the film's sound track do in fact come from any of several hundred archival sources, including LPs, 78s, newsreels, archival radio broadcasts, sound tracks of classroom educational or feature-length fiction films, etc., there is a significant portion of the narration that is in fact original. It is not always apparent to the audience which is which. Much of the narration written specifically for *Ruins* was recorded in a studio with a voice-over artist, and then run through one of several digital filters to simulate the hiss, low fidelity, clipping, and other particular audio qualities of a 1940s-era newsreel, a midcentury didactic film with an optical sound track, or any of the other recognizable filmic styles being paraphrased. Together with the mimicking of certain rhetorical forms, modes of delivery, and so on, these conspire to blur the distinction between original and archival audio, though the content often gives away a particular voice on the sound track as one or the other. Here surface noise, clipping of the frequencies beyond the midrange, and other technical flaws are misleadingly deployed as markers of age. The layers of noise, like the strata of deposits employed in *varve* chronology dating, give an impression of age. Knowing this, the filmmaker, who is not always to be trusted, can replicate the particular audio qualities of anything from the synchronously recorded magnetic track of super-8 film to a World War II–era radio broadcast, all for the purposes of deception.

In *Ruins,* the character of María Elena Pat is another strategic fake. This character was developed in collaboration with the actress who plays the part, the Chicana performance artist María Elena Gaitan. Essentially, this character functions as a device to respond to the statements made by the two distinguished forbearers of Maya archaeology, Sylvanus G. Morley and Sir Eric Thompson. The critique she offers is to a great extent derived from the model developed by the current generation of Mayanists, archaeologists like Mary Miller, Jeremy Sabloff, and so on. The intention is not that hers is the authentic voice of the indigenous—in a sense, she's the phoniest thing in the whole film—but rather that hers is the interpretation currently in vogue, one likely to be replaced subsequently by some other model.[6]

The film does not mean to celebrate the forger as a heroic or unproblematic figure. Nor is the forger's practice equated with those of the archaeologist charged with reconstructing the ruins or the artisan who manufactures the plethora of commodities for the tourist trade for sale at the site: paperweights in the shape of a miniature rendition of Chichén Itzá, for example. The viewer should not mistake the forger's statements as unadulterated truth. As is the case with so much of what takes place in the shady world of forgers, it's difficult to know how to evaluate the statements that Lara makes. Corroborating his claims of authorship has proven no simple matter. In the Metropolitan Museum's Michael C. Rockefeller Memorial Collection of Art of Africa, Oceania, and the Americas, there is a spectacular, three-foot-tall, hollow ceramic figure of *Ehecatl,* the Mesoamerican wind god, which Lara claims to have made. It is illustrated in the coffee-table book *Masterpieces of Primitive Art.*[7] Fluoroluminescence and other laboratory tests attempting to date the piece have yielded ambiguous results, and expert assessments on the basis of style reach no consensus. Lara, who has never been to New York, knows a great deal about the piece and its construction, enough to suggest that at the very least he was witness to its manufacture. But other details seem to contradict this conclusion. Before being exhibited in the Metropolitan Museum's Rockefeller Wing, the object was part of the permanent collection of New York's (no longer existent) Museum of Primitive Art. Before that, it was in Nelson Rockefeller's private collection. When Rockefeller purchased the object, Lara was eight years old. Classified as a "masterpiece," it does not look like the work of an eight-year-old. When pressed for details, Lara explains that he made the *Ehecatl* figure "many years ago." Could Lara have been the apprentice to an older, master forger, making him the latest, most notorious representative of a tradition of *Veracruzano* forgers? Lara emphatically denies this, claiming to be an autodidact. His training was in the fields as a child in Loma Bonita, Oaxaca, and in Mixtequilla, Veracruz, where he grew up. Both towns are located in areas rich in archaeological artifacts. He would study, he says, the fragments of ancient objects that peasant farmers would turn up while plowing their fields. From these he would extrapolate the form of the entire object. Meanwhile the Metropolitan Museum has taken the piece off display. Whether this *Ehecatl* is a "fake fake," that is, an authentic object falsely labeled as a forgery, remains an open question.

Although the objects Lara claims to have made are unquestionably of aesthetic value, aesthetics are only part of the reason (real) pre-Columbian objects are valued. For the archaeologist, the object provides information about a (no longer existent) worldview. Not being an eleventh-century Totonac, Lara is not privy to this worldview. When he manufactures the representation of a Totonac divinity, he does so without the knowledge of which elements are associated with which gods. One can imagine that if members of that ancient culture had a chance to evaluate Lara's creations, they would have rejected them, just as William Henry Holmes, writing in the magazine *Science* in 1886, dismisses some of the more inept forgeries he encounters as "compositions made up of unrelated parts (derived, maybe, from ancient art), and thrown together without rhyme or reason."[8] To the extent that archaeologists have used his objects to draw inferences about the ancient world, Lara is guilty of adding misleading data to the pool of available evidence. Given the extent to which Lara's creations are so convincing and have been so widely disseminated, it is difficult to share Holmes's assuredness when he writes "doubtless in time most of the spurious objects will be detected and thrown out."[9]

Although *Ruins* does not aim to celebrate the forger as a postmodern hero, neither does it damn the forger as a villain. The latter position has, perhaps not surprisingly, been the rule within the archaeological establishment. In 1910, Leopoldo Batres published his *Antiquedades Mejicanas Falsificadas: Falsificación y Falsificadores,* the first book-length study of the subject. There, he provides reproductions of numerous objects of dubious authenticity, his rationale for claiming certain celebrated objects are inauthentic, and an eyewitness account of a workshop of forgers located near the pyramids of Teotihuacan, forgers whom Batres claims to have reformed.[10] The depiction he creates of the forger is unflattering: typically both a victim of unscrupulous middlemen and an alcoholic "who spends his time in taverns."[11] Although information on the subject is scarce, Batre's evident contempt is consistent with most of the published accounts of forgers and their motivations. Almost without exception, the most celebrated and accomplished forgers of the twentieth century—Lara's peers—are depicted in the available literature as a despicable bunch. Cleared of the accusations of collaborating with the Nazis, his "Vermeers" purged from the art museums, Hans Van Meegeren goes down in history as a resentful failure, stung by the critical rejection of his own mediocre paintings: the kitschy oils of fawns and overblown allegorical scenes exhibited under his own name in his youth. More recently, John Myatt, forger of "Picassos," "Matisses," "and Giacomettis," is invariably portrayed as a hapless loser, manipulated and bullied by his own collaborator, the more intelligent and conniving John Drewe.[12]

In contrast, Lara's story is not one of an aggrieved aspirant stung by the art world's hostility to his own production, a greedy four-flusher in search of profit, or the patsy of controlling co-conspirators. An affable, modest, salt-of-the-earth type from a poor, rural area, Lara is an honest forger, a man absolutely without a chip on his shoulder. At least according to his own account, he was an innocent gifted with a special talent, a babe in the woods drawn into a scheme designed by cunning profiteers. He expresses a sincere admiration for the pre-Columbian cultures that he mimics, and regrets not having lived in those times. No longer beholden to the imposed vow of silence of the forger, he signs all of his "original interpretations" and is insistent on his authorship. This points to the dilemma of the forger for whom the greatest success implies anonymity, the reverse of the experience of any other artist. Perhaps, before his arrest, Lara craved the recognition that could only come at the price of exposure. If this is so, then the outcome must be a disappointment. Recategorized as contemporary replicas, the market value of his creations has plummeted, and rather than exhibiting in the Metropolitan, he now shows at decidedly less prestigious events like the Veracruz State Fair. In art world terms, this is unquestionably several steps down, though the aesthetic content of the objects has not changed. Although he states the desire to be accepted as a "modern artist," that recognition has not been forthcoming. Is it that the authentic Totonac objects express a way of understanding the world that is otherwise lost to us, while Lara's replicas only mimic their superficial appearance, without being grounded in understanding of their significance? Are not Lara's sculptures authentic expressions of what Hillel Schwartz calls "the culture of the copy"?[13]

Lara's story also loans itself to another, more contentious interpretation. Although he makes no such claims himself, it is tempting to view Lara's life's work as a sort of comeuppance, revenge for the plague of looters that continue to carve up archaeological ruins, raid tombs, and ship off the spoils for sale in foreign markets (and for archaeologists who once behaved similarly). The illegality of this trade makes it easier for forgers to succeed, to the extent that it discourages collectors from inquiring too deeply into an object's provenance. Even after the passage of legislation protecting national patrimony, museums, universities, and other scientific institutions (and, of course, private parties) have all engaged in these activities. Edward Herbert Thompson famously smuggled objects hidden in his dirty laundry from Chichén Itzá to Harvard's Peabody Museum.[14] In the light of all this, there is poetic justice in the fact that a peasant artisan with a grammar school education seems to have fooled not only dozens of collectors but some of the world's leading archaeologists and curators as well. Lara's success does not simply call into question the expertise of the authorities; it can be seen as a subversion of that neocolonial project that continues to drain Latin America of its cultural heritage.

The theme of forging returns in my more recent film, *The American Egypt* (2001). One of the elements I incorporate here is a reference to the work of Carlos Martínez de Arredondo, pioneer filmmaker of the Yucatán. In 1915 he filmed Mexico's first fiction film, a drama of life on the sisal plantations, called *La voz de su raza*. Unfortunately, like most of the films made during that era, *La voz de su raza* no longer exists. Given Mérida's scorching climate, it is likely that the unstable nitrate print has long ago disintegrated. There are, however, synopses of the film available both in newspaper accounts printed around the time of the film's premiere and in Carlos Martínez de Arredondo's autobiographical statement.[15] Based on this description, I re-created this film and edited the footage into *The American Egypt* as a film-within-the-film.

In both cases, forging, reconstruction, the simulation of markers of age, and related strategies prove to be important techniques for questioning the authority of documentary film. At times subtle, at times blatant, these methods conspire to encourage active participation on the part of the audience, who is compelled to view the film critically, and to skeptically consider the authenticity of the images and information being presented.

◆ ───

NOTES

1. The first Mexican laws forbidding such trafficking of ancient objects were passed in the nineteenth century. To this day, such illegal smuggling continues. For a collector's defense of this trade, see Gillett G. Griffin, "In Defense of the Collector," *National Geographic* 169, no. 4 (April 1986), 462–65.
2. *Ancient Art of Vera Cruz* (Los Angeles: Los Angeles County Museum of Natural History, 1971).
3. Interview with Brigído Lara, Xalapa, Veracruz, May 31, 1996. Further quotes from

Lara are from either the same interview or that conducted the following day.
4. This practice is no longer part of restoration processes, and it unfailingly strikes contemporary audiences as dangerously close to vandalism, but it functions as a useful reminder that standards for restoration continue to change, often with each presidential administration. Styles in reconstruction (Díaz Ordaz, Echevarría, de la Madrid, etc.) are as identifiable as the pre-Columbian architectural styles (pre-Classic, Classic,

etc.) that they stand in for and upon which they are superimposed. For more about the changing tastes in reconstruction, see Elizabeth H. Boone, ed., *Falsifications and Misreconstructions of pre-Columbian Art* (Washington, D.C.: Dumbarton Oaks, 1982). My interest here is not in identifying certain styles as misreconstructions, so much as in articulating the links and the distinctions among a variety of post-Conquest neo-pre-Columbian sculptural, painting, and architectural practices.

5. Val Edwards describes this process in "Rare pre-Columbian Relics at Any Cost," *New York Times* (July 31, 1995), A7.

6. In fact, the current model seems an overcompensation for the excesses of Thompson and Morley's doctrine.

7. *Masterpieces of Primitive Art*, photographs by Lee Boltin, text by Douglas Newton (New York: Knopf, 1978).

8. William Henry Holmes, "The Trade in Spurious Mexican Antiquities," *Science* 7, no. 159 (1886): 170.

9. Ibid.

10. Leopoldo Bartres, *Antiguedades Mejicanas Falsificadas: Falsificacion y Falsificadores* (Mexico, D.F.: Imprenta de Fidencio S. Soria, 1910), 14.

11. Ibid., 15.

12. The literature on forgers is vast. See Sándor Radnóti, *The Fake: Forgery and Its Place in Art*, trans. Erwin Dunai (Lanham, Md.: Rowman and Littlefield, 1999); Mark Jones, ed., *Fake? The Art of Deception* (Berkeley and Los Angeles: University of California Press, 1990); the Nelson Atkins Museum of Art's exhibition "Treasures of Deceit: Archaeology and the Forger's Craft" (1996).

13. Hillel Schwartz, *The Culture of the Copy: Striking Likenesses, Unreasonable Facsimiles* (New York: Zone Books, 1996).

14. For more on this case, see my essay "Thompson en el cenote sagrado," *Alquimia* 5, no. 13 (September–December 2001): 23–26.

15. Carlos Martínez de Arredondo, "Yucatán, precursor del cine nacional," *Enciclopedia Yucatense*, vol. 5 (1946), 317–23.

STEVE ANDERSON

[5] *The Past in Ruins: Postmodern Politics and the Fake History Film*

> *Concern for authenticity links forger and documentary filmmaker—both create an illusion of the real through an elaborate web of artifice.*
> :: Jesse Lerner, *Ruins* (1999)

Since the late 1970s, theorists of historiography have challenged the assumption that the goal of history writing should be the progressive assembling of "larger historical truths" into grand libraries of fact and interpretation.[1] Hayden White's influential writings on narrative and historiography claim that the work of the historian has never been merely the transliteration of a preexistent past into a documentary medium. Rather, he argues, history is fundamentally constituted through the emplotment of historical data into recognizable narratives and literary tropes.[2] Although White's intervention initially proved more readily assimilable in the emerging field of cultural studies than within history proper, his privileging of narrative marked a significant challenge to the empirical pretensions of much academic history.[3]

In spite of its reputation for conservatism and discursive sobriety, the discipline of history is far from monolithic. Ongoing challenges to historical research and writing protocols have resulted in a highly diverse and dynamically self-conscious array of competing methodologies. However, until the early 1990s, it was a rare historian who was willing to consider seriously the significance of film as a discrete and fully articulated form of historiographical practice. Arguably, the tropic convergence of history and literature described by White ultimately proved agreeable to historians in contrast with the greater threat posed by the dramatic spectacle of the history film. Hollywood's historical epics were—and, for that matter, still are—known for their factual inaccuracies, character composites, and elisions of historical complexity in favor of plot-friendly contrivances centered on personality, conflict resolution, and romance. Although the value of historical filmmaking is often presumed to be its ability to bring the past "to life," a certain dishonesty attends historical narratives that undertake to present the past as an experience that may be recaptured, re-lived, or represented.[4] Put bluntly, the most interesting histories are those in which the past is fundamentally understood as a field of discursive and political struggle—a text that is open to revision and debate rather than one that delivers comfortable narrative closure.

Nonetheless, most literary and cinematic histories remain guilty of obscuring the "discontinuity, disruption and chaos"[5] of the past in favor of well-plotted narratives. The solution lies not in a retreat into more detached or objective forms, but in the complication and elaboration of existing narrative or documentary strategies. Indeed, Dominick LaCapra argues that no record of historical events, whether a personal diary or a documentary newsreel, should be considered free of its own historical consciousness. Even the most neutral among these is always "textually processed before any given historian comes to it."[6] If we consider the basic condition of historiography to be an ongoing process of cultural struggle, then we must look for meaning beyond the "footnotes, bibliography, and other scholarly apparatus"[7] of professional historians, to the way historical evidence is culturally processed, disseminated, and remembered. Although debates continue, mainstream historical scholarship has come to recognize the importance of film in mediating historical consciousness in American culture.

The resulting subdiscipline of "film and history" has carved a small but vibrant niche within academia. Beginning in 1971 with the founding of the specialty journal, *Film and History,* the past three decades have witnessed a proliferation of associations, publications, and conferences devoted to media and history. In 1978, the TV miniseries *Roots* became the most popular television event, and arguably the most powerful historiographical moment, of its time.[8] Throughout the 1980s, seminal works on film and history by Pierre Sorlin[9] and Marc Ferro[10] were translated into English, and even mainstream journals such as the *American Historical Review* introduced film reviews as a regular feature. The 1990s, in turn, witnessed a veritable explosion of book publications on the subject, with contributions from both well-known historians and film scholars alike.[11]

Perhaps the most influential and widely published figure in this movement was historian Robert Rosenstone, who, as recently as 1993, was justified in declaring himself the first to articulate the specific characteristics of historical films rather than simply to treat them as a visual adjunct to written history. Rosenstone went on to break ranks with his more conservative colleagues to focus attention on a number of films and videos that he regarded as examples of "postmodern history." According to Rosenstone, postmodern history "tests the boundaries of what we can say about the past and how we can say it, points to the limitations of conventional historical form, suggests new ways to envision the past, and alters our sense of what it is."[12] Rosenstone limited his analysis to films that share the desire to "deal seriously with the relationship between past and present"[13] as defined by more conventional modes of history. The representational strategies mobilized by postmodern history are, he claimed, "full of small fictions used, at best, to create larger historical 'truths,' truths that can be judged only by examining the extent to which they engage the arguments and 'truths' of our existing historical knowledge on any given topic."[14] Rosenstone essentially made the argument that certain films and videos may be considered works of history because they try (with varying degrees of success) to do the same things that *real* historians do. Postmodern histories, though unorthodox, may be recuperated to the extent that they point to histories that are verifiable through traditional means. Thus, ironically, Rosenstone reinscribed these film and video texts that he labeled "postmodern" into a thoroughly modernist (rational, empirical) historical epistemology.

In spite of these limitations, Rosenstone's intervention marked a turning point in discussions of film and history, which had previously focused on questions of factual accuracy in large-scale historical epics. At the same time, theories of postmodernism that were once firmly predicated on assertions about the "loss of history" gave way to the troubling admission that in order to be "lost," history would first have to be "found." Within cultural studies, more sophisticated models for understanding cultural memory emerged in response to experiments with radical history[15] and the redefining of popular memory by Michel Foucault and others.[16] The "culture of amnesia" associated with unreconstructed theories of television was gradually replaced with a notion of history and memory as fundamentally "entangled" with popular media, rather than antithetical to it.[17] By the early 1990s, proclamations about "the end of history" following the collapse of the Soviet Union revealed themselves as cynical prevarications when what Francis Fukuyama called the "triumph of liberal democracy and capitalism"[18] led to an unprecedented (and still unresolved) economic crisis in Eastern Europe. Under the tutelage of Oliver Stone and Fox Mulder, American preoccupations with history came to be dominated by an amalgam of skepticism, conspiracy, and paranoia mixed with furtive, lingering hopes in the reliability of carefully executed, scientific research methods and technology.

In documentary film theory of the 1980s and 1990s, already precarious connections between the real world and systems of representation were aggravated by the introduction and proliferation of digital imaging technologies. The popularity of Errol Morris's *The Thin Blue Line* (1988) revived once scorned strategies of recreation and simulation in historical documentaries. Soon after the Rodney King verdict put the final nail in the coffin of visual positivism, the ontological status of images as historical evidence reached an all-time low, and a renewed critical attention to ideas such as "performativity" necessitated a revision of Bill Nichols's venerable taxonomy of documentary modes.[19] With increasing access to personal computers and the Internet, databases and digital archives emerged as the primary means of storing, organizing, and disseminating historical information. The logic of the search engine, with its enabling of nonlinear and nonteleological narratives, began motivating more varied kinds of historical storytelling, resulting in a profusion of counternarratives, fantastic histories with multiple or uncertain endings, and alternative histories constructed from the point of view of traditionally disenfranchised or voiceless peoples. However, even the most hyperbolic of these works, such as the Recombinant History Project's artificial intelligence apparatus, *Terminal Time,* which generates infinitely customizable historical documentaries, rarely sought to undermine the grounds of historical understanding. Even in the midst of a culture of paranoia, the desire for coherent, historical narratives that rationalize the present remains powerfully seductive.

In popular culture, postmodernism's predilection for perpetual presentness resulted in well-known sublimations of the persistent desire for history into endless varieties of kitsch, pastiche, and nostalgia. However, new modes of cinematic historiography emerged most actively from the other end of the high/low culture divide. In his 1984 article, "An Avant-Garde for the 80s," Paul Willemen described the goal of the avant-garde in the 1980s as (paraphrasing Godard) "cinema which doesn't just ask the questions of cinema historically, but asks the questions of history cinematically."[20] A few years later, Paul Arthur concurred, noting that, since the 1970s, the American avant-garde had been "increasingly infused with a historicizing energy" that represented a break with the previous thirty years of deliberate and insistent ahistoricism.[21] Both Willemen and Arthur viewed this "turn to history" in conjunction with a revitalized sense of political relevance in avant-garde filmmaking. Nearly two decades later, the revision and politicization of history and memory remain frequent obsessions among experimental filmmakers. The most interesting of these undertake an interrogation not only of the strategies of authentication deployed by documentary filmmaking, but the material and epistemological premises of history itself. The latter part of this essay investigates the range of possibilities that have come under investigation in the sphere of experimental documentary filmmaking, and looks in depth at an example of a "fake" historical documentary, Jesse Lerner's *Ruins*.

▶
_____

The Real in the Fake: Jesse Lerner's *Ruins*

It is a truism of postmodern culture that the difference between truth and fiction is not what it used to be. But in Jesse Lerner's *Ruins*, this is more than an empty slogan: it's a point of departure. *Ruins* is a self-proclaimed "fake documentary" that exposes the persistence of colonialist ideology in prehispanic histories of Mexico and calls into question the processes by which the disciplines of archaeology and art history are constituted. In *Ruins*, Lerner is as much concerned with historiography—the processes of writing history—as with history itself. The film mobilizes a multiplicity of historiographical and documentary strategies, ranging from archival footage compilation and hidden camera interviews to cutout animation and fictional recreation. *Ruins* puts forward a scathing revelation of the racist and colonialist underpinnings of ancient Mesoamerican historiography and offers in its place an enlightened critique and alternate vision of the region's past. The film succeeds brilliantly in snatching Mexican history from the jaws of colonialist discourse, while simultaneously interrogating the conventions of authenticity and authority in the historical documentary.

    Ruins is constructed in three movements. The first poses the basic questions of Mesoamerican historiography, debunking both the colonialist naiveté of nineteenth-century accounts and the arrogance of the "definitive" archaeological histories written in the 1920s and 1930s. The second part of the film illustrates what is at stake in the history of this region, and the ongoing instrumentalization of Mexican history in the interests of growing U.S. internationalism during World War II, followed by tourism and other corporate incarnations of Manifest Destiny. The final movement consists of a sustained meditation on questions of originality, authenticity, and competing discourses of art and culture, as refracted through the practice of forgery. The film's visual syntax is a blend of American avant-garde and essayistic documentary, combining strategies of found-footage collage with a handheld, home-movie vernacular. The structure of *Ruins* is fundamentally intertextual, referencing other historical texts as well as fiction films, advertisements, music, newsreels, and

Ruins (Jesse Lerner, 1999)

Hollywood feature films. Audiences must work to make meaning out of the diverse juxtapositions and layers of historical revision embedded in the film, a process that is consistent with the film's implicit critique of dramatic narrative historiography.

The opening sequence in *Ruins* presages the film's pedagogical intent. Title cards identify the setting as the Yucatan Peninsula in 1931, where Sylvanus G. Morley, a somewhat legendary figure in Maya archaeology, is teaching a Maya woman to speak English. The young woman, dressed in traditional Maya garb, stands in front of a pyramid and phonetically pronounces the words "We are dressed as our ancestors were, who lived here in peace and contentment seven hundred years ago." The scene ends with a somewhat awkward bow toward the camera, followed by another title card announcing the film to be a "Fake Documentary." The next shot is a pan from the ancient Maya pyramids of El Rey to the pyramid-shaped hotels of contemporary Cancún. This opening sequence functions as a metaphor for the historiographical strategies of the entire film. Past and present are dialogically imbricated in relations of space, time, language, and ideology. To truly understand the past, one must first grapple both with the desires of the present and with the awkward mechanisms through which historical discourse is rendered.

Following this preamble, a feature-film-style credit sequence introduces each of the film's major "characters," thereby announcing one of Lerner's guiding ambiguities—the fluidity of fact and fiction in terms of performance, evidence, and documentation. *Ruins'* "elaborate web of artifice" begins with a sequence of crude, cutout animations, accompanied by voice-over narration from several nineteenth-century histories of Mexico and Central America. The animations depict events for which no documentary record exists—the expropriation of ancient Mexican objects and their installation in North American and European art museums.[22] The animations are accompanied by inconclusive speculations on the origins of the Maya people (with theories ranging from the lost tribe of Israel to Vikings and Pygmies). These histories attempt to reconcile the reputed savagery of Maya rituals with the magnificence of this people's architectural and artistic accomplishments. A final voice-over admits that, in the absence of definitive evidence, all historians can rely on is "probabilities and conjectures"—while, on-screen, the pages of a history book are systematically shredded, another metaphoric rendering of the historical revision that will be enacted in the film.

Ruins borrows its overall rhetorical strategy from postcolonial theory to highlight the power relations implicit in the gaze of ethnographers and in the cultural narratives that are their stock in trade. The film implicitly argues that the act of viewing and theorizing "primitive" cultures cannot take place outside the paradigms of colonialist ideology. And the film argues that appropriating the past to render it in a coherent, linear narrative is equivalent to the cultural appropriation undertaken by the colonizer. By labeling the film a "fake," Lerner distances himself from the problematic histories of visual anthropology and ethnographic filmmaking. *Ruins* proceeds to mobilize discourses of documentary accuracy and historical authenticity along divergent trajectories, a destabilizing gesture that leads to a reflexive questioning of the filmmaker's own process. Interestingly, Lerner's disruption of the fact/fiction binary is only a temporary rhetorical strategy that allows him to distinguish his project from the outmoded pedantry of the racist predecessors seen in the film, while eventually coming around to articulate his own revision of the historical record. In spite of repeated proclamations that the film is a "fake," by the end of *Ruins,* a senile old history has essentially been replaced with a smarter, newer one. The difference is that *Ruins* functions as an open rather than a closed text—a text that suggests fissures and contradictions in its own argument and ultimately stretches beyond the critique of historiography to pose an indictment of tourism, colonialism, ethnography, and documentary itself.

Voices of Authenticity

The story told in *Ruins* is dispersed into a multiplicity of voices, some are linked to on-screen characters and texts while others are presented as disembodied fragments, quotations, recreations, and fakes. Lerner's role as filmmaker thus comes to resemble that of a ventriloquist rather than a unifying consciousness.[23] Indeed, Lerner speaks from a position of omniscience only in rare moments, through the voice of a female narrator who ruminates on the similarities between documentary and forgery, and occasional inter-titles that remind viewers they are watching a "fake documentary" made in 1999. In the latter half of the film, *Ruins* becomes increasingly idiosyncratic in the range of voices it presents, eventually quoting figures as disparate as Orson Welles, Margaret Mead, Rod Serling, and Allen Ginsberg. This panoply of voices metaphorically references an associative montage of historical consciousness and creates a web of textual connections and collisions. Lerner thus establishes a contract with the viewer that is based not on the belief that he is presenting reliable information, but on a tacit agreement to collectively investigate and draw meaning from a range of historical perspectives, images, artifacts, and documents.

The first and last sections of the film are anchored by contemporary interviews with two individuals representing opposite ends of the spectrum of historical authenticity. The first interview is with a woman named María Elena Pat, who is identified as an eyewitness to the mid-twentieth-century excavation of Maya cities by archaeologists Sylvanus G. Morley and Eric Thompson. Speaking to the camera, Pat refutes and ridicules the accepted histories of Maya culture, arguing that Morley and Thompson fundamentally misunderstood Maya language, culture, and politics. Pat speaks as a cultural insider but also as a well-informed critic of Morley and Thompson's outmoded research methods. Her monologue is intercut with archival footage of Morley and Thompson presenting their theories as well-established archaeological facts. In juxtaposition with Pat's critique, however, Morley and Thompson's once authoritative accounts appear preposterously speculative and transparently rooted in projections of their own cultural anxieties.

Interestingly, however, Pat's analysis is not simply presented as an unproblematic correction of the historical record. To undermine the authority of her (somewhat unlikely) testimony, Lerner positions Pat against a rear-projection screen on which appears a series of images by Laura Gilpin depicting scenes of Maya civilization. This strategy[24] lends a highly constructed, performative feel to the interview, suggesting that Pat's testimony may be as much of an artificial construct—a potential fake—as everything else in the film. This layering of discourses of authenticity and artifice underscores *Ruins'* operating premise that the past is accessible only through accumulated layers of historical sedimentation[25] and competing interpretation. Historical consciousness, as Walter Benjamin argued, does not move forward through "homogenous, empty time."[26] The nonlinear structure and contradictory discursive strategies of *Ruins* function as a metaphor for historical sedimentation and the need to sift through layers of evidence and interpretation to understand both the past and the construction of history.

In the latter part of the film, Lerner's interest in the relation between reality and artifice is most clearly embodied in the heroic, but ultimately tragic, figure of the forger. *Ruins* tells the story of an art forger named Brigído Lara who, in the 1960s and 1970s, reputedly created thousands of sculptures that came to define the art of the Totonac culture, a pre-Aztec society in Mexico's Gulf Coast region. Lara's forgeries were so convincing that many were sold to museums as ancient artifacts and Lara was arrested and temporarily jailed as a looter (rather than a forger) of antiquities. Many of Lara's pieces are now in New York's Metropolitan Museum of Art and other high-profile collections—an unintentional joke at the expense of connoisseurs of "primitive" art. In one remarkable sequence, Lara looks at images of his own work in a coffee table book called *Masterpieces of Primitive Art* and proudly presents some of his sculptures to the camera, caressing them lovingly while the narrator ruminates on the nature of forgeries. Are they "worthless embarrassments or treasured pieces of art?"

Unlike the clearly staged interview with Pat, Lara is shot vérité-style, on location in his studio and in the field as he meticulously seeks out exactly the right kind of clay, tools, and conditions for creating his sculptures. Lara tells the story of his life as a forger in an earnest voice-over, noting that, although his intention was not to deceive, his work has significantly shaped museums' definitions of authenticity. Lara is ultimately unapologetic about his role in the falsification of Totonac history, remarking simply, "It's their problem if they were fooled. I suppose it is a healthy experience." Like Lerner's film, Lara's forgeries transcend the presumed limitations of their inauthentic origins. What is under investigation is not simply questions of truth vs. fiction, but the institutions of authority and authenticity exemplified by the art museum and its self-perpetuating—sometimes self-serving—curatorial practices. Expanding beyond questions of historical value and authenticity, *Ruins* thus articulates a withering indictment of the art world's systems of authority and its claims to cultural relevance.

The latter part of *Ruins* also presents etymological exegeses of words such as "reproduction" and "replica," distinguishing them from "forgeries" by their relation to deception and their embeddedness in the power dynamics of cultural appropriation. The trade in replicas and reproductions (presented as an important part of the tourism industry in contemporary Mexico) operates through a tacit agreement between buyer and seller that the objects offer primarily symbolic or sentimental value. By contrast, the collecting of original artifacts by wealthy foreigners (including Nelson Rockefeller, whose private plane was reputedly so heavily laden with Maya sculptures that on one occasion it was unable to take off) constituted a clear gesture of economic and cultural exploitation. The irony that an unknown percentage of the artifacts collected under these circumstances were forgeries is not lost on Lerner, who positions this fact among other discourses of resistance and tactical response to U.S. cultural hegemony. In what appears to be a hidden-camera interview, a replica seller insightfully theorizes that U.S. residents are interested in the indigenous cultures of Mexico because the former are a nation of immigrants with no real history of their own. This fleetingly incisive moment of nonexpert analysis throws into relief the convolutions and pretenses of academicized history and its endless revisions.

In *Ruins*, the overt parallels between the art forger and the documentary filmmaker suggest that fiction and artifice may come closer to "staging the real" than to the faithful reproduction of documentary facts. The film argues implicitly that histories that are not subject to revision and debate are thereby drained of their dynamism and cultural relevance. More, static histories are removed from the arena of politics, where meaning is formed in relation to the needs of the present and desires to transform the future. The conception of historiography deployed in *Ruins* does not simply recover or preserve a factual history, but actively engages in the conflicts and uncertainty of the past. Historians should not understand themselves to be constrained by the impossibility of total historical preservation. Rather, *Ruins* demonstrates, they may be equally freed by this apparent shortcoming to construct a relationship with the past that is imperfect and improvisational, and to understand "history" as constituted through multiple voices and cascading layers of meaning.

It is axiomatic to this discussion that most commercial history films have asked too little of their audiences, presumed too little knowledge and sophistication, and offered too little in the way of insight and relevance about the past. Most Hollywood films, to put it bluntly, construct their audiences primarily as consumers—both in the obvious economic sense and ideologically—as the generators of predetermined emotional responses: receptacles and spectators rather than producers, actors, or agents of history. As films like *Ruins* show, the first step toward a more sophisticated conception of historiography lies not in reforming narrative cinema's historical epics or the unapologetic empiricism practiced on the History Channel. Those who care about the construction and dissemination of history on film should begin by articulating strategies of counter-reading for the histories most deeply embedded in contemporary society. And, perhaps most important, they must cultivate an awareness of long-marginalized experiments with historiographical form so as to come to recognize the potential for a politically engaged, postmodern historiography.

◆————————————————————————————

NOTES

1. See Robert Rosenstone, *Visions of the Past: The Challenge of Film to Our Idea of History* (Cambridge, Mass.: Harvard University Press, 1995).
2. See Hayden White, *Tropics of Discourse: Essays in Cultural Criticism* (Baltimore, Md.: Johns Hopkins University Press, 1978).
3. Of course, debates over the relationship between fact and fiction in historiography are much older than that. In Western universities, the discipline of history was not fully articulated until the early nineteenth century, concurrent with, and in response to, the rise of the historical novel. See Leo Braudy, *Narrative Form in History and Fiction: Hume, Fielding, and Gibbon* (Princeton, N.J.: Princeton University Press, 1970).
4. Rosenstone, *Visions of the Past*, 3.
5. White, *Tropics of Discourse*, 50.
6. Dominick LaCapra, *History and Criticism* (Ithaca, N.Y.: Cornell University Press, 1985), 34–35.
7. Robert Rosenstone, *Revisioning History: Film and the Construction of a New Past* (Princeton, N.J.: Princeton University Press, 1995), 11.
8. Although the unprecedented commercial success of *Roots* underscored the power of both historical fiction and televisual history, critical attention remained focused disproportionately on film, as opposed to television.
9. Pierre Sorlin, *The Film in History: Restaging the Past* (Ottowa: Barnes and Noble, 1980).
10. Marc Ferro, *Cinema and History* (Detroit: Wayne State University Press, 1988).
11. See, for example, Robert Brent Toplin, *History by Hollywood: The Use and Abuse of the American Past* (1996); Peter C. Rollins, *Hollywood as Historian: American Film in a Cultural Context* (1983); Rosenstone, *Visions of the Past*; George MacDonald Fraser, *The Hollywood History of the World: From "One Million Years B.C." to "Apocalypse Now"* (1988); Vivian Sobchack, *Persistence of His-*

tory: Cinema, Television, and the Modern Event (1996); Rosenstone, *Revisioning History*; Leger Grindon, *Shadows of the Past: Studies in the Historical Fiction Film* (1994); Mark Carnes, *Past Imperfect* (1995); Marcia Landy, *Cinematic Uses of the Past* (1996); Maria Wyke, *Projecting the Past* (1996); Michael Lynch and David Bogen, *The Spectacle of History* (1997); Marcia Landy, *The Historical Film: History and Memory in Media* (2001).
12. Rosenstone, *Revisioning History*.
13. Ibid., 3.
14. Ibid.
15. This is evidenced in the legacies of "history from below" and oral history movements of the 1960s and 1970s.
16. See, for example, Michael Bommes and Patrick Wright, "The Public and the Past," in *Making Histories*, ed. Richard Johnson et al. (London: Anchor, 1982).
17. See Marita Sturken, *Tangled Memories: The Vietnam War, the AIDS Epidemic, and the Politics of Remembering* (Berkeley and Los Angeles: University of California Press, 1997).
18. Francis Fukuyama, *The End of History and the Last Man* (New York: Avon, 1992), 44.
19. See Bill Nichols, *Blurred Boundaries: Questions of Meaning in Contemporary Culture* (Bloomington: Indiana University Press, 1994).
20. Paul Willemen, "An Avant-Garde for the 80s," *Frameworks* 24 (Spring 1982): 68.
21. Paul Arthur, "The Four Last Things," in *The End of Cinema as We Know It*, ed. Jon Lewis (New York: New York University Press, 2002), 342.
22. The "exhibition" depicted in the animation is loosely based on William Bullock's display of Aztec objects at the Egyptian Hall in London in 1824, a display that included a live Indian, a facsimile of the Codex Boturini, and a possibly fake stone serpent. For more background on this exhibition,

see Ian Graham's essay, "Three Early Collectors in Mesoamerica" in *Collecting the pre-Columbian Past*, ed. Elizabeth H. Boone (Washington: Dumbarton Oaks, 1993).

23. This authorial dispersion stands in contrast with comparable works such as Cheryl Dunye's *Watermelon Woman* (1997) and Marlon Fuentes's *Bontoc Eulogy* (1997), in both of which the filmmaker appears as an on-screen character and provides a focal point of the narrative.

24. This sequence is reminiscent of the rear-projection performance sequence in Straub and Huillet's *The Chronicle of Anna Magdalena Bach* (1969).

25. This idea of historical sedimentation is developed in George Lipsitz, *Time Passages: Collective Memory and American Popular Culture* (Minneapolis: University of Minnesota Press, 1990).

26. Walter Benjamin, "Theses on the Philosophy of History," in *Illuminations*, ed. Hannah Arendt (New York: Schocken, 1985).

II Double-Cross Cultural Filmmaking

LUIS BUÑUEL

[**6**] Land without Bread

*This essay was originally delivered by Luis Buñuel at a conference at
Columbia University, New York, 1941.*

Before you see the film which has been announced for this meeting, I should
like to tell you very briefly something about this district of Spain which you
are about to visit, especially about some aspects of it which do not appear in
the film.

When I made this film, my intention was to give the bare facts, not
to interpret them or to invent new ones. I was drawn to this place because
of its drama and awe-inspiring poetry. The little I had read of it had made
a deep impression on me. I knew that there, for centuries, human beings
had been struggling against a hostile land, where nature gave them no
hope of ever overcoming her. Travelers and geographers alike pronounced
this place as uninhabitable.

And yet the climate is gentle, the water plentiful, and vegetation there
is all around. But climate, water, vegetation, the earth itself seem to stifle
human life instead of encouraging it. There are bees, and they make honey,
but the honey is bitter. The water is pure, but its very purity is harmful, for
it is completely lacking in those mineral salts essential to health. In fact,
this water is a breeding ground for the terrible Anopheles mosquito, and all
the inhabitants of this district suffer from malaria.

You will want to know the name of this region—it is called Las Hurdes,
and it is in the west of Spain, very close to the Portuguese frontier.

Until very recently this district was completely cut off from the rest
of the world—separated by the huge labyrinth of hills which none but
climbers could penetrate. There was no means of getting in touch with
these mountain vastnesses, and even within the region itself communication was almost impossible between the different villages. And this is not

surprising; men make roads only when they want to get somewhere, and Las Hurdes does not lead anywhere. It is a lost land, far from all human succor. Not only is it unfriendly to man; it is opposed to all human traffic.

So cut off are these villages from one another that one of the inhabitants once told me that it was twenty years since he had seen his daughter, who was married to a man from the next village. This village was six miles away. But to get there meant a tramp of several hours through thick undergrowth and over sharp craggy paths, and this man simply could not spare the time. He needed all his strength, every moment of his time, for the hard daily toil on this ungrateful land, from which it was difficult to scratch his bread.

The majority of Spaniards knew nothing about Las Hurdes until 1922, when some publicity was given to it by the visit of the former King Alfonso XIII. It was said then that the existence of such a place was a disgrace to Spain. Personally, I do not agree. The problem of these people is so deep, so intangible, that action by a government could not get at the root of it. Our great Unamuno has said, perhaps paradoxically, that Las Hurdes is the glory rather than the disgrace of Spain. Is it not worthy of our admiration as well as our pity, that a handful of men are striving, and have striven, to eke out a livelihood toiling hour after hour, century after century, without ever giving up in their hopeless task? And even supposing that the existence of such a place were a disgrace to Spain, what of it? Let that country that has nothing to be ashamed of cast the first stone.

The first historical document proving the existence of Las Hurdes is a comedy by the prince of Spanish geniuses, Lope de Vega. He did not ever go there, but he had heard of it as a primitive, pastoral region. It is interesting that the discovery of this place by the Spaniards should coincide with the discovery of America—the everlasting paradox of the Spanish mind: it discovers at the same time the Lost Land of Las Hurdes and the Promised Land of America.

It is believed that it was at the beginning of the sixteenth century that this region was first inhabited. Jews, fleeing from persecution under Ferdinand and Isabella, sought refuge in this deserted country. As time went on, there were added to its numbers outlaws fleeing from justice. And in the ensuing years few people ever ventured into this savage place, where it was unbelievable that human life should exist at all.

There is no time in this brief introduction to tell you of the various additions to the inhabitants, which helped to put new blood in their veins, and which prevented their total degeneration. You will see something of this in the film itself. Both Spaniards and Frenchmen have studied the problem. But we must mention the most valuable of all the documents,

Land without Bread (Luis Buñuel, 1932)

which is also the most accurate one—it is the book written in [1927] by the French professor Maurice Legendre. For twenty years he went to this place every year to study it, and his book is remarkable for its objectification and accuracy. Professor Legendre says that Las Hurdes is unlike any other place in the world, for two reasons: its wretchedness and its tragedy.

We know that there are many groups of people in the world who live under wretched and precarious conditions: in the Atlas Mountains, in Chinese villages, in Hindu settlements. But usually, if the conditions become impossible—that is, permanently impossible—the population emigrates en masse to subsist in less desperate surroundings. Not so in Las Hurdes. If by chance one of them should leave, he returns almost at once. It is a living death to be there, yet it is a living death too until they can get back again. I have met some who can talk French. They had worked in France as laborers, but as soon as they got together enough money, they hastened home again. I have even met one who had been to America.

Usually, people who are permanently in want emigrate all together, or slowly disperse, leaving the village empty and deserted. It is the opposite in Las Hurdes. The population does not disperse, in fact it has greatly increased, and at present the district is overpeopled. How is it possible to explain so unexpected a phenomenon?

And so, it is not wretchedness which makes Las Hurdes unique in human society, but the fact that this wretchedness is permanent. It is not the tragedy, but the fact that the tragedy has no end.

There are a number of strange ideas about Las Hurdes. The most persistent is that the people are savages. Nothing could be further from the truth. If these people are unlike *anyone,* they are unlike savage tribes. Among savages, life is not nearly so hard. Man has only to reach out his hand to gather the fruits of nature. There is no spiritual conflict between the savage and his circumstances. A primitive civilization has a primitive culture. But in Las Hurdes a primitive civilization goes with a modern culture. These people have the same moral and religious principles as we have. They speak our language. They have the same needs as we have. But in their case the means for satisfying those needs are hardly better than those of the caveman.

I do not know whether there is any human society which has fewer utensils than these people. Though they live in an age of such frighteningly complicated mechanization, their tools are scanty and primitive. In the upper region, there are no ploughs, no beasts of burden, no firearms, no steel weapons at all. There are hardly any domesticated animals; for example, there are no dogs and cats. You will see in the film what sort of animals do exist there. There is nothing on wheels. There are no jars, no bottles, no forks. I could go on with the list indefinitely.

So you can imagine my surprise when one day I discovered that in one of the villages there was a sewing machine—an out-of-date model, very rusty, but a real Singer.

The few utensils which are seen have been brought in from Castile or Extremadura by some who went off begging in those regions. In the district of Las Hurdes, nothing is made. There is no skilled labor. I once met a man who said he was a baker, but he had had to give up long ago because he had no dough to make into bread. This is the secret of their great poverty: the soil produces only briars and brambles—hence they have no means of procuring raw materials, and in consequence there is no craftsmanship.

What do they wear? Much the same thing as we do. The men wear jacket and trousers, the women bodice and skirt. But so patched and darned that you can hardly see the original cloth. I once counted seventy-two different places where one garment had been mended.

Another point hard to believe is that there is no folklore. The whole time that we were there, we never heard one song. The men are silent at their work, and have no songs to make their task a little lighter. But even their silence is different. It is not the silence of death but the silence of life. This is not so poetic, perhaps, but it is much more awe-inspiring.

Nor did we see drawings on rock or wall. Yet, just where this district begins, in Las Batuecas, there is one of the finest examples of cave-drawing in existence. In other words, thousands of years ago this place was the heart of human culture, and now the men who live there know nothing of artistic expression.

The character of these people is very gentle. When they talk, they lament their misfortunes, their slavery to this cruel land. Their customs are simple. Their grim daily toil makes any relationship impossible unless it serves some useful purpose. There is no gaiety, no joyful recreation. Because of the smallness of their dwellings, a whole family is obliged to live in a single room. There is no doubt that this leads to incest, of which some cases do exist. This is perhaps the only moral defect of which they can be accused; and we might say with St. Thomas, "To be virtuous it is necessary to have a minimum of material well-being." And in Las Hurdes even this minimum is lacking. Many suggestions have been made for the solving of this crying social problem. We cannot go into these now. All that we can say is that, although some have been tried, none has proved effective. Perhaps the only solution is the one which an old woman suggested one day when we met her on an indescribable path. When she saw us, she put down her bundle of wood and came to us. "You are engineers," she said, "and you are coming to improve our poor lot. Well, I can tell you there is no cure. If you want to rescue us from this hell, take us out of here by force. We cannot leave here now of our own free will."

And she is right. To solve their problem, we should have to drag them away by force, send them out into other parts of Spain, and destroy completely their wretched homes.

Professor Legendre supports the opinion of the old woman when he says "Las Hurdes is what it is because of its isolation. It may be that by drawing people back into the world by making roads for them, it will gradually cease to be." Yet a road has been made, and these people have not flocked out along it. They are still there to confound the philosophers and the sociologists.

If Las Hurdes is unique in human society, because of its extent and the number of its inhabitants, there are nevertheless other parts of Europe where similar conditions of life exist—in France, in Italy, in Czechoslovakia. But these are isolated cases which up to the present have not roused the interest of men of science. Besides, they are gradually disappearing. In the French Alps, for example, in Savoy, about twenty years ago there were two villages of this type. Today there is only one of them left, and it will probably disappear very soon. And this one, like Las Hurdes, is cut off from human contact, and for six months in the year it is entirely inaccessible owing to the heavy snows. The inhabitants make bread only once a year, and this, with a few vegetables and some starchy foods, is their principal diet. Almost all the inhabitants of the French village are dwarfs or cretins, and if by chance one of them should develop normally in body and mind, he soon leaves the village. In this respect, it is already different from Las Hurdes.

As we have seen, one of the things which is unknown in Las Hurdes is idleness. In the village of French Savoy, however, there is a terrible period during the winter when the whole population is idle for six months, unable to leave their wretched hovels. Under such circumstances, relationships within the same family are common.

In Czechoslovakia and Italy, it appears, there are also examples of similar conditions. But my information about them is very scanty because there is scarcely anything scientific written on the subject. I have never seen these places. I had hoped to accompany the psychiatrist Dr. Lacan, of the hospital of St. Anne in Paris, on an expedition to these scenes of retarded civilization still existing in Europe, but my professional duties and the political situation completely ruined our plans. But I still hope it may be possible to go some day.

I should like to end this introduction by recalling those friends who worked so unselfishly to produce this film with me. Our work was the fruit of love for this unhappy country. I had been able to find public and private support for my other films, but for this one I could not find anything like enough. In Europe, there are hardly any of those cultural groups or patrons of art which in America are willing to finance educational films. It was a humble Spanish worker, Ramon Acín, who made it possible for me to make this film: he gave me all his savings—a thousand dollars, which is all the film cost.

By one of those strange tricks which the Censorship plays, a few incidents were suppressed by the French authorities, particularly in the first reel; so you are about to see it in a slightly reduced form. In the first reel there are two details I wish to correct. They were actually corrected in the second version, which was shown in several European countries, but by mistake [they] sent me a copy of the earlier one. These mistakes are, first, in one of the captions: it says that the film was made under the First Spanish Republic; it should be, of course, under the Second Spanish Republic. Apart from a few sound errors, there is only one more correction to make; in Europe the film was not known by the title given here, *Unpromised Land*; it was called *Land without Bread*.

As we had so little money, we had to adjust the technique of the film to the possibilities of my budget.

We possessed two old cameras lent by a friend who was an amateur film enthusiast in Paris: an old Éclair camera with a crank-handle, and an old Eyemo made when they didn't yet have a turret for installing different lenses. This apparatus had a defect; when you started shooting there was a sudden jolt which can still be seen in some shots.

The problem of unused film stock was also delicate, because we had brought almost exactly the footage that the film would come to. So, after studying the area for three days, we decided to shoot only scenes that corresponded to a previously prepared synopsis. In a documentary, generally you take not only the shots in the screenplay drawn up beforehand but also odd shots that crop up by chance and that may be useful for inserting into the film afterwards. I didn't do anything like that. I divided the script into various sections—for example, what the Hurdanos ate, school, making fields for cultivation, burials, etc. And every day I carried on with completing those sequences.

The work was extremely hard as a result of the lack of mechanical resources and adequate staff. During the month and a half that we were there, we got up at about four in the morning and reached the locations that we had chosen previously at close on midday. We worked until three in the afternoon, when we had to start the journey back to Las Batuevas, where we were staying. We prepared only one meal a day, when we got back from work, and we devoured it like lions. Physical exercise and the morbid desire to eat because we were in the land where people did not eat contributed to this. During the first few days, we tried to have lunch at the place where we were working, but everyone came out to watch us eat. They stared at us eagerly, and the children dashed forward to pick up the peelings of salami or scraps of bread that we let fall. So we decided not to eat while we were working.

All the shots that you see in the film had to be paid for. Our budget was slender, but fortunately it was sufficient for the meager demands of those poor people. The population of Martilandrán, one of the poorest villages, placed themselves at our disposition in return for a couple of goats that we got them to kill and cook, and twenty large loaves of bread, which the people ate all together, with the meal directed by the mayor, who was possibly the most famished of them all.

Once we found a boy herding some goats and asked him to walk in front of the camera again. He looked at us with what seemed like fright. So I put my hand in my pocket and showed him a peseta, a small silver Spanish coin equivalent to a dime. The boy looked at it suspiciously. In my hand I also had some copper coins and he eyed them enviously. As an experiment, I offered him one that was worth a cent. He snatched it from my hands and immediately allowed himself to be photographed with the goats.

The only lesson that I think can be drawn from this picture is that, although sufficient money is one of the most important conditions to make a film, the film can be made just the same when one loves the work.

CATHERINE RUSSELL

[**7**] *Surrealist Ethnography:* Las Hurdes *and the Documentary Unconscious*

Evidently a different nature opens itself to the camera than
opens to the naked eye—if only because an unconsciously
penetrated space is substituted for a space consciously
explored by man.
:: Walter Benjamin

Luis Buñuel's 1932 film *Las Hurdes* (a.k.a. *Tierra sin pan*) may be the
only actual example of a surrealist documentary film, and its experimen-
tation provides an important example for understanding more contemporary play with documentary representation. The very possibility of documentary veracity is put in question by Buñuel, partly by working within
the terms of ethnography and challenging its humanist conventions, and
partly by pushing an aesthetic of realism into the realm of the absurd.
Produced within the modernist context of interwar Europe, Buñuel's
film coldly calculates the cruelties of history, delimiting the realm of the
European ethnic repressed.

For James Clifford, ethnography and surrealism are two faces of a
modernist fascination with the familiar and the strange, the exotic and
the banal. When they are brought together, ethnography and surrealism
provide important strategies for overcoming the universalizing tendencies of anthropological humanism. Clifford argues that "an ethnographic
surrealist practice . . . attacks the familiar, provoking the irruption of
otherness—the unexpected."[1] Analysis of *Las Hurdes* should further suggest how this defamiliarization in the cinema implies an unsettling of the
truth claims of documentary representation.

The conjunction of ethnography and surrealism can be traced to the
journal *Documents,* edited by Georges Bataille, of which seventeen issues
were published from 1929 to 1930. Its contributors included anthropologists,

surrealists, former surrealists, and future anthropologists. Its title, and one of its main objectives, was the promotion of an anti-aesthetic mode of representation, which meant, in part, an attraction to the grotesque and the "dirty," and equally to the collection and description of objects and practices that resisted the marketplace logic of use and exchange value. Stripped of "beauty" and "good taste," the journal challenged bourgeois humanist norms of art and museology. As Denis Hollier explains, "The official ideological contract was an aesthetic of the irretrievable."[2] The collusion of ethnologists and artists was not without friction, but *Documents* was in all respects grounded in "an aggressive realism." The status of the document was the nemesis of poetic metaphor: "Photography takes the place of the dream." Objets trouvés, appropriated and recontextualized, like the related Duchampian ready-made, were the aesthetic predecessors of found footage. But the dream is never completely banished, nor is the dream-work, when the accumulation of cultural detritus is reassembled into a phantasmagoria. "Heterogeneous and foreign, [the document] has an impact, it shocks (it has shock-value) as a trauma would."[3]

Documents included written texts, some as short as a paragraph, photographs, and so-called dictionary definitions. Its technique of juxtaposition, creating ironic effects of cultural collision, brought together the "high" and the "low," the familiar (European) and the strange (mainly African). The journal included film reviews—of *Hallelujah* ("a hallucinating realism")[4] and *Fox Movietone Follies* ("not the slightest hint of an aesthetic in this spectacle")[5]—that placed popular cinema side by side with Picasso and African musical instruments. Europe was perceived as being as worthy of ethnographic study as were Africa and other distant colonial sites. Clifford describes *Documents* as a "subversive, nearly anarchic documentary attitude" that constituted "an epistemological horizon for twentieth-century cultural studies."[6] Its techniques of collage and juxtaposition, and its transgression of cultural purities, involved the recognition, on the one hand, that nothing was uncollectible, and, on the other, that the values implicit in classification and categorization were entirely arbitrary. In many ways, *Documents* is the originary moment of subversive cultural criticism.

Ethnographic surrealism was a short-lived moment, out of which ethnography, art, and surrealism "emerged as fully distinct positions."[7] And yet their blurring occurred at a moment of crucial historical conjunction when the avant-garde embraced everyday life and ethnography was reoriented toward cultural pluralism and hybridity. Alongside *Documents*, Walter Benjamin's cultural criticism of the period provides an intellectual context for Luis Buñuel's startling perspective on ethnographic representation.

An Antihumanist Documentary

In 1932 Luis Buñuel shot one of the most shocking ethnographic films ever made. Variously titled *Land without Bread, Unpromised Land,* and *Las Hurdes,* it is shocking because of its profound lack of sympathy. Images of the Hurdanos, a destitute population settled in a remote region of Spain, are accompanied by Brahms's Fourth Symphony and a voice-over commentary that is condescending, sarcastic, and brutally blunt. Although the film is well known, *Las Hurdes* does not fit well into any particular film-historical narrative, and tends to be marginalized in most accounts of Buñuel's oeuvre, as in most accounts of surrealist cinema, documentary cinema, and experimental cinema. In fact, the film refers back to thirty years of protodocumentary filmmaking, as well as forward to a subsequent history of collusion between the avant-garde and anthropology.

The *Documents* group represented a splinter group of the surrealist cadre, and Buñuel himself had an uneasy relationship to the surrealist project. James Lastra has situated Buñuel and *Las Hurdes* within the historical context of divisions within the surrealist movement, to conclude that his strategies of representation come closest to Bataille's heterology. Buñuel, says Lastra, develops "a form that respected the otherness of Hurdano life without recuperating it for reason, nationalism, or even humanism."[8] In 1931, the surrealists in France mounted an anticolonial exposition in France, deploying many of the tactics of the *Documents* journal. Neither project was, however, free of an orientalist tendency to idealize the Other as a site of alterity. Lastra argues that Buñuel aimed to counter this approach with a text that could not be recuperated in any way. "Buñuel's corrosive critique is of no use to the dominant culture. The Hurdanos do not become symbols of anything."[9]

Las Hurdes was originally screened in Madrid in 1933 with Buñuel delivering the narration "live" in the manner of a silent film lecturer.[10] *Las Hurdes* was first received by an extremely displeased audience, which of course was precisely the response Buñuel was aiming for. In the various versions of the extant film in English, the narration has been recorded slightly differently, and the version currently available on video has toned down what was originally described as a combination of "insolent indifference" and "apparent objectivity."[11] The newly recorded tone of voice adopts the conventional soft edges of contemporary documentary style, but by doing so has made it more difficult to read the film's ironies.[12] *Las Hurdes* is an extremely ambivalent and ambiguous film that has provoked at least one recent critic to move against the dominant critical grain, in an

article in *Third Text*: "I suggest that *Land without Bread* is distinctly colonialist in its reduction of a hinterland people to the status of freakshow
exhibits for the Parisian avant-garde and that this is because, rather than
in spite of, its ethnographic and surrealist character."[13] This reading is not
simply a response to the toned-down narration; it is a very literal interpretation that is certainly warranted by the film. Its exemplary status lies in
its blatant *in*correctness, its shocking transgressions of the humanist mode
of colonialist ethnography.

A necessary context for *Las Hurdes,* in addition to the surrealist one,
is that of the transition to sound that the cinema was completing in 1932.
Although neither music nor commentary were recorded on the film until
1937, it was essentially Buñuel's first sound film, and, as such, constitutes
a remarkable parody of the voice-over documentary that did not yet exist.
Buñuel may have been working within the conventions of the travelogue
lecture, but he delivered his original monologue from the projection booth
rather than from a podium.[14] Like most travelogues, the film is framed by
the arrival and departure of the narrator-adventurer-ethnographer, clearly
marking off the boundaries between here and there, us and them.[15] The
narrator's attitude of condescension and matter-of-fact description is very
much that of the tourist displaying the sights of his travels.

Like the illustrated lecture, Buñuel's voice-over is "impersonal" in
its lack of empathy with the Hurdano culture, and yet it is authorized by
the "person" of the traveler-ethnographer: s/he-who-has-been-there. The
narration furthermore adopts the first-person "we," referring perhaps to
the film crew, but invoking the familiar dualism of "us and them." In *Las
Hurdes,* the voice, perhaps for the first time, is disembodied. The voice-
of-God has not yet been officially born, so Buñuel invents Him, along
with His infinite powers of making meaning. It may be fair to say that
the film could not have been made much later than 1932, after which the
Griersonian voice-over became institutionalized as the preeminent documentary form. Even in the context of the silent film lecturer, the parody
was horrifying in its blatant use of discursive power.

Caught within the imperious, disembodied discourse of the narrator,
the bodies of the Hurdanos are furthermore photographed in a most sub-
missive manner. Not only are they objectified by the camera in their poses,
but Buñuel's montage makes no attempt to develop a realist, diegetic, narrative space. The ordering of quick-paced shots has been compared to a
slide show, which is indeed the precursor of the cinematic travelogue.[16]
What movement there is, in the pro-filmic, and of the camera, is minimal.
With very little depth of field, even the landscape shots appear cramped
in a very flat pictorial space. The effect is one of extreme fragmentation, a

series of glimpses of people, animals, landscape, and architecture, each shot subject to the narrator's cursory explanation.

Music, like spoken commentary, was an integral part of silent film; since 1927, sound tracks had begun to be physically attached to films, becoming an important component of the text. In *Las Hurdes* the role of music in the fixing of meaning and the production of knowledge is made evident through its failure. The function of Brahms' Fourth Symphony is to provide a radical juxtaposition of a classical, highly developed culture with the primitivism of the Hurdanos. The music's transcendent, triumphant, dramatic hyperbole is completely incongruous with the ethnographic imagery. Together with the commentary, this sound track may be one of the most successful instantiations of the famous 1928 Soviet manifesto in which the contrapuntal use of sound is advocated for avant-garde cinema.[17]

Buñuel uses the sound track as a "montage element" building the film on three separate discursive levels—music, image, and narration—fully exploiting the scope of the audiovisual medium. The power of the sound track, the impact of narration on the way images are read, and the effect of music on how they are "felt," is laid bare in *Las Hurdes*. Most critics and commentators on the film—and there have been many perceptive and articulate ones—agree that the film foregrounds and throws into relief some basic prejudices and conceits of anthropological cinema. As Vivian Sobchack says: "We can see neither as an Hurdano nor as the narrator—nor even as our once unselfconscious selves. Rather, we are led to question our own devious prejudices always ready to surface and distort the world in every glance. Even though we are doomed to failure, we are asked to strain and squint and peer through our own history, our own culture, to get a glimpse of some adorned and shadowy reality which can never be made clear and visible but which will forever lurk in our peripheral vision."[18]

As an exemplary instance of experimental ethnography, the film engages with numerous issues that go to the core of the politics of representation in anthropological cinema. In addition to the strategic use of the sound track, three further aspects of the film need to be identified: the (un)reliability of visible evidence, the discourse of primitivism, and the role of sacrifice and death.

▶

Unreliable Visible Evidence

The tension between voice and image in *Las Hurdes* plays a key role in undermining the potential role of film as visible evidence. For example, over a shot of a woman who looks about seventy, the narrator says, "this woman is thirty-two years old." Doubt immediately enters the contract between narrator and viewer, a doubt that spreads insidiously throughout the entire film. Can we believe anything he says? Can we believe that he could be deceiving us? And if he is telling the truth, of what use is truth to the woman or to the viewer? The doubt is compounded by sarcasm: the narrator says, over a shot of the interior of a village home where a few unidentified objects are tacked on the wall, "Note the efforts at interior decorating."

Despite its authority, the voice-over does not completely close down the meaning of the images. In a key sequence in a schoolroom, when the music has momentarily died away, our attention is drawn to an *infanta* on the wall. The narrator says, "What is this fair lady doing here?" These comments on representation break the more objective, matter-of-fact mode of address that dominates the film, puncturing the veneer of authority and inviting the viewer to participate intellectually.

The commentary on visible evidence in *Las Hurdes* is extended to a demonstration of ethnographic cinema as a scientific instrument. In one early sequence, a young girl is examined by a member of the film crew, as the narrator explains that she has a mysterious illness that afflicts many of the Hurdanos. A close-up of her open mouth underlines the role of the

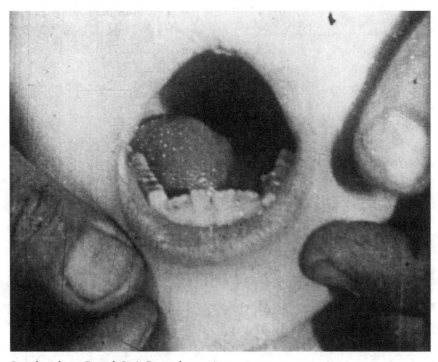

Land without Bread (Luis Buñuel, 1932)

camera as a tool of examination and penetration, a tool with the cool detachment of a medical instrument. The narrator says, after the cut to the next image, "We were told that the girl died two days later." At another point, illustrations from a scientific book on mosquitoes are inserted as the narrator explains that the Hurdanos suffer from malaria. The scientific drawings are followed by a man shaking (apparently) from the disease, so that the anthropological and entomological discourses are suddenly aligned. Malaria, like the anopheles mosquito, is "easily recognized," but not by the Hurdanos.

The alignment of visible evidence and scientific method is also their failure. The Hurdanos keep dying, in a persistent resistance not only to the interventions of science, but equally to the ethnographic impetus toward abstraction. The narrator's rhetoric consistently refers to individual Hurdanos as "typical" of the various social and medical disorders with which the film is obsessed—a common strategy of ethnographic film by which the individual social actor becomes an illustration of an ethnographic principle.[19] These people may be "typical," but they are contradictorily individuated by their deaths. The failure of the film is its failure of aesthetic redemption, compounded by the failure of scientific discourse, to save—or even help—the Hurdanos. In aligning these two failures, Buñuel also aligns the structures of visual culture with those of social science as discourses of power and subjugation.

Bill Nichols has suggested that the desire for knowledge that governs ethnography is a desire that parallels pornographic desire; both demand a certain diegetic coherence in the representation of the Other. The viewer needs to be able to fantasize his or her role in the spectacle as one of mastery,[20] so the codes of narrative cinema are often deployed for the creation of a closed diegetic space from which the viewer is categorically absent. *Las Hurdes* eschews any pretence of transparency, addressing the viewer directly as a voyeur for whom the Hurdanos are being presented as specimens. The great gap between the known and the knower, the viewed and the viewer, is the shock of *Las Hurdes*. Its greatest transgression is in its inhumane refusal to even try to close the gap, or to cover it up, and this is closely tied to the film's failure to create a closed diegetic space.

The disjunctive cutting of *Las Hurdes*, within scenes and between scenes, prevents any kind of spatial orientation for the viewer. Despite the premise of the entry and exploration of the Hurdanos' villages and environment, Buñuel has respected few conventions of continuity editing. In conjunction with the double-layered, contrapuntal sound track, the film might be described as an "open" modernist text. And yet this formal playfulness is inappropriate to its subject of lived poverty. Radically overstepping the boundaries of avant-garde "art," Buñuel has taken his art film strategies into the realm of social science. Thus, the subversive quality of *Las Hurdes* has everything to do with the expectations of "appropriateness."

▶

Primitivism, Regression, Repression

Las Hurdes has an equally "inappropriate" view of primitivism. The film's inversion of ethnographic conventions reveals the ideological and representational structures that are embodied in the myth of primitivism. Although the Hurdanos are very likely descendants of Jews fleeing the Spanish Inquisition, Buñuel makes no mention of their ethnicity.[21] The Hurdanos are not represented as victims of history, but as a regressive enclave, an exotic curiosity. The narrator's explanatory commentary implies an infinitely regressive cultural process, so that the Hurdanos come to represent an inverted modernism in which their relations with nature and government are increasingly devastating. Every cure, every attempt at bettering their lives, makes them worse. Death is the logical and inevitable outcome of every endeavor, and haunts the film as a recurring event with no redemptive power.

The rhetoric and diction of the narration is largely responsible for the sense of regressive social decay. For example, "Although the Spaniards are naturally given to song, never once did we hear anyone singing in these dreary streets." Or, over shots of children eating bread, "Until very recently, bread was unknown to the Hurdanos. The bread these children are eating was given to them at school. The master usually makes them eat it in front of him for fear that it will be taken from them by their half-starved parents." Over a two-shot of a man and a woman eating some berries, we are told: "May and June are the two hottest months of the year for the Hurdanos. By that time the stock of potatoes has long been exhausted. They have nothing to eat, nothing but these unripe cherries. If they wait till the cherries ripen, they will starve, so the Hurdanos have no choice but to eat them and so they suffer from chronic dysentery." Another passage concerning the search for food is illustrated by a series of images that move from observation to analysis to confrontation:

> Here at last are the precious strawberry trees [triumphant music, landscape], but their trials are not yet at an end, for this apparently harmless plant [a woman fills a sack held by a man] is the haunt of the deadly adder. The peasants are frequently bitten [frontal close-up of a man holding up his bandaged hand for the camera]. This is seldom fatal in itself, but [extreme close-up of the hand] the Hurdanos generally infect the wound by their unhygienic

efforts to cure it [close-up of man's face, glancing up at the camera and back at his hand].

In each of these examples, the mode of address uses the referential language of the lecturer's pointer: "these children," "these unripe cherries," "here at last." The man's glance in the last example plays a similar role, pointing to the hand proffered to the camera. Layers of discourse are the effect, layers in which the image is at once prior and inert. As a mode of primitivism, the regression is implicit in the cinematic medium: the logic of documentary realism pushes the referent back historically, precluding any possibility of "catching up." If ethnography and the cinema are two aspects of a single culture of colonial modernism, *Las Hurdes* deconstructs the logic of primitivism that has tied them together.

As an ideology, primitivism is a construction of Western modernism, arising in conjunction with an industrialized society that began to see itself in terms of a loss of innocence. Primitivism denotes a highly conflicted desire to retain a sense of the premodern without losing faith in the principles of "civilization." Other cultures become fetish objects that represent the childhood of humanity. Only in their infantilized form can these others be linked to the colonial form of "us," the human race. However, the myth of primitivism also has a utopian aspect, and represents a progressive impulse of modernism insofar as it challenges the norms of industrialized society. If postcolonial theory has focused on the ideological effects of primitivism, the avant-garde has been preoccupied with the latter, progressive, impulse.

In his 1941 lecture on the film, Buñuel noted that in *Las Hurdes* "a primitive civilization goes with a modern culture."[22] Buñuel may be understood as calling the bluff on the myth of primitivism by identifying the coexistence of disparate stages of development within contemporary Europe. But he does so precisely by invoking a documentary mode drastically ill-equipped to grasp the reality of these premodern inhabitants of modern Europe. The inadequacy of the cinema becomes especially clear in light of this lecture in which he describes the landscape and the people as "awe-inspiring." He admits to a deep admiration for the Hurdanos, an attitude that is far removed from the film itself. His surrealist approach to ethnography needs to be recognized as an antihumanist (perhaps even postmodern) critique of the colonialist tenets of anthropological cinema.

In *Las Hurdes*, Buñuel effectively deconstructs the two-sidedness of primitivism, foregrounding the "unhygienic conditions" of the Hurdanos as both symptom and cause of their misery. The only happy Hurdanos are the group of village idiots who stare down the camera in a brief challenge to the film's caustic and condescending gaze. Although this brief lapse into the irrational may be the film's most obvious nod to surrealism, Buñuel's strategies echo many of Bataille's in the pages of *Documents*. Denis Hollier describes the confluence of ethnography and surrealism as an uneasy alliance, in which topics such as "spitting" had different significance for different writers. For the ethnographers, "Dirtiness is proper to man, from which it follows that the less a thing is clean, the more human it is."[23] But the impoverished conditions of the Hurdanos embody a principle of excess that was especially significant for Bataille. As Hollier explains, "Everything must be said, yes, but on the condition that not everything can be said . . . The avant-garde has no use for the right to shock proffered by the ethnographers: where, if anyone takes offense, one simply shows one's permit. Ethnographer's license? But what would a sacrilege be within the limits of mere reason?"[24]

The ethnographic perspective of *Las Hurdes* defies reason, pushing its shock-value beyond the limits of humanism. Buñuel takes advantage of his "license" as a filmmaker, but he also maintains a strict separation between "reason" and "reality." The regression of the Hurdanos is unspeakable and unknowable except as a shock to the system of civilization. The sheer hopelessness of their situation situates the Hurdanos as not just stuck in the past like most "primitive" cultures, but an inversion of human progress. Their future of infinite decay and regression is the mirror image of modern progress, an inversion implicit in the contradictory myth of primitivism.

It is not incidental that the Hurdanos are a European people. The film exemplifies Trinh T. Minh-ha's observation that "there is a third world in every first world,"[25] and in 1932 this would have been an especially striking subversion of ethnographic otherness. The Hurdanos are an extreme instance of an impoverished peasant class hidden within industrialized Europe. Lastra has suggested that "the Hurdanos . . . play the same role in Buñuel's national body that the big toe plays in Bataille's physical one,"[26] referring to Bataille's essay "The Big Toe" about the challenge this "base" appendage poses to the integral body. Surrealist ethnography is a means of resisting cultural imperialism—the subsumption of all cultural differences within a standard of "the same." If the specific intervention of Las Hurdes pertained to the Spanish nation state, the film's formal innovations are equally significant to the ideology of humanism. As an anthropological method, humanism also embraces otherness as a means of transcending cultural difference—as Roland Barthes pointed out in his critique of "The Family of Man."[27] *Las Hurdes* proposes an otherness that cannot be recuperated.

Cultural difference is announced in the opening titles that evoke the "first contact" mystique of ethnographic purity along with the romance of survival that Flaherty had exploited ten years earlier with *Nanook of the North*: "The Hurdanos were unknown, even in Spain, until a road was built for the first time in 1922. Nowhere does man need to wage a more desperate fight against the hostile forces of nature . . . In light of this, the film may be considered as a study in 'human geography.'" This introduction is followed by a voice-over and a map of Europe indicating the so-called primitive communities (Tchecoslovaquie, Savoie, Italie, Espagne), which is then dissolved into a map of Spain with major cities marked, and then to a more local map of Las Hurdes and its surrounding towns. The narration posits the Hurdanos themselves as typical of an antithesis to "civilized" society: "In certain hidden and little-known parts of Europe, there still exist remnants of the most primitive type of human life. A typical example is to be found in Spain. Only sixty miles from Salamanque with its old university, famous for its literary and scientific traditions, live the Hurdanos. They are cut off from the rest of the world by a lofty range of mountains. To reach the Hurdanos we were forced to pass through the village of Alberca . . . "

By withholding the history of the Hurdanos and refusing to acknowledge their ethnic or cultural specificity, Buñuel assures that they are apprehended as an element of the Spanish national unconscious. Sure enough, it was Jacques Lacan with whom Buñuel had hoped to visit comparable regions in Europe.[28] If the imagery of the Hurdanos, gathered in glimpses, is a return of the repressed inequities within a manifestly democratic and ethnically coherent culture, the layering of discursive registers in *Las Hurdes* replicates the Freudian structure of consciousness. Where the Brahms represents the most systematic formal aesthetic language, the Hurdanos are depicted as grotesque and monstrous, manifestly without form. Bataille attacked architecture as a straitjacket that could only be escaped by way of a path "traced by the painters—toward bestial monstrosity."[29] And if the Hurdanos are being "used" in this avant-garde enterprise, they are not contained by it. As "an aesthetic of the irretrievable," *Las Hurdes* renders the cultural otherness of the Hurdanos as monstrous and therefore unrecuperable as either Jewishness or a victimization by history. These people are not the primitive Other, but the primitive within.[30]

▶ ───

The Discourse of Cruelty

At the heart of the film is a scene in which a goat falls to its death from a rocky cliff. The narration seems to precipitate the accident by saying, "Goat meat is only eaten when this happens": cut from a medium shot of a goat on the cliff, just when it is about to jump or slip, to a long shot in which the goat falls, striking the rocks on its way down, to a third shot of it falling past the camera and rolling down until finally it stops, already dead. In the second shot, a puff of smoke can be detected on the right side of the frame. The last shot is taken from a camera position located somewhere on the cliff itself. The scene is obviously set up—in terms of montage and narration, and even within the pro-filmic. Tom Conley has described this sequence as a "photographic ritual and an exemplary sacrifice."[31] The goat is, in effect, murdered for the film, in the same way as the rooster decapitated earlier in a village ritual (censored from most prints of the film).

The give-away puff of smoke betrays the documentary contract of authentic reality. As a spectacular sacrifice, this scene may evoke Bataille again, who identified sacrificial ritual as a transgression of the bourgeois sense of self.[32] The ritual sacrifice of animals has come to be a familiar trope of ethnographic film. Death plays a crucial role, both as narrative event and as indexical marker of cinematic truth, an irreversible sign of the once-only of documentary realism. The camera as witness of ritual sacrifice binds the filmmaker to "the field," and authenticates the realism with a historically specific event. However, it is difficult to see any redemptive power in this sacrifice in *Las Hurdes*. The film spectator is hardly the "collective," and, as Tom Conley notes, the Hurdanos are not represented anywhere in the film as a real mass or collective.[33] One could even argue that the cinema deadens the redemptive potential of any ritual sacrifice by making it infinitely repeatable. Death on film was an "obscenity" for Bazin because it reversed the irreversible.[34] By staging such a ritual sacrifice, Buñuel renders spectatorship a matter of witnessing without the erotic charge of the religious ritual, and identifies a particularly sadistic aspect of colonial culture.

In Lastra's reading of *Las Hurdes,* the killing of the goat has a further allegorical significance insofar as the film bears witness "to an exemplary moment of cultural scapegoating."[35] In the context of 1930s Europe, when neither Left nor Right offered clear ideological tactics, Buñuel's invocation of the scapegoat was bound to the contemporary discourses of anti-Semitism, as the European Jews were forced into such a role. The scapegoat served "to symbolically rid a community of an inner threat."[36] Although the Hurdanos are identified as Christians in the film, it is evident from his lecture that Buñuel was well acquainted with the history of the region and the legends of their ancestry. Given the (subsequent) fate of European Jews in the decade of *Las Hurdes'* production, Buñuel's statement concerning the only solution to the Hurdanos' fate is especially loaded. An old Hurdano woman, he says, proposed a plan of radical social engineering, "take us out of here by force."[37] The deadly scene of the mountain goat plunging to its death takes on yet another layer of tragic significance, as does the English title added in 1941, "Unpromised Land."[38]

The goat's death radically interrupts the film's pedantic discourse, challenging the documentary register of the contingent flow of everyday life. As a staged event, it splits apart the contract of authenticity, already weakened by the arbitrary, incredulous mismatching of voice-over and image track. However, Buñuel's comments on the production of the film can perhaps shed another light on this sacrificial scene: it is entirely possible that the slaughter also provided food for the Hurdanos. The film was made in a regime of scarcity, a context in which every goat counts. Buñuel says that he and his crew starved themselves each day rather than eat in front of the hungry Hurdanos; he also indicates that, given his own meagre resources, he did not waste precious film stock on random shots, but planned every single sequence carefully before shooting. If, in fact, two goats needed to be killed to produce the "reverse shot" from above of the animal crashing down the cliff, and if a "couple of goats" were killed to procure the participation of one of the poorest Hurdano villages, it is entirely possible that the dead animals served to underwrite the production costs of the film.[39]

Buñuel's comments nearly ten years after the film was released effectively draw the Hurdanos back into the spheres of humanism and cultural capitalism from which they are so radically excluded by the film. Even if he refrains from explaining his idiosyncratic strategies, Buñuel's comments confirm that the fundamental deceit at the heart of his "fake documentary" is his refusal to admit these people into a cultural economy in which they had no previous role. He might have provided them with a role, briefly, during the production of the film by paying them for their images, but by disallowing any trace of that offscreen exchange into the finished text, the harshness of these people's exclusion is doubly underlined.

▶

The Nightmare of History

The killing of the goat in *Las Hurdes* is a shock of the order of Walter Benjamin's dictum that "there is no document of civilization which is not at the same time a document of barbarism."[40] By 1940, when Benjamin had come to this conclusion, the progressive project of the surrealists had long since dissipated. Many of Benjamin's most important essays were written contemporaneously with the *Documents* journal and with *Las Hurdes*. He seems not to have commented directly on either of these enterprises, nor was he interested in the emerging field of ethnology. Yet his remarks on surrealism and on cinema are extremely pertinent.

Shock, for Benjamin, was a condition of modernity that needed to be mobilized by the avant-garde. Surrealism came close to realizing the potential of shock as an awakening from history, but Benjamin also criticized its nihilistic inability to "bind revolt to revolution."[41] *Las Hurdes* may ultimately fall to the same critique, and yet it exemplifies Benjamin's observation that the revolutionary potential of surrealism lies in its blasting open of the image sphere. In the aftermath of "such dialectical annihilation," he argued, "this will still be an image space and, more concretely, a body space."[42] Benjamin saw in surrealism a means of awakening a marxist materialism in danger of becoming a stale orthodoxy in 1929. His description of surrealism as "profane illumination" distinguishes its redemptive power from that of religion and grounds it in "a materialistic, anthropological inspiration."[43] Benjamin's own study of the Paris Arcades constitutes a form of surrealist ethnography, and was indeed inspired by the surrealist's collecting of urban phenomena. The textual strategies of *Las Hurdes* indicate the significance of the surrealist project to ethnography in the film's radical ambivalence and equivocation, its absolute refusal to accommodate the Hurdanos into any aesthetic or ideological system of thought. Buñuel's materialism consists of a rejection of humanist models and a reduction of cinematic representation to a collision of competing discursive voices.

Las Hurdes is shocking because its antihumanism allows no position from which to judge; there appears to be no ethical perspective within the film. There is no *we* with which the viewer can identify, no comfortable subject position. The film belongs to a very specific moment in history when the surrealists mobilized such social transgression for a politicized aesthetic practice, which Benjamin realized early on was really only a matter of playing with bourgeois codes of morality and changing the rules. As the only cinematic example of surrealist ethnography produced in this period, *Las Hurdes* goes beyond this play with decorum and pushes its transgressive practice onto a materialist plane. "The study in human geography" shows how the construction of cultural difference is a sadistic colonial practice. Its use of a modernist technique of fragmentation exploits the potential of the shock effect in a horrifying depiction of social decay. The imagery and references to death that haunt the film are inseparable from the uncanny familiarity of its structure. The exploitation of the Hurdano people resounds as the repressed memory of "civilization" surfacing in the form of a scientific object.

Buñuel's modernist techniques of fragmentation and textual discursiveness cut through any conception of lost aura. His irony is Benjamin's allegory, insofar as the authenticity of the Hurdanos, sealed only by their deaths, is inaccessible to the medium of cinema. The Hurdanos are surrounded by references to Christianity that are traces of a luxury unavailable to them, mere spiritual commodities in Buñuel's treatment. Neither ritual value nor cult value can be attached to the images of these people; the failure of such aesthetics is only underlined by the killing of the goat. Phenomenological perception and its corollary of "exhibition value" are both cause and symptom of the horrors of *Las Hurdes*.

Hal Foster claims that "the political in surrealism lies less in its stormy party affiliations and isolated anarchistic gestures than in its uncanny ability to oppose to modern rationalization its other face."[44] Foster may be referring to industrial mechanization, and yet "modern rationalization" is equally characteristic of colonialism and its techniques of domestication and assimilation. If, moreover, "the usual definition of the Surrealist image as a coupling of different elements in space can be read in terms of a working over of different memories and/or fantasies in time, a working over of trauma,"[45] surrealist ethnography proceeds by the juxtaposition of radically different realities.

The benevolence of humanism is ultimately a condescension toward the Other,[46] and it is this convention of anthropology that is challenged in *Las Hurdes*. Surrealist ethnography might therefore be a means of denoting the strategic roles of ambivalence, cruelty, *and* empathy in refiguring the ethnographic relationship in postcolonial culture. Buñuel evokes the dangers of the photographic image and its implicit historical structure, marking the deep divide between those "out there" in the real, and those who watch "in here," in the auditorium.

In his own surrealist-inspired text, *One Way Street* (1928), Benjamin compared the status of the document to that of the artwork in an aphorism, "Thirteen Theses against Snobs." Where the artist makes a work, he says, "The document's innocence gives it cover." On the side of the document, he locates the primitive, public education and the "dispersal of forms." In the document, "subject matter is the outcome of dreams . . . The more one loses oneself in a document, the denser the subject matter grows."[47] Buñuel's contribution to the "fake documentary" lies precisely here, in his understanding of the filmic document as having the primary status of the dream state awaiting secondary revision. His crude manipulation of the image takes the form of the artwork, as Benjamin describes it: "The artist sets out to conquer meaning . . . The masculinity of works lies in assault."[48]

For both Benjamin and Buñuel, the document offered a way out of the bourgeois artform, and a way back to the public sphere. Neither was prepared to embrace the positivism of the document; instead they apprehended it as the raw, unfiltered material of the social unconscious: "the bare facts" free of interpretation, stripped down precisely through an aggressive assault of meaning. In this respect, *Las Hurdes* lays the groundwork for Resnais' *Night and Fog* (1955), a film in which the trauma of the Holocaust challenges our ability to apprehend the filmic document as a record of civilization. The astonishing thing about Buñuel's Hurdanos is that they are not retrieved from an archive, nor are they relegated to memory. They retain a certain presence despite everything that is thrown at them, most especially the rhetoric of humanist anthropology.

◆ ————————————————————————————————

NOTES

1. James Clifford, *The Predicament of Culture: Twentieth Century Ethnography, Literature, and Art* (Cambridge, Mass: Harvard University Press, 1988), 145.
2. Denis Hollier, "The Use-Value of the Impossible," trans. Liesl Ollman, *October* 60 (Spring 1992): 21.
3. Ibid.
4. George Ribemont-Dessaignes, *"Hallelujah,"* trans. Dominic Faccini, reprinted in *October* 60 (Spring 1992): 47–48.
5. Michael Leiris, "Fox Movietone Follies of 1929," trans. Dominic Faccini, reprinted in *October* 60 (Spring 1992): 43–46.
6. Clifford, *Predicament of Culture*, 134.
7. Ibid.
8. James F. Lastra, "Why Is This Absurd Picture Here? Ethnology/Heterology/Buñuel," in *Rites of Realism: Essays on Corporeal Cinema*, ed. Ivone Margulies (Durham, N.C.: Duke University Press, 2002) 196.
9. Ibid.
10. Francisco Aranda, *Luis Buñuel: A Critical Biography*, trans. David Robinson (London: Secker and Warburg, 1975) 93. Buñuel had thoroughly researched his subject, and the film and his narration are partially inspired by a 1926 study by Maurice Legendre (see Aranda, *Luis Buñuel*, 89), and by a 1922 travel essay by Miguel Unamuno. According to Lastra, these two writers attempted to rehabilitate the *Hurdanos* as Spanish citizens in response to earlier accounts of them as savages (Lastra, 34). Buñuel rejects these authors' romanticization but adopts their self-serving anthropological voice.
11. Aranda, *Luis Buñuel*, 93.
12. The version of the film that my analysis is based on is released by Interama Video Classics (New York). The English narration is credited to Pierre Unik. Although other versions are still in circulation, a detailed comparison is beyond the scope of this paper.
13. Nicholas Thomas, "Colonial Surrealism: Luis Buñuel's *Land without Bread*," *Third Text* 26 (Spring 1994): 26.
14. E. Rubinstein, "Visit to a Familiar Planet: Buñuel among the Hurdanos," *Cinema Journal* 22, no. 4 (Summer 1983): 8.
15. Nichols describes these conventions of ethnography in *Blurred Boundaries: Questions of Meaning in Contemporary Culture* (Bloomington: Indiana University Press, 1994), 67.
16. Rubenstein, "A Familiar Planet," 9.
17. "A Statement on the Sound Film," by Eisenstein, Pudovkin, and Alexandrov, in *Film Form*, ed. and trans. Jay Leyda (New York: Harcourt Brace & World, Inc., 1949), 257–60.
18. Vivian Sobchack, "Synthetic Vision: The Dialectical Imperative of Buñuel's *Las Hurdes*," *Millennium Film Journal* 7/8/9 (1980–1981), 149–50.
19. Bill Nichols, *Ideology and the Image: Social Representation in the Cinema and Other Media* (Bloomington: Indiana University Press, 1981), 238.
20. Bill Nichols, *Representing Reality: Issues and Concepts in Documentary* (Bloomington: Indiana University Press, 1991), 218.
21. Rubenstein, "A Familiar Planet," 5.
22. Luis Buñuel, "Land without Bread," conference talk given by Buñuel at Columbia University, New York, 1941. Reprinted in the present volume as chapter 6.
23. Hollier, "Use-Value of the Impossible," 19.
24. Ibid.
25. Trinh T. Minh-ha, *When the Moon Waxes Red: Representation, Gender, and Cultural Politics* (New York: Routledge, 1991), 148.
26. Lastra, "This Absurd Picture," 194.
27. Roland Barthes, "The Great Family of Man," in *Mythologies*, trans. Annette Lavers (London: Paladin, 1973), 100–102.

28. Buñuel, conference talk.
29. Georges Bataille, "Architecture," entry in "Critical Dictionary," *Documents* 1, no. 2 (May 1929), trans. Dominic Faccini, repr. in *October* 60.
30. The film was banned in Spain and foreign embassies were instructed to keep it from being shown abroad because authorities felt it was injurious to Spain (Aranda, 90), an instruction indicating a level of guilty identification with Hurdanos as Spaniards.
31. Tom Conley, "Documentary Surrealism: On *Land without Bread*," in *Dada and Surrealist Film*, ed. Rudolf E. Kuenzli (New York: Willis Locker & Owens, 1987), 185.
32. Georges Bataille, *Erotism: Death and Sensuality*, trans. Mary Dalwood (San Francisco, Ca.: City Lights Books, 1986).
33. Conley, "Documentary Surrealism," 186.
34. André Bazin, "Mort tous les aprés-midis," in *Qu'est-ce que le cinema?* vol. 1, *Ontologie et langage* (Paris: Editions du cerf, 1969).
35. Lastra, "This Absurd Picture," 209.
36. Ibid.
37. Buñuel, conference talk.
38. Lastra, "This Absurd Picture," 210.
39. Buñuel, conference talk.
40. Walter Benjamin, "Theses on the Philosophy of History," in *Illuminations,* ed. Hannah Arendt, trans. Harry Zohn (New York: Schocken Books, 1969), 256.
41. Walter Benjamin, "Surrealism: The Last Snapshot of the European Intelligentsia" [1929], trans. Rodney Livingstone, in *Walter Benjamin, Selected Writings,* vol. 2, *1927–1934,* ed. Michael W. Jennings, Howard Eiland, and Gary Smith (Cambridge, Mass: Harvard University Press, 1999), 215.
42. Ibid., 217.
43. Ibid., 209.
44. Hal Foster, "Exquisite Corpses," in *Visualizing Theory: Selected Essays from V.A.R., 1990–1994,* ed. Lucien Taylor (New York: Routledge, 1994), 169.
45. Ibid., 159.
46. The best example of the condescending aspect of "humane" ethnology may be seen in the fundamental similarity between National Geographic documentaries about animals and people. See my *Experimental Ethnography* (Durham, N.C.: Duke University Press, 1999), 119–56, for a further discussion of the relation between animals and people in ethnographic representations.
47. Walter Benjamin, "One Way Street," trans. Edmund Jephcott, in *Selected Writings,* vol. 1, *1913–1926,* ed. Marcos Bullock and Michael W. Jennings (Cambridge, Mass: Harvard University Press, 1996), 459.
48. Ibid.

MARLON FUENTES

[8] *Extracts from an Imaginary Interview: Questions and Answers about* Bontoc Eulogy

Q: What was the impetus in making this film?

A: My work in photography was being generated by an increasingly narrative subtext, ideas about duration and the use of history and ritual and their artifacts. I was also fascinated by how certain bodies of knowledge and their representational strategies were codified into structures and surfaces that had their own intrinsic valences and ways of reception. For example, anthropology and, specifically, ethnographic film had historically contained epistemological assumptions about the Other. These are deeply embedded in a historical tradition that can be traced to the early eighteenth century. On a personal level, I wanted to locate myself within the historical narratives that define the Filipino in America. Art for me has always been an orienting device, and I thought that film was a good medium that could capture the process of passage through the membranes we navigate. It is only in retrospect that a lot of the events that happen to us make sense. In this context, narrativizing discrete yet incomplete fragments of our memories becomes a vital way of knowing where we fit in the grander scheme of things. Growing older necessitates looking back, if only to reassure oneself that the increasing velocity by which we experience the passage of time has some meaning. Film has the power to impose a sense of order, purpose, and interconnectedness onto this vortex of events.

Q: The film straddles fact and fiction, mixing imagination and interior dialogue with history. Why did you use this particular approach?

A: The technique of conveying the event that occurred utilized the fictional character of Markod, a young Bontoc warrior designated as the Narrator's grandfather. The name is borrowed from Bontoc lore; it is the name of the mythical narrator invoked at the end of an oral story transmission—"thus said Markod"—without which one is bound to be haunted in sleep. There were several Bontocs who died at the 1904 St. Louis World's Fair, and I envisioned the Markod character as a composite of the group, encapsulating their experience of the Fair. It was through Markod's eyes that the viewer saw the events that unfolded. More important, it was also through him that the events were interpreted. At times, the Narrator's voice and Markod's voice became interchangeable.

I wanted to make an *anti-illusionistic* piece, in the Brechtian sense of the word. I wanted the seams and sutures to show, and the process of the movie unfolding as a movie was a critical element. In a sense, the effect I wanted was synonymous to viewing an optical illusion, for example, the one with the profile of two human faces melding into contours of a vase, or, for example, the old woman/young woman picture. Depending on how long or intently you looked, the ground of the picture changed to reveal the other figure. In the film, the oscillation between the "fictionality" of the story (as clued in by liminal references or subtle sleights of hand) and the historical authenticity of what was transpiring, was a formal tension necessary to the theme: history as memory and vice versa. This oscillation was achieved by the juxtaposition of archival footage and photographs with the recreated footage of the children and the actor playing Markod. It was also complemented by references to early cinema, as in the jump cut that occurs in the scene of the rabbit being pulled out of the hat. This was fair warning to the viewer that here was, after all, a bungling Méliès incapable of tricking the audience. It was the incompetence that would lay bare the tricks of the trade, the porosity and unreliability of the cinematic language being used. These devices—i.e., the oscillation between implausibility and authenticity, the movement between past and present, using the children as narrative fulcrums of this temporal seesaw, the realistic foregrounding of the texture of the Narrator's voice—were all aspects I wanted the viewer to be aware of. Of course, in the absence of a familiarity with the references, the film could be read strictly as a realistic personal story about the events of the Fair. I crafted the film with the intention that it can present a straight historical story of what happened in 1904, regardless of the intertextual references embedded or the sophistication of the viewer. In a sense, the audience is really bimodal: the Filipino-American viewing the film for its historical and political interest, and the cineaste interested in strategies of ethnographic representation, early cinema, and formal/narrative issues relating to the documentary form.

Q: When you talk about an anti-illusionistic film, are you referring to a certain kind of realism?

A: In a sense, yes. The Hollywood model, in its classic form, aims for narrative totally driven by the dramatic world of the characters. The studios therefore simulate, by techniques such as invisible editing and a musical score that "is not heard," the world of the characters while simultaneously obliterating the presence of the narrator/filmmaker. Even early fake documentaries such as Jim McBride's *David Holzman's Diary* (1968) present a hermetic surface that is subservient to the portrayal of the character's world. The film's difference is that this time it uses the documentary (i.e., the personal diary), compared to traditional dramatic narrative, as a form to explore the story. Both examples are illusionistic in purpose. *Bontoc,* however, aims to engage the viewer with the process of story telling itself, by foregrounding the elements I have mentioned earlier. Bontoc's presentation is akin to an Indonesian shadow puppet performance *(wayang kulit),* where one can watch on either side of the screen. Watching the puppeteer's side shows the movements of the craftsperson concurrent with the unfolding narrative. In the film, the narrator's "search" and performance become part of the dramatic and thematic subtext of the story. The challenge was to be able to convey the story, while presenting the intentionality and the artifacts of cinematic effort, without losing the viewer. After all, the story still had to have the basic function of "historical" text. As an aside, materialist film has always struck me as the most realistic cinema one can make, because, after all, it is an exploration of the properties of the film. One of the most radical things one can accomplish is to direct the viewer toward the process of his/her perception at the very moment of perception. It is a special kind of mindfulness that the cinema is capable of facilitating.

Q: It is interesting that you did not pursue a Brechtian arc by diegetically revealing the fictional construct employed, i.e., providing a denouement (or frame) that overtly transforms the film into a formal orchestration of narrative deconstruction.

A: I seriously thought of that alternative, but in the end I opted for a solution that implicated the viewer more in the bidirectionality of the act of observing. Breaking the "ethnographic" surface by disclosing the fictional device within the film would have dissipated the emotional momentum generated by the historical gravity of the actual story. It could have been an aesthetically satisfying direction to take, but it could have trivialized and deflated the tragedy of the nine Filipinos who died during the exposition, and the hundreds who endured the ordeal.

Q: What about your choices of archival footage, such as the Edison re-creations? It seems that they add one more layer of tension to the narrative surface of the film.

A: The scenes representing the Philippine-American War—for example, the trench shots of "Filipinos" retreating from the advancing American soldiers—were obtained from the Library of Congress collection. They were, as you said, re-creations for Edison's Biograph Company. In the particular reel I mentioned, the Filipinos were played by African Americans. These are of course pieces of archival footage that are filmed simulations of the real thing, passed off as newsreel at the time the footage was shown. The "truth" really depends on who, or where, or when the information was shown, and for what purpose. Another good example in the film is the Battle of Manila Bay sequence. The boats were scale-sized models of the 1898 battle, and the model setup itself was exhibited in St. Louis. So the scene is 1904-vintage simulation (i.e., an authentic Fair artifact of an actual Fair event) of a recorded event. I cut in the actual newsreel footage of the ship's guns from the actual battle, so the perversity could be complete. I actually considered slowing the boat speeds to realistic speed, but I decided against it because the illusion of the boat model as real ships would then simply become seamless, thereby destroying the Brechtian scaffolding I was trying to create.

Q: Certain viewers, visual anthropologists, for example, have received *Bontoc Eulogy* as an ethnographic film. I have heard you and other critics refer to it as an autoethnographic film. Did you originally see the piece as having this specific reception?

A: I have a very keen interest in ethnographic filmmaking. It is a specialized genre that is a useful and dynamic way of communicating stories about the human situation. It is primarily observational in style (i.e., it communicates an authoritative claim in relation to its "objective" uninflected surface), and for that reason, it can be subject to a lot of politically derived criticism. Another reason this is so is because the choice of its subject has traditionally and historically been the Other.

As a filmmaker who wanted to explore history in a personal way, I found ethnographic film presented a stylized and codified syntax that in certain ways preempted content. I wanted to participate in the discourse of ethnographic representation by using and appropriating the idea of the "native filmmaker." This idea stems from an anthropological practice of handing over cameras to native peoples (as subjects of ethnographic research) as a way of capturing a unique insider perspective on the culture under study. More often than not, the assumption is that of a tabula rasa "recorder" of cultural facts. My case, of course, is a little different, but it is still a logical extension of the original idea.

Another reason for using the ethnographic form was actually based on logistics and availability of materials. My goal was to create a story from the bits of information I could unearth here in the United States, without going back to the Philippines. For many painful reasons that I shall not go into here, I was still not prepared to visit "back home." Thus I consciously confined myself to the materials available in archival sources such as the Library of Congress and the Smithsonian. Fortunately, some interesting "salvage footage" existed in these archives (These items are footage taken by nonanthropologists such as U. S. Army camerapersons, home moviemakers, etc.). I found this footage (much concerning the Cordillerans) extremely appropriate for what I had in mind.

I believe that history is really an art of memory. The gaps and ellipses are just as important as the materials we have in our hands. If they are missing for certain reasons, whether by accident or force of omission, perhaps these irregularities force us to reflect on the nature and origins of our own situation.

Q: So, in a sense, your film is about the display of the fragment. I would like to quote a section from B. Kirshenblatt-Gimblett's article "Objects of Ethnography" (1991), because I think it is particularly relevant:

> The artfulness of the ethnographic object is an art of excision, of detachment, an art of the excerpt. Where does the object begin and where does it end? . . . Perhaps we should speak not of the ethnographic object but of the ethnographic fragment. Like the ruin, the ethnographic fragment is informed by a poetics of detachment. Detachment refers not only to the physical act of producing fragments, but also to the detached attitude that makes that fragmentation and its appreciation possible. Lovers of ruins in seventeenth- and eighteenth-century England understood the distinctive pleasures afforded by architectural fragments, once enough time had passed for a detached attitude to form. Antiquarian John Aubrey valued the ruin as much as he did the earlier intact structure. Nor were the ruins left to accidental formation. Aesthetic principles guided the selective demolition of ruins and, where a ruin was lacking, the building of artificial ones. A history of the poetics of the fragment is yet to be written, for fragments are not simply a necessity of which we make a virtue, a vicissitude of history, or a

response to limitations on our ability to bring the world indoors. We make fragments.[1]

The article proceeds to make a distinction between *in situ* and *in context,* which are the two approaches to the display of the object.

A: These are terribly important distinctions because they can be applied to a wider context beyond the strictly museological implications of displaying the object.

Q: Metonymy and mimesis are the essential ideas behind the notion of *in situ.* Continuing Gimblett's line of argument:

> the object is a part that stands in a contiguous relation to an absent whole that may or may not be recreated. The art of the metonym is an art that accepts the inherently fragmentary nature of the object. Showing it in all its partiality enhances its aura of its 'realness.' The art of mimesis, whether in the form of period rooms, ethnographic villages, recreated environments, reenacted rituals, or photomurals, places objects (or replicas of them) in situ. In situ approaches to installation enlarge the ethnographic object by expanding its boundaries to include more of what was left behind, even if only in replica, after the object was excised from its physical, social, and cultural settings . . . In situ installations, no matter how mimetic, are not neutral . . . Representational conventions guide mimetic displays, despite the illusion of close fit, if not identity, between the representation and that which is represented . . . The notion of in context, which poses the interpretive problem of theoretical frame of reference, entails particular techniques of arrangement and explanation to convey ideas. In addition to labels and commentary, objects are also set in context by means of other objects, often in relation to a classification or schematic arrangement of some kind, based on typologies of form or proposed historical relationships. In context approaches . . . establish a theoretical frame of reference for the viewer, offer explanations, provide historical background, make comparisons, pose questions, and sometimes even extend to the circumstances of excavation, collection, and conservation of the objects on display. There are as many contexts for an object as there are interpretive strategies.[2]

The reason I have cited this discussion is that I thought that these perspectives were specifically relevant to the display that was the Philippine Village, as the subject of your film. It is obvious that, in the Philippine display, the approaches of *in situ* and *in context* were integrated: there was a "brick by brick" mimetic display, but there was also a direct mediation afforded by the anthropologists' presence. In fact the Anthropology Museum beside the Village offered an extensive frame of reference for the Fair-goer. Gimblett's observation throws useful light on the primary diegetic subject of the film, which is the Filipino display in 1904. But it seems to me that the Narrator himself (as a character in the story), and the filmmaker (meta-diegetically) implicate themselves in the process of "displaying" the fragment—albeit in a temporal, cinematic "installation," so to speak.

A: This is a subtle point, but it is actually central to the whole idea I mentioned earlier about the film serving as an autoethnographic project. Gimblett's display dichotomy can actually be used to frame the film as a personal reconstruction project. One can look at the "inert" salvage footage as being relocated *in situ* (temporally and spatially) into the film's domain/setting. And one can view the Narrator as the interpretive commentator facilitating an *in context* site, if you will. Looking at it this way is really interpreting ethnographic film as a logical extension of the living exhibit approaches that preceded it historically.

Q: In both instances—that is, in 1904 St. Louis and in the film itself—one can posit that the image of the Native is still utilized as a sign. Do you think this is problematic?

A: The problem really is not whether a particular signifier essentializes or totalizes (as becomes the nature of objects chosen to represent some thing or idea); rather it is the way the process of representation perpetuates whatever oppressive power relationships may exist. This is the acid test.

The ideas of power, conflict, and marginalization are inherently embedded in the ideas of display, whether that display takes the form of folk festivals, of rituals, or of ethnographic film. The operative goal, I think, may be two-pronged: illumination of and opposition against further suffering and dehumanization. The problem with market-induced manic pluralism is that it neutralizes everything in its path, to the point where we become passive anaesthetized receptors of difference and cultural marginalia, transformed apathetic digesting organisms waiting for the newest jolt to register to confirm our existence.

Q: Do you think that, like its cousin, scientific categorization, aestheticizing the ethnographic fragment co-opts it and robs it of its potential to "illuminate and oppose?"

A: Every activity is vested with its own motivation, regardless of whether the latter is conscious or unconscious. Categorical or taxonomic imperatives follow some master narrative, one way or the other. It is the nature of the grid. Likewise, specific aesthetic programs have corollary objectives, whether the distillation of the sublime or the baring forth of "what-is." I can only speak of art, because it is the practice I am engaged in. I think that there is actually a moral imperative that generates art practice, regardless of how it is manifested. This engagement has to exist in the maker to begin with; one simply makes the best of what one can do based on the degree, sophistication, and energy of one's moral commitment and position.

Q: The basic challenge of curation is the use of objects to illustrate an idea: to textualize objects, and objectify texts. If we were to view *Bontoc Eulogy* as an end product of curatorial activity—since, after all, it is an archaeology of sorts—how are we to read its underlying schema?

A: There are numerous interrelated thematic strands, and their respective visibility or materiality really depends on where the viewer is situated. The optimal viewer hopefully gets to digest most, if not all, of it. These thematics are entered into through their emotional doors. *Bontoc Eulogy* is not a theory film. Instead it is a film that deals with issues of race, difference, voyeurism, science as ideology, spectacle, memory, time—as the particularities of one's existence in the here and now.

Filmmaking is as much a question of problem solving as it is of artistic creation. And I don't mean just the logistics of narrativizing, but striking balance points (as you proceed on the story path) between, let's say, respectful cultural "preservation" and continued exotization of a group.

Q: Let's focus on the film in terms of its construction. I'd like you to talk more about the visual surface of the film, which blends archival footage with re-creations, and about the sound track, i.e., the voice-over and the music.

A: The primary source of the tribal footage was the Human Studies Film Archives at the Smithsonian. Jake Homiak was kind enough to lead me to the right sources, specifically the Hillman footage on the Northern Luzon tribes. It turned out that most of these were Cordilleran tribes. The Prints and Photographs Division of the Library of Congress was a main source of photographs, as was, of course, the National Archives. The only 1904 vintage film footage that I was able to recover consisted of the panoramic shots at the exposition grounds, the fairground shots, the gondolas, and the extended crowd and parade scenes. There were no shots of the native Filipinos at the Fair, except the sequence of marching and exercising Scouts. There is probably extant footage of the tribes, but I haven't found it. My research was done primarily in the Washington, D.C., area.

The present day re-creations, including the Narrator on the benches, Markod in the jungle environment: these were all taken in San Diego's Balboa Park. This was also the site of the Panama-California International Exposition of 1915–1916, incidentally.

Q: The scenes where the Narrator refers to visual memories of the homeland, in the beginning part of the film, were really not consistent with the approximate age of the character. They appear pre–World War II vintage.

A: It is interesting that you pointed out this inconsistency because not many people have noticed this, maybe because they didn't have a local knowledge of how Manila looked, or maybe because these scenes were consistent with their vision of what the Third World was supposed to look like—a frozen, romanticized version of provincial quaintness and repose. This temporal misallocation was part of the Brechtian pastiche I was using. It really emphasizes the Narrator's nostalgic longing for the homeland, tarnished with the patina of a long physical absence. In other words, his childhood there was so long ago that he had to physically raid the storehouse of memories to concretize its topography. The result was a corrupted vision, a floating fragment transmogrified by the passing decades, the reluctantly surviving images of stories passed down to him during his formative early years. By default, it represents the Narrator's unreliable memory of his dim lacunar landscape.

Q: Which brings up the topic of the Narrator's credibility . . .

A: The authorial voice of the Narrator clues the viewer into the potential fissures of the tale. This idea is introduced in the first sequence of the film, with the three successive shots of him listening to an ancient victrola, reminiscent of "his master's voice." This prologue suggests the possibility that the whole film, the whole story about to follow, is really a concoction of the character's imagination—a fleshing out of the sound artifacts he has heard. Right from the beginning, the possibility of a cinematic Piltdown is offered to the viewer. The tension created by the Narrator's credibility is a central one in the film. It is this very characteristic that becomes a trope for the fallibility and fragility of memory, and hence of history. The film has the initial aura of an omniscient narrator, which is quickly challenged by the "cracks" that follow as the story proceeds. It is probably the momentum of "wanting to believe," or perhaps more precisely "wanting to know what happens next," that propels the viewer onward.

Q: Or perhaps this occurs through the innate power of the historical images with intrinsic truth claims in their wake . . .

A: Absolutely. And it is the characteristic truth claim that after all is the subject of the film's deconstructive thrust. The re-creations, e.g. Enrico Obusan's Markod, served as the "fragments" that further "authenticated" the historical images, and vice versa. The children's performance, Markod's turntable display, were there to allow the viewer passage into the "historical" world of the Fair. They allowed the viewer a starting point in the oneiric re-creation, and prevented him/her from simply dismissing the visual world and surface of the film as an inert and petrified source of information. If you look at the whole narrative dynamics of the film as a membrane, often the viewer is caught in the membrane itself, bisected by it, with the left eye on one side (viewing the construction scaffolding) and the right eye on the other (absorbing the "content" of the text).

Q: A form of dichotic listening, so to speak . . .

A: Which is probably how the process of memory works. We are viewing the corruption of our recollections at the same time we are filtering, evaluating, and making note of what we think is important in the present. The problem is that conscious effort and intent only works to a certain extent. More often it is the preexisting gestalt of all our previous moments that really exerts the power to organize and select what we are going through.

Q: The archival patina of the film's hermetic visual surface seemed to extend to its sound as well. What processes were involved, particularly in the creation of the music and text?

A: The three basic elements of the film, the visuals, sound, and text, were organically, and precariously linked. My composer, Doug Quin, created the music simultaneous to my writing of the text. He did not have any preconceived notion (since I hadn't even done a first cut of the film) of how the piece was going to materialize. He saw the footage, I talked to him about my general intentions in terms of story, and that was that. We continued to talk about the formal, theoretical, and thematic issues that hovered around the film, but he never created a score in the traditional sense of the word. His work functioned as a sonic text for me, just as the archival images served as a visual text. When I wrote the Narrator's voice-over, the availability of images and sound (i.e., Quin's music) "dictated" what the Narrator had to say. I sort of threw everything into the subconscious pot, and let things emerge. I knew what I wanted, analytically, as an objective observer of the process, but I didn't know exactly how it was going to be accomplished, or how the three strands were going to be woven together. I immersed myself fully into the world of the Fair, reading newspaper accounts, first person descriptions of the event, essentially saturating myself with any and every arcana available about the exposition. This even included complete inventories (in one instance, even, in Tagalog) of the objects on display, down to the taxonomic categories. I began to recognize the faces from the collection of photographs I had copied, and even had a mental map of the Fair's physical layout.

It was at this point that I began to write the text that was to be the Narrator's lines, after I had become intimately familiar with the music and of course the footage. Structurally, I had a basic idea of what I wanted. I was making a rough visual outline with the Steenbeck, while wrestling with the form and content of the Narrator. I was also trying out certain recreations that I thought could serve as the shift points (e.g., the children's scenes) for the story.

There were four types of music I was working with. The first was the group of field recordings of actual Cordilleran music, primarily percussive pieces using indigenous instruments, recorded live in their respective locales. The second was a recording of live performances by the Ramon Obusan Dance troop musicians, interpretations of tribal/village music. The third type was Doug Quin's compositions, partially based on local music documented and transcribed by ethnomusicologists in the Philippines. Quin also created musical pieces that were interpretations of the intermingling between the tribal cultures and turn-of-the-century cultural and musical ideas as represented by Ives, Sousa, etc. Quin's personal work is very much influenced by the sounds of animals in their local habitat and the sonic structures found in nature (he is also a recordist of rare and disappearing species, and has worked in the Amazon and at the North and South Poles). So he was eminently suited for the project, and I was very lucky to work with him. The music that you hear in Markod's later escape to the "jungle" encapsulates the interior space of the character using, quite appropriately and authoritatively, sounds from a natural forest habitat. So the idea of the resurrection of the fragment, which we have earlier touched on, even has relevance to Quin's essentially musical archaeology.

The fourth type of sound I used is composed of the marching band (Sousa) music and 1904 (or earlier) vintage recordings, including the classic original recording of *Meet Me in St. Louis*.

Q: What about Markod's passages? The Narrator was translating for us what seemed like very old, degraded recorded audio. Was this in the Bontoc dialect? Was it an original archival recording?

A: The original source of Markod's voice-over is an English transcription of an interview conducted with a certain Chief Famoaley of Bontoc. This was dated 1906, two years after the Fair, at Coney Island in New York. You know, of course, that the Igorot contingent was so profitable and popular in St. Louis that the Fair authorities created a traveling road show that traveled across the United States in subsequent expositions and display venues.

From this document I selected certain passages that I thought were appropriate for the film. (Chief Famoaley was part of the original St. Louis group.) Afterward, these were retranslated (into old Bontoc) and read by Fermina Bagwan, a Bontoc elder based in the Los Angeles area. The wax cylinder hiss was added later, after changing the pitch of Mrs. Bagwan's recording to make it sound more androgynous.

Q: I'm surprised that you did not find original recordings, given the amount of ethnolinguistic investigations being done at the exposition's Anthropology Museum.

A: I'm sure there are cylinders remaining from the period. But I could not locate any in the course of my research. I wasn't working as a scholar, but as an artist. Therefore my own definition of authenticity was somewhat

Bontoc Eulogy (Marlon Fuentes, 1995)

flexible. There were realistic economic and time constraints to my fetishism for historical accuracy.

Q: How accurate was the ethnographic information embedded in the film?

A: It was accurate, for the most part, in terms of the images matching what was stated in the text. In certain sections, I have deliberately provided a false lead, a misdirection. This happens when "Antonio" is introduced, a Visayan (so the text says) who talks to Markod, yet the screen's image of Antonio is actually a Negrito. This is directed at a Filipino audience who can readily see this subterfuge as a critical (albeit humorous) statement on intertribal mind sets. This kind of putdown is not uncommon. In *arnis* (the Philippine martial art), for example, I have heard certain practitioners criticized as coming from Batangas (a Tagalog province) yet moving in a "Visayan" way. There are certain other references to intertribal hostility, most apparently in Markod's antagonism against the Scouts. There is a particular distaste reserved for collaborationist elements back home. There are even certain geographic groups that have traditionally been associated or accused of being collaborationists or worse, traitors to one cause or another. I will not name names here, but this is semi-common knowledge among Filipinos.

Q: It seems that even in the homeland (and by extension, in the diaspora), the idea of Toni Morrison's "serviceable other" still applies. Morrison (*Playing in the Dark,* 1992) examines how white authors construct blacks as the kind of person required for the whites to have the identity they desire. In a similar vein, Johannes Fabian (*Time and the Other,* 1983) provides an analysis of how the European preserves his or her identity by the construction of a serviceable primitive as his Other.

A: Cultural distortions are produced when certain groups have the power to define reality and construct serviceable others. When this definition eventually dominates the environment where the groups reside, the problem begins in earnest. The solution, in my opinion, becomes a political process that starts with understanding the dynamics of social perceptions and how images of the other are created and perpetuated.

Q: There seems to be an interesting parallel between the narrative machinations in the film (its mixture of dissimulations and embedded truth claims) and the necessary history of an imagined homeland.

A: Philippine history is in itself a continuing process of identity formation in the context of its colonial past. Its geographic, ethnic, and class fractures are suffused with a hybrid nostalgia, nostalgia doubtless overshadowed and affected by the country's colonial hybridization. When one talks of Philippine American history, and in a larger sphere, the Philippine diaspora, one begins to see hidden interaction effects: love–hate, stranded identities, mutant longings, self-flagellations, cultural camouflage, serendipitous belongings, defibrillating communities, phantom pain, social anesthesia, cultural amnesia: the absence of true north. The alien in America is constantly being bisected by this membrane of passage that does not melt away. Caught in the remnant of this time machine membrane, some of our limbs atrophy (they are after all, stuck in the side of the past, arrested and unable to follow the rest of the body in its tropic search for the father). Some of us, reptilians in your midst, shed our limbs, regrowing them in the new land. Others, more unfortunate, never regenerate; their only reminder is the painful phantom limb whose tremor wakes them in a sweat-drenched delirium. The rest choose to live with the vestigial remnants of their passage, living neither here nor there. It is easy to spot us: we walk in circles, while we console ourselves with the belief that, after all, our children will have better lives.

Q: There is a palpable wistfulness in the character of Markod, as well as in the persona of the Narrator, that encapsulates what you have just said. There is a difference, though, in their respective longings. Markod seeks redemption in the return to his terrain and by the decision of taking a head. The Narrator simply continues to dig until he reaches a dead end.

A: Markod represents the necessity and triumph of the imagination; the Narrator, the reconstitutive potential of an archaeology that is never finished: art and science stripped bare, floating downriver at twenty-four frames per second.

NOTES

1. Barbara Kirshenblatt-Gimblett, "Objects of Ethnography," in *Exhibiting Cultures: The Poetics of Museum Display*, ed. Ivan Karp and Seven D. Lavine (Washington, D.C.: Smithsonian Institution Press, 1990), 388.
2. Ibid., 389.

ROBERT F. REID-PHARR

[**9**] *Makes Me Feel Mighty Real:*
The Watermelon Woman *and*
the Critique of Black Visuality

The conceit of Cheryl Dunye's 1995 feature *The Watermelon Woman* is that the archive of the lived reality of black lesbian women is so scattered and fractured that it becomes necessary for the artist to weave the historical narrative herself, to uncover through the practice of her art bits and pieces of usable evidence, remnants of an early version of liberated black lesbianism. The film follows the character Cheryl, played by Dunye herself, in her search through videos, books, and the memories of an odd collection of characters, and as she looks for incomplete and compromised narratives, stories, and clues about the Watermelon Woman, a stunning black female character whom Cheryl encounters in a 1937 feature entitled *Plantation Memories*. Dunye uses these clues to produce a very satisfying conclusion in which the "mystery" is revealed. A black lesbian twist is added to the typically American story of a girl, Fae Richards, played by Lisa Marie Bronson, who struck out to make it big and who eventually ended up back at home surrounded by family and friends. Dunye produces a tight, clever, and archly comic film in which the artist's ability to recreate black lesbian history is associated with her ability to piece together her own chic, sexy identity. The film then deals its audience a walloping blow: *The Watermelon Woman* reveals itself as not so much a documentary as what Dunye calls a mockumentary. There is no Fae Richards. The lovely clip from the feature *Plantation Memories* has been produced from scratch by Dunye and her production team. Or, to put the matter as straightforwardly as possible, the Watermelon Woman is a phony.

   This odd tendency to juxtapose the seemingly realistic with the obviously fake makes the film difficult to read. Although Dunye seems ready to concede when she announces, "Anyway, [here's] what you all been waiting for; the biography of The Watermelon Woman, Fae Richards, Faith Richards." This rather innocuous sentence comes close on the heels of

Cheryl's self-consciously instructive address to her audience in which she takes control of the work's narrative threads and announces that her version of Fae Richard's life is in some ways quite distinct from the version offered by Fae's older, black butch lover, June Walker. Here, Dunye cleverly casts the black lesbian poet and feminist Cheryl Clarke in the role of Walker. Unlike the older character, however, Cheryl insists on maintaining all available narratives. Faith Richards, a pretty, talented black girl from Philadelphia; Fae Richards, a seasoned actress attempting to have a meaningful and dignified life and career; the Watermelon Woman, an individual sophisticated and resourceful enough to get herself to Hollywood and to find a powerful white female lover, but not so resourceful as to be able break out of the trap of having to recreate the most stereotypical black characters: all of these narratives are acknowledged and drawn together in the biography that Cheryl narrates.

Meanwhile the audience is treated to a delicious montage of stills, shot by Zoe Leonard, that documents Fae Richards's many lives. We see her as a sepia goddess á la Dorothy Dandridge, as a scolding mammy, a black mobster, a lover, a party girl, a matron, and finally as the Watermelon Woman. The sequence ends with the camera sweeping slowly across the beautiful face of Fae Richards, here playing her signature role in *Plantation Memories*. Indeed it is after seeing this work that Cheryl asks the inevitable question, "How can one be so highly esteemed as an artist and yet so hated as a woman, whenever and wherever she is deemed to be one?"[1]

The biography seemingly answers this question by demonstrating not so much the profound obstacles that Fae confronts as she attempts to succeed in life and love, but instead the pleasure she took in confronting those obstacles, the contradiction of her life. At this point, the film could not be more modern, sophisticated, correct. Cheryl and Fae Richards become poster girls for late-twentieth-century celebrations of multilayered identity. And it is here, just as the film invites its audience to feel most relaxed and satisfied, that Dunye delivers her most furious blow. The film ends with a simple printed message. "Sometimes you have to create your own history. The Watermelon Woman is fiction. Cheryl Dunye. 1996."

Dunye once told me a story that I believe proves instructive here. After a screening of the film in Philadelphia, a youngish black woman made her way up to speak with the gifted filmmaker. She told the filmaker that, if she wanted the true story of Fae Richards, all she needed to do was go to North Philadelphia and talk with the Richards family. (Apparently they were still in the area.) The truth revealed by this episode is of course that many people either feel cheated by the revelation of the work's lack of verisimilitude or simply ignore it, opting instead to continue with a

The Watermelon Woman (Cheryl Dunye, 1995)

well-articulated conception of a "real" Fae Richards whose family could be scratched up with a single well-placed call to someone's grandmother. To put it bluntly, the film does its work too well. Dunye uncovers the way an essentially materialist conception of history has become so deeply ingrained in our discourses of identity that, even when audiences are told explicitly that the object they are being offered is fake, they will insist upon this object's authenticity if it is offered alongside a formulaic allegiance to the notion of a material reality behind the ephemeral image.

I should say that one of the criticisms that I have heard of my thinking here is that I do not dwell long enough on the "fact" of the lack of realistic representations of "blacks and other people of color" in Hollywood cinema. I cannot say that I do not understand or sympathize with this line of thought. I will say, however, that the formulaic manner in which this question is raised suggests both its overdetermination and its simplicity. Although I chafe as readily as anyone at the great range of stereotypical images of "blacks and other people of color" that one continually encounters on screen, I nonetheless cannot sign off on the notion that one may ever adequately represent the reality of Black America, as that reality is itself dynamic. Further, I cannot help but be stunned by the manner in which the linguistic construct "blacks and other people of color" has come to be taken almost as an ancient concept within American society, when in truth it has much less than a twenty-year shelf life among the critical apparatuses of American intellectuals. Indeed, though the polite phrase "people of color" carries with it many of the valences of "colored people," it came into common usage among critics only in the latter part of the twentieth century. More to the point, it was at exactly this moment that another mode of critical phoniness gained a sort of awkwardly chic acceptance, as any person of color came to stand in for any other person of color—but never, it seems, for those staunchly peculiar whites.

I make these points as part of my efforts to understand better the somewhat odd relation that *The Watermelon Woman* and its director hold to what we might call the tradition of Black American cinema and to the tradition of Black American cinematic criticism. *The Watermelon Woman* tells us that early images of blacks in film are infinitely available yet somehow always lacking. They are but pale and distorted reflections of the vibrant reality of mid-twentieth-century black American life and culture. One might make exactly the same argument about images of lesbians. Indeed, part of the charm of the film is that it suggests that both "the black" and "the lesbian" have been seen regularly within American cinema, but most often as demeaned, degraded, or silenced figures. Moreover, the hostile gaze that envelopes the black is one and the same with the malevolent stare visited upon the lesbian.

What strikes me as strange about Dunye's practice, then, is that, though her film explicitly references Melvin Van Peebles's 1970 feature *Watermelon Man,* and though it stakes out a position for itself in the tradition of Black American cinema, it nonetheless remains somewhat aloof from the generations of Black American film immediately proceeding it. *Watermelon Woman* treats us to a black segregated world, bursting at the seams with talent, that existed from the early part of the twentieth century through the forties and fifties. In fact, *Plantation Memories* puts one in mind of the Plantation School of filmmaking, represented by such works as *Birth of a Nation* (D. W. Griffith, 1915), *Gone With the Wind* (Victor Fleming, 1939), and *Jezebel* (William Wyler, 1938), that helped pave the way for the weepy passing films of midcentury, *Imitation of Life* (Douglas Sirk, 1959) and *Pinky* (Elia Kazan, 1949), not to mention the deeply earnest, if erotically static, films of that prototypical respectable Negro, Sidney Poitier.[2] All of these cinematic precursors were in the sights of the black American filmmakers in the sixties and seventies as they turned the very soil against which Dunye has now set her own plow. Like Dunye, they hoped to offer correctives to the tendency to present blacks only as stock characters, as subjects who would be heard in one short register or not at all: Mammy as Mammy, the Watermelon Woman as the Watermelon Woman.

I would suggest, then, that Dunye has broken with a slightly earlier tradition of black feminist cultural production and criticism, one associated with writers like Audre Lorde and Barbara Smith as well as filmmakers such as Michelle Parkeson and Ada Gae Griffin, in that her referent is no longer the radical, misogynistic, homophobic, yet infinitely promising black sixties, the generation into which Dunye was born, but instead the generations that came before. Indeed, as I will demonstrate below, the critique that *Watermelon Woman* offers is that we continue to exist within that sixties moment. Black feminists and black nationalists alike continue to articulate a conception of black American history and culture that gained cohesion in post-World-War-II American society precisely through the manipulation of culture, particularly television and film.

I would remind you that after the Second World War, black American intellectuals were met by the strangest of intellectual conundrums. The war sparked yet another round of mass migration by all Americans, so that in the postwar era it was quite clear that black Americans could just as easily be associated with the North, the West, or the Midwest as with the South. Moreover, in their new homes in Chicago, Philadelphia, New York, and Los Angeles, blacks often lived cheek by jowl with foreign-born immigrants, many of them of uncertain racial lineage, some recently arrived from the African continent. This migration was fueled by the spotty, jerky, but nonetheless substantial increase in the total wealth and income of the black American community such that today one feels sometimes as if living in a country at once absolutely beguiled and deeply disturbed by the homegrown miracle of the middle-class black. More significant still was the fact that UNESCO published in 1949 what would essentially be its final statement on race, a statement written by Ashley Montagu, in which the United Nations put to rest the notion that there might be such a thing as biological race. Add to this the marked increase in the visibility of homosexuals and interracial couples in the forties and fifties, and one easily sees that the matter of the black community's boundaries was very much open to debate. The black American was in some ways losing her ability to name herself properly, distinctly. Black identity could no longer be associated with specific region, caste, economic status, erotic affinity, or biology. Is a copper-colored man who lives in a pleasant Cleveland suburb, who drives a German car, who marries a natural blond, and who votes with regularity for conservative Democrats and liberal Republicans black?

I believe that this question seems frivolous only insofar as my interlocutor turns to a rather hackneyed conception of the essential veracity of our highly parochial modes of visuality. "Seeing is believing" becomes, in the American context, "Look, Mama. A Negro." Indeed, I would suggest that a great deal of effort is expended in our country to remind all of us of what a Negro actually looks like. We seem incessantly concerned to sign off on the notion that, though blackness, like pornography, cannot be precisely defined, one knows it when one sees it. I am still stunned, in fact, by the number of persons, black and white, who have challenged my arguments in this regard with the retort that, though my thinking might be correct or perhaps even clever, this nonetheless will not stop a white police officer from seeing me as black. I am less troubled by the clumsiness of this particular argument than by the rather pronounced desire it demonstrates to maintain a hold on a racialism that many of us proclaim to challenge. Although the statement disallows whole worlds of reality—black policemen, differences in status between individual black persons, sexual desire between men, not to mention hundreds of years of history and culture that might rightly be taken as the only proper evidence of black American particularity—I nonetheless find that what most troubles me is the way in which my interlocutors themselves engage in a quite effective form of policing. In truth, no police officer with whom I have interacted has ever specifically hailed me as a black person. Thus, each time that I have heard the idea of the policeman who makes one black with his eyes, I have had the distinct impression that what was really being expressed was a rather pronounced desire to maintain the modes of visuality with which we are familiar. Policing continues though there is no policeman in the room. You look black, thus you are black.

I would suggest that much of the reason for the resilience of this particular bit of theoretical sophistry is the way in which the black American, the black who can be seen and understood, has come to lend a certain type of ontological stability to all American identities. The phrase that I used above, "Look, Mama. A Negro," is of course a loose translation of Frantz Fanon's description of his encounter with a young French child and her mother in his classic work, *Black Skin, White Masks*.[3] And while Fanon works rather assiduously in this passage and elsewhere within that text to represent what it means to feel oneself trapped within the gaze of the Other, to experience one's "blackness" from the vantage point of the white interlocutor, it nonetheless would behoove us, I believe, to pay much closer attention to the other side of the equation that he offers. For, as his most recent autobiographer, David Macey, reminds us, the white French citizens whom Fanon hails in this passage, even when they had little or no contact with so-called Negroes, were still quite confident about what a Negro actually was—that is to say, what a Negro actually looked like.[4] Images of the Negro abounded (and abound) in French popular culture. The notion of the loyal colonial from the "civilized" West Indies or the "developing" African colonies was deeply ingrained within the French national consciousness. Thus, when the child in the passage hails Fanon as a Negro, she does not simply trap the young black medical student in her gaze, she also rather straightforwardly articulates the racial logic that binds together her society: "Yes, mother, there are the Negroes of which I have heard so much, the ones who make tangible the fiction of my own status as European and white." The fact that the child is frightened stems not from some biologically based fear of that which is novel, but instead from the fact that this Negro, Fanon, is altogether different from what the child had come to expect. Thus she experiences a form of vertigo as she wonders if the Negro can be civilized: does this mean that the white can be savage?

I will attempt to return to the parameters of American culture and history by reminding you that, early in the twentieth century, Charlotte Osgood Mason, patron extraordinaire of the Harlem Renaissance, insisted that her protégés, Langston Hughes and Zora Neale Hurston, focus on the African and folk elements within Black American culture because she saw these as the only way to inoculate American society against the "artificial values" and "technological excess" that she attributed to Western culture.[5] Thirty years later, Mason's hope that an essentially innocent black subject would help resuscitate American culture would be repeated in a more perverse key by Norman Mailer, who found in the Negro's sexuality, his tendency toward violence, and his disdain for all things "un-hip," unbridled potential for the redemption of the country.[6] The point, of course, is that once one gives up on the Negro, the white is surely to follow. Once one can't tell the true blacks from the fakes, then all of us become a bit more dusky.

It is clear that many of the filmic and televisual images of black Americans that come to us from the 1960s and 1970s work precisely to address this largely unspoken anxiety in American culture. In the Blaxploitation genre, the black body is presented to us fully formed, in luscious technicolor, presumably only two or three steps removed from rickety shanties and blooming cotton fields. Most discussions of the representation of black bodies within Blaxploitation films argue that the black is figured as, on the one hand, hypersexual, almost animal, and, on the other, as sensual, soulful, perhaps even revolutionary. My addition here is to suggest that both sides of this argument turn on exactly the same ideological axis. In a medium in which it is infinitely possible to play with the codes of visuality that shoot through our society, we see in Blaxploitation and in the *critique* of Blaxploitation the continual rearticulation of the belief that one can know the real black body, and, by extension, real black history, when one sees them. I believe, in fact, that much of contemporary black representation within film works precisely to instruct audiences on what a black actually is, a difficult task given the wide range of individuals, communities, locations, beliefs, histories, and life situations nestled not so comfortably under the sign of blackness.

Earlier I made the argument that *The Watermelon Woman* is a film that is particularly self-conscious about the ways audiences learn and relearn how to recognize black identity and black bodies. I went on to suggest that the importance of *Watermelon Woman* may be precisely the manner in which it refuses to allow the notion that our codes of visuality are as sophisticated as we may imagine. Indeed, I believe that the general lack of a direct reference to Blaxploitation in the body of the film, even while its title gestures toward the genre, suggests that Dunye is eager to demonstrate that we exist within the same visual terrain as our most recent, if least appreciated, intellectual ancestors. We see in much the same way that Melvin Van Peebles saw in *The Watermelon Man* and later *Sweet Sweetback's Baad Asssss Song* (1971), the film generally understood to have inaugurated Blaxploitation. Thus, the sex, drugs, violence, and putative soul of blaxploitation seem mundane while the remarkable beauty of a faux 1940s black starlet appears ancient and unique.

Dunye gives her audiences what they want: talking heads, file footage, stills, letters, and voice-overs that clearly satisfy some of the most basic requirements of documentary while also suggesting that this artist, unlike Van Peebles, has captured the lived reality of black American history—not the fanciful, perhaps even perverse depiction of black life so evident in blaxploitation. She also seduces her audiences by suffusing these elements with the gritty texture of black lesbian life. The talking heads include characters ranging from Miss Shirley, a working-class stone butch who idealized Fae in the forties, to feminist bad girl Camille Paglia, to a local gay male film buff played by Brian Freeman, an aging white society matron, Dunye's mother, and Dunye herself. The point is that *The Watermelon Woman* taps the great wealth of black lesbian common sense, the knowledge not only that there is historical continuity between generations of black lesbians but also that this continuity might be revealed by asking a few questions, puttering about in libraries, and generally educating oneself about the past. The shock for *The Watermelon Woman*'s audiences is not simply that they have been given a case study in the ways that documentary can be woefully inaccurate and even misleading, but also that they are being told that their own ideas about how one might mitigate this reality, how one might see and *know* that one is seeing images of real black lesbians on screen, are quite vulnerable to manipulation. When Dunye informs us that the Watermelon Woman is a fiction, she simultaneously reminds us that all of our attempts to recapture the past, to produce narratives of "forgotten" or "lost" histories, are exercises in fiction.

I would like to focus for a moment on what I take to be one of the most delicate and complex scenes in the film. Therein, Cheryl has a first date with her white female love interest, Diana, played to bubbly perfection by writer/actress Guin Turner. After dinner and long moments of heavy innuendo, Diana and Cheryl watch the film, *Souls of Deceit*, one of the few black cast films Cheryl has been able to find that feature Fae Richards. The scene cuts to the black-and-white image of Fae's character and her very fair friend, Irene. The two are framed by the large mirror that Irene uses to apply her powder, thus bringing into focus the way the scene being enacted by Cheryl and Diana mirrors the earlier, grainier scene between the two friends. Indeed, the juxtaposition of Cheryl and Diana's exchange with that between Fae and Irene allows the audience to see the repressed racial antagonism in the one and the suppressed homoeroticism in the other.

The camera cuts back to a medium shot of Cheryl and Diana sitting on a bed looking at the film on (what the audience discovers is) a television monitor. Thus the story line is once again properly framed. We are, after all, seeing the progression of history. The Watermelon Woman and her ways of seeing and being seen are in the past. Therefore they have been reduced from the grandeur of the film screen to the more intimate platform of the television monitor. This returns us rather neatly to our own present and, I believe, to the somewhat congratulatory manner in which we approach our conceptions of history. Fae Richards proves herself an insightful critic of the ways race and sex become intertwined with desire in contemporary society precisely because she is not of this society. The starkness of the world into which she was born necessitates that she maintain an aloof, "couldn't be bothered with that nonsense" attitude to those who come behind her.

After Diana and Cheryl finally kiss and thus initiate a sex scene that is much more reminiscent of the 1970s than of the 1940s, we hear Fae say to Irene, "You're a no-good lying tramp. That's what you are. Committing a sin that will surely send you to hell." Irene retorts, "I am going to hell, but not for being a tramp, but for being poor and living on the streets like I do." At this moment, Cheryl and Diana fall onto the bed and out of the frame of the camera, revealing again the television monitor. Fae, with a remarkably pinched face, looks briefly in the direction of the interracial lesbian couple almost in the act of lovemaking and then looks quickly back at her friend. She sees what is happening but cannot be expected to turn her head to such frivolity while her friend, a friend who lives in her own world, is in such danger. The effect is almost perfect. Dunye somehow manages to map the two scenes onto each other without dispensing with the historical specificity of either. That is to say, she suggests that the one scene represents a progression, however awkward and stilted, over the other. Racial mixing is a much less severe sin than racial passing.

But then she assaults her audience. She tells us that the Watermelon Woman, Fae Richards, Faith Richards, is a lie, a figment of her own imagination, the photography of Zoe Leonard, and the talents of actress Lisa Marie Bronson. She draws outside the margins. Once this particular cat is let out of its bag, once we know that the delicately grained and faded black-and-white stills are fakes, as are the interviews, the books, and most especially the remarkable clips from two films featuring Fae Richards, *Plantation Memories* and *Souls of Deceit,* we are left with the sense that indeed all our remnants might properly be understood as fakes. The process of stitching together the history of a community necessarily involves a somewhat idiosyncratic interpretation and representation of the cultural artifacts that one encounters. I believe this is a matter on which we all may agree. I think that *The Watermelon Woman* takes us a step further down this particular path, however, by not attaching differential values to the various levels of evidence, the many remnants, on display. Dunye tells us that film, photographs, documents, gossip, storytelling, and her own narration are all suspect, open to interpretation. Moreover, she brings her audience up short by leading us down a deliciously appealing narrative path only to reveal to us in the end that our own conceptions of what constitutes a "real black lesbian history" are just as manufactured as the other ideas and media that Dunye critiques.

I will bring these comments to a close by making what some will undoubtedly believe a rather odd turn. I would like to suggest that Dunye hardly produces her work in a vacuum, though she does have few intellectual or creative peers. Still, I am reminded of the now infamous work of artist Kara Walker, who utilizes paper cutouts to represent images of a racially and erotically charged American past but who was also severely criticized by other black American artists for her use of "unrealistic" and "stereotypical" imagery.[7] The very fact that Walker utilizes such a frivolous medium, the silhouette, suggests, I believe, that she, like Dunye, is struggling to capture the essence of a profound intellectual paradox within her work. The histories that we construct, even at their most lush, are always fashioned from the thinnest of materials: faulty accounts, flimsy documents, grainy images. Thus we will never come to have a truly complicated or thick conception of black or American history until we begin to seriously consider the frail and ephemeral nature of the evidence that we have at our disposal.

This problem doubles upon itself once film becomes a part of the evidentiary archive. Although we assume that documents can be falsified, we know that films are of necessity "faked." Indeed one can rightly make the argument that modern filmic practice derives from the production of the fake documentary as evidenced by Robert Flaherty's 1922 *Nanook of the North*. That is to say, even though we may no longer regularly see the wholesale manipulation of fact that we now know was part of the making of *Nanook,* all of us should be aware that the production of film, including documentary, involves staging scenes, manipulating environments, and, most important, editing. Understanding this may help us to better understand not only Flaherty's work but also that of Walker and even Ralph Ellison, whose posthumously published novel, *Juneteenth,* tells of a "white" child happily ensconced in a "black" community until the day he sees a movie and comes to yearn for the fake world that he witnesses on screen. Indeed the child, Bliss, is warned by his adopted father, Daddy Hickman, of the danger of precisely the "transparent insubstantiality of a cinematic image," but to no avail. The child comes to prefer the lie ("I am white and you are black") to the truth ("We are one").[8] This then is the difficult intellectual ground on which Cheryl Dunye has produced her fake documentary, *The Watermelon Woman*. And by doing so she reminds us that our work is never more artificial, more fake, than when it comes freighted with all the trappings of the real.

◆

NOTES

1. This is a paraphrase of James Baldwin in *Just above My Head*. Baldwin writes, of his character Sonny Carr, "He bows his head before their silent wonder that he can be so highly esteemed as a performer and treated so viciously as a man: whenever, and wherever, he is esteemed to be one." James Baldwin, *Just above My Head* (New York: Dell, 1978), 102.

2. For more on the history of black Americans and film, see Donald Bogle, *Toms, Coons, Mulattoes, Mammies, and Bucks: An Interpretive History of Blacks in American Films* (New York: Continuum, 1973); Ed Guerrero, *Framing Blackness: The African American Image in Film* (Philadelphia: Temple University Press, 1993); Valerie Smith, ed., *Representing Blackness: Issues in Film and Video* (New Brunswick, N.J.: Rutgers University Press, 1997); and James Snead, *White Screens, Black Images: Hollywood from the Dark Side* (New York: Routledge, 1994).

3. Frantz Fanon, *Black Skin, White Masks,* trans. Charles Lam (New York: Pluto Press, 1952).

4. David Macey, *Frantz Fanon* (New York: Picador USA, 2000).

5. See Wilson Jeremiah Moses, *Afrotopia: The Roots of African American Popular History* (New York: Cambridge University Press, 1998), 214.

6. Norman Mailer, *The White Negro* (San Francisco: City Lights Books, 1957).

7. For more on the controversy surrounding Walker and her work, see Robert F. Reid-Pharr, "Black Girl Lost," in *Kara Walker: Pictures from Another Time,* ed. Annette Dixon (Ann Arbor: University of Michigan Museum of Art, 2002).

8. Ralph Ellison, *Juneteenth* (New York: Random House, 1999).

III Deception

CATHERINE L. BENAMOU

[**10**] *The Artifice of Realism and the Lure of the "Real" in Orson Welles's* F for Fake *and Other T(r)eas(u)er(e)s*

*I'm interested really in the myth of the past, as a myth. Jack Ford is one of the myth-*makers.
:: Orson Welles

The question, filtered through so many cultures, through so many different captions of the same picture, is how do you know the truth, when you see it?
:: Bob Brown, commenting on television coverage of the war in Iraq, ABC News, March 26, 2003

F for Fake (1973) is one of the last films that Orson Welles would complete and release (although certainly not his final project of significance) before his career was cut short by his death in 1985.[1] In essence, it is a film about the pitfalls of the art market, about how, in advanced capitalist modernity, the commodification of art inevitably undermines claims to authenticity, even as such claims are avidly established and pursued by the market's arbiters (gallery owners, museum curators, and auctioneers) and beneficiaries (collectors) as a measure of cultural and monetary value. The trouble is, Welles suggests, that this pegging of value to authenticity has taken precedence over and above any emphasis on meaning and satisfaction for the artist, as well as any aesthetic "quality" or pleasure for the viewer. In the current market climate, such a bias favors the enrichment and empowerment of those institutions whose mission it is to support, preserve, and disseminate "good art," and also provides both the need and the opportunity for forgers to infiltrate the market. As a result, the art "expert," whose status depends on this market logic (that is, on the theoretical and actual existence of "fakes" as opposed to "originals"), has come to displace the artist, the members of his/her appreciating public, and even the art forger, as a determining force in artistic expression and consumption.

While s/he may not be the largest monetary beneficiary of art market dynamics, the "expert" is thus able to accumulate and retain considerable amounts of personal cultural capital, while safeguarding the cultural capital and material wealth of the museum/collector.

As if in direct response to this state of affairs, in *F for Fake,* Welles chooses not to dwell on those who have putatively been duped or conned by imitation and fakery, namely art dealers (often willingly) and the viewing and buying public (usually unwittingly), so as to focus instead on the fate of the artist-fakers and the works they forge or fabricate. (As Welles's documentation of forgery at work shows us, to become a great forger, one must first possess a modicum of talent and acquire some experience as an artist.) By denying a screen appearance to the institutional victims and accusers (who at the same time are, in their own way, "fakers" of knowledge, since they have allowed themselves to be duped by the forgers), Welles notably avoids the usual balanced approach to controversial subjects in U.S. television documentary, according to which both sides of a question and their representatives are given equal screen time. And, while this film's narrative is "character centered," he also resists privileging any individual viewpoint or line of reasoning, preferring to weave into the peripatetic, transatlantic itinerary he pursued during the latter part of his career, the equally nomadic itineraries of the film's featured protagonists: the infamous master art forger Elmyr de Hory; his biographer Clifford Irving, who is also the alleged forger of the autobiography of airline magnate and movie studio impresario Howard Hughes; and Croatian actress-writer-sculptress Oja Kodar. Included in these core plot elements are guest "appearances" by Hughes, Pablo Picasso, and Kodar's Hungarian "grandfather." Welles is assisted in the overall task of reconstructing the past and teasing out the "truth" about these acts of forgery by actor-collaborators from his Mercury Productions days: Joseph Cotten, who starred in *Citizen Kane* (1941) and other early Welles films; Richard Wilson and Paul Stewart, both of whom had cameo roles in *Citizen Kane* and collaborated with Welles on the 1938 *War of the Worlds* radio broadcast; and French filmmaker and former art dealer François Reichenbach, who started his own film on art forgery starring de Hory. Reichenbach passed that project on to Welles, who incorporated some of the footage into this film and expanded its scope to include digressions on the celebrity publishing industry (which, like the art world, is so lucrative that it encourages falsified biographies like the one published by Irving on Hughes), and on his own professional capers as a self-denominated "charlatan."

Traveling along and across these itineraries with Welles himself as our guide, we learn how de Hory, a Holocaust survivor who has assumed scores of different legal identities, became an art forger out of socioeconomic desperation; how Howard Hughes, failing at his dream invention, a mammoth airplane curiously named the "Spruce Goose," sentenced himself to obscurity and professional inactivity; how the writer Clifford Irving succeeded in bringing Hughes back into the limelight by fabricating secret encounters with Hughes that allegedly led to a book manuscript, the authenticity of which was supported by forged documents that could have been signed by Irving's wife, who might also be Hughes's former wife, Helga; how Welles himself "faked" his way onto the legitimate stage in Dublin, Ireland, and then into the Hollywood studio system; and finally, how Oja Kodar got herself into a suitcase, and then into a jam with the painter Picasso, the sole artist in the film who steadily profited from the art market while sticking to the making of his own art. In open defiance of the plot formulas of the popular genres of the biopic, the mystery, and the documentary exposé—all of which were dear to Welles as a director, and which this film, like his earlier *Mr. Arkadin* (a.k.a. *Confidential Report,* 1955) compellingly evokes—none of the dramas emanating from these predicaments are ever "resolved," nor are any of the protagonists' stories fully told.

However, if one follows the line of argumentation presented in *F for Fake* closely, it is possible to learn that the late modern shift in the basis of artistic value bears consequences not only for the *orientation* of artistic practice and modes of consumption, by encouraging imitations ranging from "benign" reproductions (posters, postcards, museum store replicas, and the stylistic homages seen in popular art fairs) to the "malignant" (expert fakes passed off as originals), but also, echoing Walter Benjamin, for the cultural and ontological *status* of art as a creative act of representation. I stress this distinction because for Welles, as for Benjamin, once art begins to circulate and become accessible to more than one set of viewers at one time, there is a shift in emphasis from tangibility and localized control over phenomenal objects toward mediation and the broadening of art as a form of social experience.[2] The physical object is only the first step in the mediative process involving technological reproduction, which in and of itself contributes to a diversification in the types of objects and experiences that can be considered art. On the one hand, this signals the democratization of art; on the other hand, it opens the way for cultural and economic hegemonies sustained by reproduction and imitation. Assuming the position of the skeptic, Welles quotes Rudyard Kipling on this latter point more than once: "It is pretty, but is it *art?*" If these observations do not sound new, it should be remembered that *F for Fake* was produced within a decade of the pop art interventions by Andy Warhol and others, which endowed ordinary industrial products with art market value by way of their recontextualization as contemporary cultural symbols; and the film was contemporary to the *fluxus* (open-ended performative art) experimentations, as well as to the appropriation of some of these experimentations by a Hollywood cinema that was seeking to reinvent itself in the television age.[3]

Cinema, of course, epitomizes for Benjamin the mediated artistic experience,[4] and so the question inevitably arises as to the status of *F for Fake* as a work of art (it's *not* pretty, but it does look like art) with regard to the trends of the art market and the embedded quandary over fakery vs. authenticity, which pivots in turn around claims of authorship. Does *F for Fake* demystify the fakery at the heart of the art world so that a modicum of verifiable authenticity and public confidence can be restored to the museum collection? Or does it aid and abet that fakery by transforming the culprits into credible and sympathetic documentary subjects? On the other hand, should a creative object's "authenticity" as the unique handiwork of a certain individual (preferably verified by the fine art "expert") remain so central to the workings of the art market in a modern age of mediated representations? And what of art when it has become "inherent in the technique of the film [as Benjamin phrased it] that . . . everybody who witnesses its accomplishments is somewhat of an expert"[5]? Welles's initial answer to this question appears to be the ambivalent "yes" and "no."

As its French title, *Verités et mensonges (Truths and Lies)* suggests, *F for Fake* contains a mixture of factual and confabulated material, and, since Welles does not establish any infallible boundary between the two, the audience is advised to remain on guard against any temptation toward gullibility (normally encouraged, it is implied, by documentary discourse). The deliberate blurring of the boundary between actual and staged events is facilitated by Welles's choice of the essay format, which, as Timothy Corrigan has pointed out, is itself located aesthetically "between the categories of public realism and formal expressivity, and so becomes a critical wedge within the very idea of filmic categorization."[6] Thus, regardless of its ideological positioning on the issue of art forgery, *F for Fake* appears designed to elude any easy valuation and classification by film "experts." The film unfolds in its narration like a photojournalistic exposé, combining archival newsreels, stills, and newspaper clippings with pro-filmic interviews and observational footage, yet, as I've suggested, Welles is quite careful to leave us with more questions than solid answers, and not all of these questions pertain to, or are to be explained by, the characters in the film. The overriding structural principle is that of a mosaic, constructed from multiple points of departure for investigating the theme of fakery, along with more than one blind alley, a strategy that ultimately undermines the "neat" separation Welles has devised and promises the viewer that he will uphold: one hour of material based on the "available facts," followed by seventeen minutes of fiction and a brief coda to demystify that fiction and provide biographical exposés of some of the film's main characters. This is in effect a *warning* by Welles that the film's representational strategies can move imperceptibly, as if by sleight of hand, between "documentary" and "fiction," and the device not only augments the reflexivity already induced by the mosaic structure and the aesthetic hybridity of the source material, but also lets us know that on the question of fakery, Welles is not about to let either the film, or himself as *one* of its makers, easily off the hook. Moreover, himself a "forger" of Reichenbach's project, cobbling together pieces of footage, both "found" and newly fabricated, Welles leaves the traces of this appropriation by including Reichenbach as a "real life" character in the film.

The result of this augmentation is that, more than simply a topical exposé about hypocrisy and pettifoggery in the art world, *F for Fake* is a metacritical film that investigates the possibilities of delivering truth in documentary (the mosaic and labyrinthine structure indicates that there is no simple formula here), while self-consciously raising the question of authorship and its increasingly less covert relationship to documentary representation. Whereas today, documentary directors such as Errol Morris and Michael Moore have made it nearly impossible to ignore the presence and identity of the documentarist, the prevailing discourse of "fly-on-the-wall" transparency during the years of direct cinema, which were tapering off when Welles made *F for Fake,* begged the question of authorship (manifested at that time in distinctive shooting and editing styles) in close association with the question of "objectivity."

The remainder of this essay will be devoted to an examination of these metacinematic themes, as well as of the ultimate position taken in the film on art fakery (if there is one), by pursuing the thematic and stylistic resonances between *F for Fake* and earlier works by Welles, including the infamous *War of the Worlds* radio broadcast and *Citizen Kane,* with its "News on the March" mockumentary, both cited by Welles in *F for Fake* as examples of his own charlatanry, paralleling that of de Hory, Irving, and Kodar's "grandfather." At the center of these resonances are what can be called the "lure" of the real for the spectator, its location on the margins of the screen image where the resourceful spectator might catch a glimpse of it, along with the dilemma of realism for the director. Realism translates into practice as a maximization of the possibilities afforded by modern film technology (like all "good fakery," on the one hand, yet at its best achieves a measure of honesty and parity in the relationship among narrator, spectator, and screen subject, on the other). Here, I am interested in how the recurrence of these themes and preoccupations in Welles's films over time can illuminate, if not reconcile, apparently contradictory tendencies in his work that have fueled a timeworn debate between the pop mythology attached to his public persona as the master of audiovisual deception (a mythology initiated by the *War of the Worlds* broadcast) and the selective, if eloquently argued, portrayal of Welles as a consummate "screen realist" (advanced most forcefully by *Cahiers du Cinéma* critic André Bazin in response to *Citizen Kane*).[7]

Concomitantly, I hope to smooth the edges of a historiographical schism that has been devised between Welles's film work in the studio system in the forties, and the films he completed after exiling himself to Europe in 1947. This schism, premised on an attention to mode of production, an adherence to romantic views of authorship, and an American exceptionalist reading of film culture, had palpable consequences for Welles as a filmmaker (could he be "trusted" to direct another commercial film for U.S. release after *The Lady from Shanghai* [1946]?), and certainly for the critical evaluation of his later works. It has also paved the way for some to champion *F for Fake* as an eschewal of modernism in art (encompassing Welles's own film practice up to that point), or alternately as a paean to poststructuralist approaches to cultural critique and linguistic decoding, especially where questions of authorship, authenticity, identity, and the instability and uncertainty of signification are concerned.[8] This view is ostensibly supported by the spoof in *F for Fake* on Pablo Picasso, the one significant character who does *not* make an actual appearance in the film, and who, during the seventeen minutes of "fiction," is so enamored by his putative model (Oja Kodar) that he allows her to keep twenty-two paintings of herself (which she then switches with Picasso "fakes" painted by her grandfather for the purpose of turning a profit). One well-meaning critic has even gone so far as to refer to *F for Fake* as Welles's "swan song,"[9] even though the film was succeeded by *Filming Othello* in 1978 as well as by a score of works in progress, including two major film projects, *The Other Side of the Wind* (begun around 1970) and an adaptation of Shakespeare's *King Lear*.

In order to avoid lapsing into the dichotomies created by Welles's "fall from Hollywood grace," or by the "modern, radical realist" versus the "postmodern, montage-happy" auteur, and to bring into focus the continuities between earlier, seminal works, such as *Citizen Kane,* and later, reflective works, such as *F for Fake,* it is methodologically fruitful to build on the precedent set by Jonathan Rosenbaum, who has reintroduced Welles's lost or incomplete films into a consideration of his work as a whole. In his article "Orson Welles's Essay Films and Documentary Fictions,"[10] for example, Rosenbaum exposes how these two discursive forms cut *across* the full length of Welles's filmography and complicate any distinctions we may wish to make between fiction and nonfiction cinema, not to mention the ideological effects of combining those categories. Likewise, Michael Anderegg has examined Welles's adaptations of Shakespeare's plays, and the symbiotic relationship Welles was able to strike up between the task of adapting literary "classics" and an active engagement with popular culture, from his radio to his mature film works.[11] More than help to establish the organicity of Welles's oeuvre as an auteur (does this still need to be established?), the intertextual continuities between *F for Fake* and other works, especially as regards points of style, strategy, and philosophy, bring into relief the resilience of Welles's commitment to media enfranchisement and accountability toward the general public, as well as the practical corollary of this enfranchisement and accountability: the spectator's active engagement with various modes and *means* of representation. It is this multiple engagement, it can be surmised, that guards against the total equivalence between phenomena that, although similar in appearance, might be ontologically distinct (or quite simply, as in the magical act or detective story, a warning is served to the audience not to allow themselves to be overly "fooled" by the semblance of presence).

In order to make this commitment stick, Welles needed to keep pace with the changing discourse of popular cinema, as well as with the ideologies and strategies pertaining to realism, especially in the realm of documentary. As in the early forties, this did not necessarily mean that he needed to buy in to the dominant discourse: *F for Fake* reflects the spontaneous camera work and immediacy of human interaction of the eminently portable, direct cinema of the period, yet it breaks with the voyeuristic position reserved for the spectator in that cinema by introducing a heavier than usual role for the on-screen narrator. Let us examine more closely the disruption (or displacement) in Welles's oeuvre of conventional realism in favor of what might be more precisely described as a ritual exercise of wonderment for the viewer and of bewilderment—and simultaneous entrapment and compassion—for the character-subject, and of confession and self-irony on the part of the filmmaker.

▶
_____

". . . about Trickery, Fraud, about Lies"

At the center of the play between documentary and fiction in *F for Fake* is Welles's general interest in the equivocal relation between the audiovisual signifier and its historical referent—without the intervention of metaphysical forces, as in traditional magic—as a modern dilemma intensified by the fact of technological mediation. For Welles, the cinema simultaneously represents a channel for playing on this equivocation—in effect, becoming a modern form of magic[12]—(as illustrated by his testing and teasing of the audience by openly challenging them to detect the fiction in the film), and an efficacious means of disclosing it, thereby staving off the nefarious effects of equivocation when it devolves into sheer illusionism. These effects, as suggested by Welles in various works, from his radio days through *Citizen Kane* to the 1956 television pilot "The Fountain of Youth,"[13] include the manipulation (as opposed to persuasion) of public opinion, the detachment from lived reality (to the point of denial), and, perhaps most significantly for him, the loss of sociopolitical agency for the spectator.

Welles invokes his longstanding popular association with media deception in *F for Fake,* and he capitalizes upon it for the sake of irony in other films in which he makes on-screen appearances as narrator, such as the mystery shorts *Scene of the Crime* (directed by Walter Grauman, 1984), *A Vote for Murder,* and *The Medium Is the Murder* (both directed by Harry Falk, 1985),[14] in which he asks the audience to trust him regarding their chances of uncovering the incriminating clues to murder. As a household name in the United States, he is perhaps best known for the spasms of public panic he triggered nationwide with his 1938 CBS radio broadcast, *War of the Worlds,* a phenomenon that attests as much to the confidence inspired by the artist-announcer's voice for his listeners, as to his skill at manipulating story content and narration to fit a live news story format. From the beginning of his media career, Welles actively encouraged this confidence: earlier in 1938, he had developed a *First Person Singular* radio series, in which the main narration was delivered in first person monologue by a fictional protagonist (played by Welles), creating an aura of intimacy between disembodied voice (easily identified as Welles's own) and listener; and Welles customarily signed off from his radio programs with a humble verbal bow (not quite offsetting his evident predilection for lead roles, center stage), "obediently yours."[15]

Not all of his listeners were "fooled" by the announcement and chronicling of a Martian invasion in the infamous *War of the Worlds* broadcast (based on H. G. Welles's eponymous story), a manipulation that, Welles insisted at a national press conference the following day, had never been his intent. The show was cobbled together from an improvised excerpting of the Welles story, combined with a parody of what Bill Nichols has referred to as the "discourses of sobriety"—in this case, science, military defense maneuvers, and politics, as well as "documentary"—appearing in the form of "live" news and weather bulletins.[16] After delivering the opening narration, Welles's distinctive voice breathes life into Richard Pearson, an astronomer at Princeton (a shift in role that easily could have unmasked the charade for the attentive, habitual listener), whose mathematical calculations regarding the possibility of life on Mars are contradicted by the phenomenally observed appearance of aliens in the New Jersey countryside. Pearson tenaciously continues to disbelieve the "empirical" evidence before him, since it fails to conform to existing scientific logic, and his explanatory authority is rapidly displaced by a news reporter's excited observations regarding the mysterious features of the extraterrestrial landing, eyewitness testimony from local residents, and finally, the radio listener's own ability to discern the audible "signs" of an alien presence seemingly transmitted by the roving and indifferent radio apparatus. The persuasive power of these remarkably verisimilar reports issued "live" and direct from the sites of the invasion resides partly in the periodic returns to "regular programming" at the local New York station—an unsettlingly bland, instrumental dance number played by a local orchestra, which, lacking lyrics or dialogue of any kind, is the perfect foil to the increasingly frantic attempts of the sober characters to verbalize the incomprehensible and unpredictable conduct of the Martians. It is also the uncanny effect of the *instability* of a reliable viewpoint through which to understand the events, as the microphone is tossed from a CBS station announcer, to a radio reporter (Carl Phillips, who, we learn, is killed by the Martians while on duty), Professor Pearson, military personnel, and the Secretary of the Interior.

At the close of these partly improvised performances, Welles assures those listeners who are still within earshot (many had already panicked and fled from their radios) that the invasion was a mere prank performed on the eve of Halloween: the Mercury Theatre's way of "pulling sheets over our heads and saying 'boo.'" Thus, the show, with its dialogism and masquerade, including that of Welles himself, can be read as a carnivalesque exercise in poking fun at publicly revered sources of institutional authority—academia, the government, the news media—the coordinated efficiency of which in an emergency is nonetheless demonstrated, and the historical continuity of which is confirmed by Welles at the close of his narration.

The fan mail Welles received on the broadcast—a significant portion of which remained unopened until long after his death—reveals evenly divided responses: some listeners complained that such willful deception, even if playful, produced gravely disastrous consequences: "if only we had known" and "how are you going to compensate me?" Others were disgruntled that so many listeners could have been so naïve as to allow themselves to be duped by (and thus failed to appreciate) the Mercury's demonstration of stylistic mastery in radio narration. The longer view of these listener responses is that the broadcast counterposed, and in the end subverted, both the semblance of intimacy Welles himself had achieved over the airwaves and the power of public institutions (often in the service of private interests) to form opinion and structure people's attitudes toward their daily lives. A Baudrillardian concern with the effects of the simulacrum (or almost-simulacrum, in the case of this analog radio montage) appears fused here with the Frankfurt School's concern with the impact of culture industries on how the individual is positioned in relation to the collectivity.

From this angle, Welles's self-reflexive collage of fictional and documentary radio genres might have signaled (to any listener who wished to take notice) the degree to which, by the mid-twentieth century, the media had become a contested terrain that could just as easily facilitate conversation among members of a democratic society (a scenario suggested by the "day after" scene in which Professor Pearson mulls over life's options with a lone survivor of the invasion in Newark), as it could serve as a major source of profit for media moguls or a propaganda machine for fascist dictators. (Indeed, the broadcast occurred just two weeks before Kristallnacht, a fateful night during which Jewish property was branded and destroyed in German cities, in collective actions that could easily have been fueled by Goebbels's propaganda machine.) Thus, it was not merely the sense of having been fooled, of driving until one ran out of gas at an inconvenient location, or of having broken a leg trying to jump out of the nearest window that was disturbing to the complainants in the audience; even more disconcerting was the notion that the media as an institution could be so easily appropriated and manipulated, its codes of representation mimicked and rendered unreliable. If nothing else, the program instructed listeners not to take for granted their access to, and reliance upon, radio communication during an historical period when radio provided the most significant source of news for the majority of the U.S. population. Significantly, this more reflective response appears to have been generated only after the fact, rather than during the broadcast itself. Nevertheless, the seeds were planted for Welles to develop the notion of reflexivity in compatible rather than contrary relation to realism in his media work. Two strategic dimensions of the "War of the Worlds" broadcast are worth noting here: the shift in the spectator's perspective on "what is really happening" in New Jersey in response to a series of shifts in narrative viewpoint and, concomitantly, in narrative authority; and the parodying and combining of documentary and entertainment genres for dramatic *effect*.

Similar doses of realism, fabrication, and narrative discontinuity can be found in Welles's first feature film, *Citizen Kane,* produced two years later, also within a powerful media enterprise, RKO Radio Studio. In the film, a markedly parodic newsreel, "News on the March," modeled on the contemporary *March of Time* (in which Welles occasionally performed),[17] is followed by a series of personal testimonies, illustrated in flashback and punctuated by scenes in which, as cinematographer Gregg Toland eloquently explained, deep-focus images are combined with long takes and the visible inscription of the physical boundaries of the set (ceilings, walls, and floors) so as to approximate the manner in which physical reality is perceived by the naked eye.[18] To Welles's credit, this hybrid construction was achieved at the expense of Hollywood conventions of cinematic narration when they were at the peak of their development, only to slip by the scrutiny of most RKO studio executives, who fixated instead on the economic impact of a publicity boycott imposed on the studio by Hearst newspapers. The boycott was rooted in allegations of a noticeable resemblance between the biographical profile of the film's main character, Charles Foster Kane, and that of William Randolph Hearst, and it delayed the release of the film by nearly three months.[19] Welles himself downplayed the resemblances in statements made to the press, yet was surprisingly modest where the film's aesthetic innovations were concerned; in a statement made to the Brazilian press nine months after *Kane*'s U.S. release, he stated: "In and of itself, *Citizen Kane* is nothing extraordinary. It's just a film in which I decided to apply old rules of filmmaking, giving them a new twist and adapting them to modern techniques."[20]

Considered from the standpoint of the modernist axiom that there is no way to tamper with the form without interfering with the dimensions and interpretation of the content, Hearst's allegations clearly ignored not only the agency of the viewer in reaching a Hearst-oriented conclusion, but the question of whether or how this complexly structured film would necessarily *dispose* the hypothetical spectator in favor of a narrow reading of the narrative's allegorical possibilities. Whereas Hearst and company were obviously content to dismiss the double-edged role played by mediation in film (even though they themselves were masters of mass mediation with highly profitable results), for Welles, the representational processes (and opportunities for creative expression) touched on by this controversy—that is, the variable gap between cinematic representation and physical and historical reality as a coeffecient of the alternate intrusion and effacement of the apparatus, coupled with shifts in narrative viewpoint and authority—would provide grist for textual exploration well into his film career. In *F for Fake*, for example, Welles appropriates the controversy over the historical model for Kane, and substitutes Howard Hughes for Hearst, with a twist: he uses actual newsreel footage of Hughes, but packages it as a film within the film, as a mockumentary, then has Joseph Cotten, who played Kane's sidekick in *Citizen Kane,* tell the spectator that, this time, he would be cast in the role of Hughes.

A key aspect of the representational strategies of *Citizen Kane,* and of several other of Welles's films, is the manner in which the foregrounding of the fact of mediation becomes linked to the themes of excessive power and misrecognition (and their antithesis, clarity of vision and the leveling of power). One finds this linkage echoed in Welles's *The Magnificent Ambersons* (1942), the unfinished *It's All True* (1942), *Mr. Arkadin, Touch of Evil* (1958), and *Chimes at Midnight* (1966). Thus, in *Citizen Kane,* the opaque and equivocal nature of the (respectively) visual and verbal signifier is transformed, from a plausible plot element linked to the theme of yellow journalism, into a reflexive motif. As Cory Creekmur has aptly observed, the hyperbolic and often spurious headlines slapped on the front pages of Kane's newspapers within the body of the text "clearly warn us of the possible manipulation of truth when money, power, and the media are allowed to intertwine."[21]

The upshot of this warning for the spectator (if not for the reporter-investigator who is implicated in the completion of the mockumentary) is that the oxymoronic copula of "citizen" and "Kane" does not hold for long once the opening titles have faded. Rather, much of the film's plot is obsessively devoted, in the fetishistic and stereotypical manner of the yellow press, to Kane's *individual* story of narcissistic power and loss. Relegated in spirit and in substance to the margins of the plot as a *casualty* (or, if you will, the "losing" end of the oxymoron) of that story, the theme of citizenship becomes a preferred position from which the spectator may engage with, even judge, Kane's character. The significance of this "marginal" and, for the filmmakers, historically emergent, position should not be overlooked, since it runs counter to the preferred spectatorial positions designated by the dominant modes of media discourse (Kane's tabloids, the newsreel) featured within the diegesis. Read superficially, the tabloids and the newsreel involve the fictionalization of real events to the point of verisimilitude, as well as the mollification of the viewer into accepting the conflation of fiction with fact. Upon closer scrutiny, and within the larger framework of Welles's realism, which (as I have suggested) includes an element of reflexivity—an element that is more tangible in *F for Fake* precisely because of its "real," as opposed to "fake," documentary component—what had to be achieved formally in *Citizen Kane* to effectively get the critique of media manipulation across to the spectator, by stirring her/him out of that mollified position into activity as a citizen, was interference with diegetic realism as an accessory to narrative integration.

Dating back to the early narrative films of the silent 1910s, narrative integration depends historically, as Tom Gunning has shown, on the development of a visual language, such as that developed by D. W. Griffith, capable of providing enough cues for the viewer to become directly involved in the "unfolding of the story" without the assistance of an off-screen or extradiegetic narrator. As a result, with "narrative integration," Gunning notes, "the narrator system seems to 'read' the images to the audience in the very act of presenting them. This narrator [system] is invisible, revealing its presence only by the way images are revealed on the screen."[22]

By the early 1940s, following the disappearance of inter-titles and silent acting techniques, and with improved mobility of the camera, more sensitive film stock, versatile lighting equipment, and a broader range of editing options, this narrative integration, supported by diegetic realism, had become the industrial norm. What is most interesting is that Welles, having just mastered the available cinematic vocabulary and grammar of narrative integration, would have sought to control and subvert its effects on the spectator-narrator relationship, and by extension on the spectators' sense of their own positioning in relationship to the events, characters, and space of the diegesis.

How, specifically, does Welles preclude the mesmerizing effect on the spectator of diegetic realism as a vehicle to narrative integration in *Citizen Kane*? Through heterodiegesis (prompted by the multiple, yet partial, versions of the same story through different narrative viewpoints), simultaneously pushing the envelope of illusionism (the foggy landscape of Xanadu, the asceptic, vaulted space of Thatcher Memorial Library, the snowy Colorado homestead in winter), expressive cutting (the much-analyzed time-lapse "breakfast scene" between Kane and his first wife Emily, the abrupt shift from still photography to moving image in the *Chronicle* staff "buyout" sequence), and the parameters of photographic realism with respect to existing Hollywood practice (using shorter lenses, reverting to arc lights, positioning the tripod below floor level to show the ceiling, and so on). There is also the hybrid parody of "News on the March" (too close to *March of Time* for the resemblance to go unnoticed by the contemporary U.S. spectator), and the lack of a scene change when the projection of this "newsreel" abruptly ends in the newsroom before the titles have rolled, signaling that it is but a "work-in-progress."

Later we find, within the mosaic structure of *F for Fake,* itself, the principle of heterodiegesis in the intercalation of individual testimonials and life "stories" told from a variety of viewpoints (including that of Welles, posing as another "charlatan"). More significant is the fact that Welles, as the "man with the movieola" and the master of ceremonies, resists the pull of full "narrative integration" from the very beginning by casting himself as an extradiegetic narrator, an observer-participant, who intrudes at will into the space of the diegesis. Hence, it is consistently Welles's body and voice, rather than a rickety, forgotten sled named "Rosebud," that forms the fragile boundary among narrator, spectator, and character-subject, along which signification and identification can begin to take shape (or be frustrated, given the number of times that these three agencies are repositioned by both films' structural discontinuities in form and subject matter). The fluid position of Welles as narrator, combined with the fact that the film is part compilation, part diary, part travelogue, and part verité, place *F for Fake* squarely within the category of the essay film (or para- and metacinematic mode for Welles), which Jonathan Rosenbaum has traced back to the trailer for *Citizen Kane*.[23] Overall, this mode allowed Welles to combine the format of the first-person singular (a narrational style he developed in radio), with the editorial (a format he had pursued in the print media), and the staging of events through cinematic storytelling, into the idiosyncratic blend of documentary and fiction that makes subtle appearances in non-essay feature films by Welles as diverse as *The Lady from Shanghai, Mr. Arkadin,* and *Chimes at Midnight.* Yet whereas the boundaries demarcating fiction from documentary tend to be clear in all of these films, including *Citizen Kane,* in *F for Fake* they are deliberately blurred, not only by the interweaving of staged, archival, and spontaneously filmed shots, but through the fictional relations Welles establishes among characters who appear in documentary material shot at different times and in different places. This fictionalization, a paradoxical part and parcel of *any* essay film, not only results from using primary material as evidence to support the narrator's commentary, but has as its ostensible purpose the forging of dialogical relations among Welles as (extra)diegetic narrator and the character-subjects, including Reichenbach, Kodar, and former associates Cotton, Stewart, and Wilson. Quite literally, Welles's montage of material allows these people to have "conversations" with one another on a range of topics that have been distilled from reams of footage and Welles's own reflections on its contents.

Although clearly and unapologetically confusing the spectator, the intermingling of documentary and fictional material is formally expressive of the film's discursive challenge: to expose the "truth" using statements by people who are pathological liars. In effect, Welles forces us to choose between, on the one hand, a broader concept of "truth" based on human experience (some of which, as we can see in the case of de Hory, is under-

CATHERINE L. BENAMOU

standably ineffable and off-limits to both filmic representation and the social sphere), and, on the other, the "certainty" as to the historicity of events and the origin of material works, to be arrived at through logical proof and the presentation of factual evidence. This distinction is akin to the distinction made by eighteenth-century Italian philosopher and philologist Giambattista Vico between *"il vero"* (the true), discovered through knowledge of that which is "universal and eternal," and *"il certo"* (the certain), arrived at through the awareness *(coscienza)* of that which is "particular and contingent."[24] Thus, Welles introduces reflexivity in *F for Fake* only to plant doubt in the mind of the viewer as to the factual veracity of its subject matter, given an apparent excess in the film of "contingency."

At the same time, I would argue that Welles's explicit narrator presence acts as a countervailing force preventing the film from drifting into a postmodern glossing of the equivalence attained by the "copy" and the "original" in art. Without insisting on the importance of singular, incontestable authorship in art, Welles conscientiously attributes all of the works we see (with very few exceptions) to an identifiable "maker," even if that maker happens to be a forger.

On the face of it, and especially if one adheres to André Bazin's formulation in his essay "L'évolution du langage cinematographique" ("On the Evolution of Film Language"), *F for Fake* is the antithesis of a *realist* film, since its narrative discourse is almost entirely built on a "montage principle" of construction. Bombarded with the shrapnel of Welles's collage of disparate materials, the spectator has little access or time to contemplate the real spatial relations or temporal sequence of profilmic events, let alone to verify the authenticity of the performances. Hence the disruption of diegetic realism, as crucial to documentary as to fiction, is much more frequent and multifarious than in *Citizen Kane* or in any of Welles's previous works. A few specific formal strategies, most involving the innovative use of sound in relation to image, are worth mentioning. First, at several points in the character's testimonies, Welles freezes the frame of the image while he lets the dialogue continue uninterrupted, allowing the character to complete the utterance. He also replays certain shots or sections of scenes involving the triumvirate, for emphasis, either in rapid succession and using invisible cutting, or as punctuation marking different segments in the plot. He dubs his own voice into a repeated recording of testimony by Howard Hughes, in contestation of Irving's claims. Finally, he and Kodar begin a scene as themselves in conversation, yet transition into role playing, whereby Welles, taking on a Hungarian accent, plays Kodar's grandfather, defending his art forgery to an incensed Pablo Picasso, played by Kodar.

One of the bolder statements Welles makes in *F for Fake* through the blending of documentary with fiction is the notion that there can be no transparency in film, only insight at best, a pointing or nudging toward historical truth or a pushing toward emotional truth; thus realism, defined as a stylistic *effect* of the creative use of audiovisual technology, as well as (whenever possible) the decision to work with unadorned physical spaces and nonprofessional actors, is no less constructed in documentary than it is in fiction film. Indeed, it is not difficult to claim that the documentary portions of *F for Fake* involve a greater manipulation of physical reality and actual sequence of events than do either the film's fictional (i.e., fully staged) sequences or the realist scenes in *Citizen Kane*. Moreover, very few lines of dialogue in the de Hory/Irving/Hughes section of the film are given in their entirety; by way of Welles's movieola's sleight of hand, each of these "fakers" is constantly being quoted "out of context" (i.e., as part of a montage, rather than shown in a scene in real time); if most news-paper reporting is any example, the spectator is keenly aware of the sort of manipulation and distortion that can take place under such circumstances (as an omnipresent element within the film's mise-en-scène, news clippings call attention to the shaping of information to fit institutional agendas).

Even as *F for Fake*, as an essay film, resists the trappings of genre, Welles stresses the effects of style or genre on the spectator's interpretation of events by using a montage strategy in the fictional "Picasso sequence" that resembles the shot-reverse-shot constructions in the "girl watching" documentary sequence at the beginning of the film. In doing so, he brings into relief the codes at work in diegetic realism, and underscores the extraordinary lure, for the spectator, of the real in cinema. It is this lure, experienced as what Bill Nichols has called "epistemophelia" (or the desire to know), operative throughout documentary cinema, coupled with the shreds of documentary style, that causes the viewer to overlook the transition from researchable fact to sheer fiction in this sequence, even though our scopophilic impulse (operative in much of fictional cinema, and especially in the mystery genre) is frustrated in that sequence—frustrated because it is the extreme close-ups of Picasso's eye behind a grid (a window?) in black-and-white stills that catch our eye, more than the medium long shots of Oja Kodar flitting by on the path to the beach, or the fragmentary zoom shots of the curvaceous portions of her anatomy. Hence, documentary, like the mystery-detective genre or the striptease (even in its embellished fine art setting), risks providing the spectator with the reward of incontrovertible "evidence," that moment of teleological transparency that can calm curiosity and desire, thereby letting both filmmaker and viewer off the hook of sociohistorical need and responsibility, a hook that requires more than a presentation of "facts."[25] Welles takes that risk, then tries to avert it by showing the spectator that these moments in the film are just whiffs of pungent smoke, not the real cigar.

It is perhaps these two undoings of the cinematic appeal to the spectator's drives that, like a joke without a punch line, have prompted Scott Bukatman to consider the film void of pleasure. Perhaps in the place of conventional sources of cinematic pleasure, the audience is asked to derive pleasure from subtle, if ephemeral, ironies produced by unseemly juxtapositions, and from the knowledge that we are going to be duped at some point in this exercise, we just don't know exactly when. Admittedly, these are pleasures that will most definitely be lost on the more passive spectator, just as the spectators of the *War of the Worlds* broadcast and *Citizen Kane* who took their news material at face value missed the suspense and punchlines of the supratextual commentaries on the contemporary world and the media's approach to positioning us within it.

In the end, the effectivity of the critique in *F for Fake,* as in *Citizen Kane,* of how the media and fine art can each be used to promote public illusion and self-delusion within capitalist modernity (aptly illustrated in Kane's building of an opulent opera house to showcase the questionable talents of Susan Alexander in *Citizen Kane*) partly resides in the fact that each film bears traces of its moment (deep focus and trick cinematography in *Citizen Kane,* the hand-held verité camera style of Christian Odasso and the seventies frocks and miniskirts donned by the fashionable Oja Kodar in *F for Fake), and* openly addresses that moment's pressing dilemmas. In the national sphere *(Citizen Kane),* we are confronted with the blurring of the boundary between private and public domains, and with the political stakes attached to the *image* of moral rectitude, owing to the very real power of the press; in the international sphere *(F for Fake),* we find the hypervaluation (in both cultural and economic terms) of marketable art whether in simulacral or original form, coupled with the devaluation of the living artist, owing to the power of the art dealer and the "expert." Both of these films must be located in their contemporary contexts if one is to seek the connection in Welles's work between a cultural politics (involving the stakes attached to artistic innovation and integrity) and political ideology (involving the crucial connection between media and democracy in a free society, the prosecution of institutional as opposed to individual crimes), at different points in his career.

At the same time, the historical referentiality of the events in films like *Citizen Kane* and *F for Fake* is more complex than their linear periodization in either film history or Welles's career allows, especially if one considers Welles's sustained ambivalence toward modernity, coupled with his penchant for allegory. The synergistic relation between these two elements—one thematic, the other formal—courses through Welles's filmography, but is expressed with particular poignance in his Shakespearean adaptations, especially *Chimes at Midnight* (a hybrid amalgam of Shakespeare's *Henry IV,* parts I and II, *Henry V, Richard II,* and *The Merry Wives of Windsor*),[26] his opening narration to *Othello* (1952), and his essayistic meditation on both this adaptation and Shakespeare's play in *Filming Othello*; the same relation is palpable in other works, such as the unfinished *It's All True* and *Touch of Evil.* In some cases, the ambivalence translates into retrospective historical glances, as in *The Magnificent Ambersons,* which, produced in the thick of World War II, focused on the irreversible changes wrought by the automobile on what was mostly an agrarian society in the United States at the turn of the twentieth century. *Citizen Kane* devotes most of its substantive plot to the decades preceding the forties, when major structural changes occurred within the U.S. political system and mass media. In *Mr. Arkadin,* a mysterious and eccentric millionaire sends a young American pretender (obviously unscathed by recent world history) into an ever-widening net of the people and places of his checkered past only to kill the witnesses, including himself, thereby sparing his only offspring from the truth of his crimes, and leaving the private eye bewildered and empty-handed. By contrast, in *F for Fake,* these vectors of temporality are both reiterated through Welles's own reminiscences of his early career, and inverted, as he makes every attempt to literally cut short the nostalgic impulses of his interview subjects by repositioning them in the flow of screen time and thrusting them into the spotlight of the present.

For the sake of discursive periodization, then, I would agree with Scott Bukatman that *F for Fake* is a "profoundly modernist document on the postmodern moment."[27] At the same time, produced as it was toward the end of Welles's career, and notwithstanding its use of irony to ward off fetishism and nostalgia (of precisely the sort indulged in by Charles Foster Kane), this film is shot through with melancholy—triggered, we can surmise, by the effects of commercialism on artistic practice in the modern world, paralleled by the uneven path taken by a film career full of lost opportunities and exile, interspersed with the striking cinematic breakthroughs that placed Welles sporadically in the spotlight.[28] *Citizen Kane* ultimately ends on a note of progressive optimism, and proffers a secure position in the historical present from which to speak of the recent past, during which older forms of power (of the "robber baron" variety) associated with unbridled capitalist expansion at the turn of the twentieth century ultimately have become exhausted and discarded (with a little help

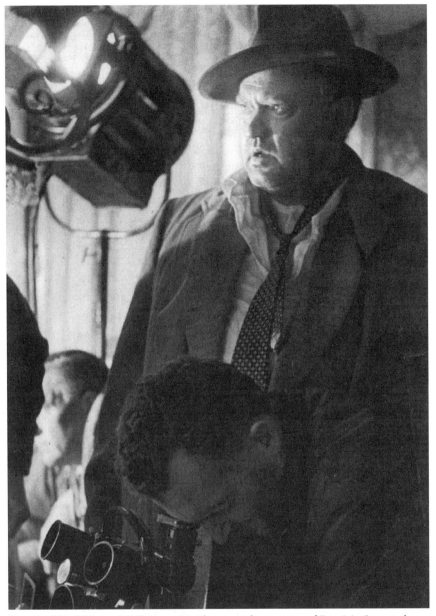

Touch of Evil (Orson Welles, 1958). Photograph courtesy of Rogério Sganzerla.

from Franklin D. Roosevelt's New Deal) by the very machinations they set in motion. In contrast, *F for Fake* is caught in a series of frustrated returns to the past which, taken at face value, provide only feeble lessons for the present. The pursuit of the "mystery" of Howard Hughes, the last tycoon to obtain controlling interest in RKO (the film studio that prematurely severed Welles's three-film contract in 1942, leading to the latter's precarious and frictive relationship to the studio system thereafter) prior to the sale of its property (including some of Welles's film elements) to Desilu in 1958, leads only to a respectful, multi-angled stare of the camera at the indifferent hotel room windows and bungalows that Hughes is reported to own and inhabit, along with the perhaps trivial discovery that Hughes's trusted employees leave ham sandwiches in a tree each night for him to retrieve as needed. Unlike his "biographer" Clifford Irving, who is allowed to make frequent appearances on camera, in sync sound even when his pronouncements are punctuated with uncomfortable pauses, Hughes is only available to us in disembodied form—framed by Welles's narration (as if to ensure the reversal of power relations)—by way of a discontinuous collage of archival footage, recorded telephone conversations, and written documents, the authenticity of which Welles encourages us to question.

The spatial corollary to this contrast in the temporal vectors of plot and memory is the centripetal manner in which all of the witnesses' narratives lead to Xanadu in *Citizen Kane* (a drama that largely takes place within secure interior spaces) and to the secure position of "citizenship" for the spectator, as contrasted with the centrifugal geospatial dynamics of *F for Fake,* which place the spectator in the position of a wandering, exiled, and occasionally disoriented subject as the scenes move from location to location in the United States (Las Vegas, Los Angeles, New York), the Spanish island of Ibiza, and France (Toussaint, Normandy, and Paris), with a few transitional scenes appropriately set at the Paris Orly airport.

▶

"The Key Is Not a Symbol"

Closely related to the issue of narrative discontinuity, anti-illusionism, and spectator repositioning and engagement is the self-conscious manipulation of symbols as bait for the spectator as s/he makes a way through the mystery plot. But only as *bait*. Mystery was one of Welles's preferred genres, inflecting the narrative structure and drive of films such as *The Lady from Shanghai, Othello, Mr. Arkadin, Touch of Evil,* and *The Trial* (1962). As with the documentary exposé and the biopic, the plot pivots around the display of "physical evidence" coupled with the search for, and carefully timed revelation to the viewer and on-screen subjects (respectively) of, the "truth." It should hardly come as a surprise that Welles combines these narrative modes in *Citizen Kane,* as in *F for Fake,* since what is defined as constituting truth, the narrative agencies that lead us to it, and the consequences of its discovery vary according to the mode, thereby impeding narrative homogeneity and the envelopment of the spectator in the cocoon of illusionism.

A rather unconventional mystery, since no single, serious crime appears to have been committed, the plot of *Citizen Kane* is less about finding clues and paying attention to symbols than about the ability, for spectator and protagonists alike, to attach symbolism to the life of an enigmatic public figure. Yet, while discussing with Peter Bogdanovich the technical and narrative decisions taken while making *Citizen Kane,* Welles avows his hatred for "symbolism." Of course, he is not advocating minimalist transparency to eradicate the possibility of symbolism; but rather, he is arguing that symbols with effective narrative significance should not be fixed for the spectator, thereby promoting further narrative integration. "If anybody finds it, it's for them to find. I never sit down and say how we're going to have a symbol for some character. They happen automatically, because life is full of symbols. So is art."[29]

Yet Welles is not quite so casual about the vehicles for, and dynamics of, symbolism in *Citizen Kane.* Throughout the film's plot, he teases us with the possibility that key symbols or leads to Kane's secret have been planted for us to find, only to undo the straightforwardness of those symbols and replace them with a more circuitous path to meaning. We invest in the possibility of narrative clues as long as we are strategically identified with the narrative agency of the detective reporter Thompson. In the plot, which Welles developed with co-screenwriter Herman J. Mankiewicz, Thompson unwittingly (yet in his capacity as narrator, coyly) beckons the screen audience through a series of false leads in the drive to uncover the basis of Charles Foster Kane's innermost obsession, which is distinctly named but vaguely identified on his deathbed. We follow the intrepid Thompson to the end of his (and our) assigned labyrinth only to discover that the kaleidoscopic, flashback-filled plot is less about the unveiling of Kane's life and personality (both riddled with synecdoche and cliché rather than idiosyncracy, notwithstanding his morbid eccentricity) than about the *trickiness* of joining a verbal signifier to its subjective and allegorical, rather than circumstantial and material, referent. In other words, the solution to the mystery does not reside in locating and decodifying "Rosebud," but in unmasking Kane. Even within the ostensible mystery logic of the diegesis, Kane's last utterance, "Rosebud," does not literally refer, of course, to the snow globe that silently slips from his fingers to shatter on the floor in the first scene of the film; it is anchored in a lost world figured within that globe, a world that is still only obliquely alluded to by the sled burning in the furnace of Kane's Xanadu mansion at the film's end.

The only remaining phenomenal link to Kane's "truth" (all of the human witnesses to that world have died), the sled/boundary begins to vanish before our eyes at the edge of the film's diegesis, as background music engulfs the sound track. Having been cut loose from all but the "primary" mechanisms of identification, the camera and sound recorder, we are now free to engage in a number of possible readings of what we have just seen and heard: a subtextual, psychoanalytic reading of Kane's failed relationships and zigzagging political positioning and social involvement; or a more broadly contextualized allegorical reading of the human price of acquiring excessive, opportunistic (or ethically compromised) power (here exemplified in the mass media), which tends to entrap and paralyze rather than liberate and fulfill in a modernizing, democratic United States. The latter reading, as Laura Mulvey has pointed out, has implications not only for our view of power dynamics within a changing United States at the onset of World War II, but also for the path taken by the United States with respect to the rest of the world (as empire) at pivotal junctures for significant portions of the world's population.[30]

Or, we may simply choose to contemplate the way in which Welles has just exposed and deconstructed our habitual response to more diegetically realist, narratively integrated films, and how, in the end, such a powerful personage as Kane does not really have a story to tell, dead or alive; at least, his story is no more interesting than the stories that each of us may have to tell. Just as significantly, even if the motifs and ostensibly symbolic objects in *Citizen Kane* are either rendered moot or shown to be polysemic, Welles has not extinguished the possibility of some truth to be discovered in this film. It is just that the dimensions and weight of this truth have been surrendered in the final zoom into the fire, and are for the spectator to determine.

More important than symbols as the bait for a missing "real" that will lure the spectator through the detective plot is the notion that a cognizant spectator not only is not a dupe but can be transformed into an accomplice. The "magic" of cinematic realism, like the magical act itself, requires the complicity of the viewer who, if only she or he will suspend her or his disbelief, will share in the pleasure of illusion: like the child in the train station in the opening sequence of *F for Fake*, who from the grin on his face may even have already seen the key trick Welles is about to perform (or at least knows that Welles is about to perform a "trick" with that key) yet takes delight in seeing it done somewhat *as anticipated*. According to this logic, the dichotomy that Welles establishes rhetorically between the portion of the film that tells the truth and the portion that lies is subverted: for if we have been paying attention as mindful spectators with one eye at the edge or outside of the diegesis, we know toward the end of the film that liberties will be taken with the truth. This knowledge, which is ideally situated on the back burner of our consciousness as considerable time has elapsed since Welles's friendly warning to us, forms the basis of our pleasure as we see the lies unfold; we become knowing accomplices to the dimensions taken by the apocryphal Picasso tale, just as we are complicit witnesses to the magical levitation exercise that Welles performs with Kodar's "grandfather." At the level of cinematic discourse, and with considerable implications for the question of authorship in relation to this film, this cross-fertilization of the "true" story with the apocryphal one by way of a narrator's warning (rather than by any visible difference in audiovisual syntax or shooting style) is not only a philosophical statement on the limitations we face when trying to grasp the truth—we are, Welles insists only human—but points to the interdependence, and equal importance with respect to the delivery of the filmic message, of Reichenbach's "cinéma direct" and Welles's collage of sound-image fragments, including his own narration in direct address.

▶ ───

Faux d'Artifice/Fakes on Fire

As for the (in)decipherability of parodic constructions in *F for Fake* and its antecedents, in his book on the uses of allegory in late-twentieth-century Brazilian cinema, Ismail Xavier remarks that the "traditional vocation" of allegory is to "march from fragments toward totality."[31] One might add that such a march depends on the kind of narrative plenitude and closure provided by diegetic realism. For allegory in cinema to "work," there must be a delicate balance between apparent narrative cohesion (and integration) and strategic breaks in that cohesion, where the spectator is invited to draw different conclusions from those proffered by the primary diegesis. A film like *Citizen Kane* can be seen as successful in this regard, since it can be seen as pushing the limits of allegorical fulfillment by creating a multiplicity of narrative viewpoints and then "disappointing" the spectator with false leads. However, *F for Fake* dashes the hopes of total fulfillment from the get-go, even as it teases the spectator with a series of allegorical "leads"—Welles's neo-Benjaminian reflection on the effects of the marketplace on artistic practice, or the "hoax" of power when capitalism is personified in figures such as Howard Hughes. On the one hand, this teasing is metaphorized in the strategically placed shots of de Hory burning his forged "Picasso" and "Modigliani" masterpieces in the fireplace, echoing the burning of the "Rosebud" sled in Xanadu's furnace in *Citizen Kane*. In both cases, Welles has understood that the image of disappearing evidence is much more frustrating to the viewer than the lack of evidence; and, read against the grain, both scenes of burning objects could just as easily function as a salvaging operation (is burning a painting for the camera really *destroying* the evidence?) in much the same way as avant-garde filmmaker Hollis Frampton's incineration of photographs from an early period in his artistic career in his short film (*Nostalgia,* 1971) is as much an act of preservation (after all, it is prints, not negatives, that are being burned) as it is destruction and commitment to oblivion. When these incendiary metaphors are unpacked, taking the factor of cinematic reproduction into account, we see that it is not a physical but a symbolic bonfire that is taking place (Kane's childhood dream was burned not by fire, but by the world that Kane helped to build; and perhaps de Hory is not burning his own handiwork so much as he is demonstrating how the art market has transformed the beautiful shapes drawn by Modigliani and Picasso into empty signifiers).

On the other hand, and more resistant to any "salvaging operation," is the undeniable fact that, in spite of the carefully crafted personal essay format and the dialogical relations established among the disparate filmic elements, as several commentators have noted, *F for Fake* barely holds together as a film, and this structural fragility, combined with the constant refusal of integrative, documentary moments, has the effect of defusing some of the film's allegorical potential. This is one of the more ironic consequences of what Timothy Corrigan has referred to as the refusal of transcendent historical discourse (associated with conventional genres) in the post–World War II essay film: "its own generic discourse collapses before the fragmentary particularities of the experience that is its defining subject."[32]

This undoing of allegory poses the question, perhaps even more frustrating for the viewer, of just what Elmyr de Hory and Howard Hughes (respectively) are doing in the film, if *F for Fake* is not really "about" real-life issues? Welles teases us with another analogy, reminding us of how, in the essay film, we are constantly aware of the filmmaker as an authorial presence, even if the essayist never appears on the screen (as for example, in Chris Marker's transnational essay film, *Sans Soleil* [1983] or Godfrey Reggio's *Koyanoquatsi* [1983] trilogy). This reflexive reference to the narrator's authority in documentary is only partially deconstructive in its effects. Since our primary identification in this film is with the editing table, not with the camera or the projector lens, Welles most definitely retains rather than debunks his own authority, and one could even say that his body and voice deflect the vectors of allegory onto his own career as an artist. Some might even say that this essay film is self-indulgent, since

Welles takes the liberty of populating it with his "favorite things:" fine food and wine, painting, magic, Spain, the human loves of his own life, and of course storytelling. Yet, in the end, none of these indulgences are pretexts for sollipsism, but on the contrary facilitate his conversational engagement and his vulnerability to comparison with his interview subjects, many of whom share at least some of these passions. Moreover, Welles's blithe references to the parallels between his own experiments with illusionism and the "charlatanry" of the forgers do not quite hold up to scrutiny, a key point since the metacritique needs at least one "real" leg to stand on. His story both belongs and does not belong with that of the forgers. Welles shares with his triumvirate of "charlatans" (de Hory, Irving, and Hughes) the pain of self-imposed exile and the anguish of trying to recover from unrealized projects while coping with old age. Yet he escapes being fully entrapped by this analogy through the fictionalization of these dilemmas as a theme, which harks back from *F for Fake* to *Citizen Kane*. As Joseph McBride has noted, "like his protagonists, Welles was often tempted by pride and by the trappings of worldly power. But in the final analysis, he was big enough to acknowledge his own limitations."[33]

In this sense, *F for Fake* is partly a confessional tale, in which Welles does not exempt himself from acts of opportunism and self-delusion, yet, in relinquishing the profitability of those acts, urges empathy and tolerance (and encourages self-irony for the more fortunate of the bunch), which are necessary for the building of community. Without community, artists like Elmyr de Hory and others who bring their own forms to the canvas simply cannot survive. A moral question momentarily supplants yet does not succeed in displacing the juridical and ethical questions linked to deliberate fakery: can one truly reproach and unmask to the point of deactivating a Holocaust survivor who, lacking the proper connections, and after failing to succeed within the competitive U.S. art scene, chose to outwit that scene by applying his same passion and skill to a less honest form of livelihood? Who in choosing that livelihood, deprived himself of a bank account and a permanent address, and occasionally became subjected yet again to imprisonment (albeit under pettier circumstances)? Linked to this moral question is the proposal of an alternative documentary ethics that deliberately does not probe into overly painful zones of experience out of respect for the filmic subject, even if it disappoints the viewer.

Thus, in *F for Fake,* Welles clearly avoids the brash intrusiveness and feigned omniscience of *Cops* and other reality shows—those wayward, twenty-first century heirs of direct cinema—that yield little in the way of "certitude" or "truth" (and, in giving the socially disenfranchised a "face" or a "voice," do little to empower them beyond the limits of the screen) yet, in unleashing an elaborate sadomasochistic flirtation with the real, succeed in distilling the dichotomous pleasure of looking through, and performing for, the camera. In contradistinction to this brand of re-flexivity, and in rhythmic contrast to the compassionate brush strokes of Odasso's gently probing and patient camera, Welles opts for solitary medi-tations in eerily still places that range from the gaudy to the sublime— against a low angled shot of Hughes's curtained window at the Desert Inn in Las Vegas, a fog-shrouded corner of the Bois de Boulogne in Paris, the facade of the Chartres Cathedral near Paris—as if to measure the distance between photojournalism and painting, and to echo through architectural metaphor the oscillation of his own artistic career among the poles of "mass," "popular," and "high" culture.[34] Whereas wire fences, moats, padlocks, and tight-lipped butlers block our access in *Citizen Kane,* in this film the real is almost tangible, thinly enveloped in pathos and irony and seeping through the interstices of interview, monologue, and travelogue material.

At the same time, one must be especially careful *not* to link what Bukatman has called the "production of absence" in *F for Fake* (the defus-ing, discarding, or hollowing out of key signifiers) to legends of Welles's "fear of completion."[35] In the end, placed at the core of his solitary nar-ration, the reverence for the Chartres cathedral and the selflessness and anonymity of its makers overshadows even the "real" of Welles's own experience as mediated through storytelling and images of his "favorite things" as well as the more elusive experiences of de Hory and Hughes. For Welles, *F for Fake* opened up a new phase of filmmaking possibilities in which he was able to hold onto his convictions and his passions while tapping into an "anti-genre" that would enable him to simultaneously comment upon and reintroduce himself to a shrinking public sphere. One can only guess at where this foray might have led had Welles not died shortly before the cybernetic revolution reached the average middle-class household in the United States, bringing a new round of reflections on the ontological status of mediated representations of the physical world, the juridical, social, and phenomenal place of the author (as well as that of the user-spectator), not to mention the new opportunities for empower-ment, profit, deception, self-delusion, and sociopolitical agency within a more amorphous and laterally structured public sphere. For the moment, we must be content with the questions raised and directions suggested by Welles in *F for Fake* and his next self-reflexive essay film, *Filming Othello,* not to mention the many unfinished projects that await our scrutiny.

NOTES

1. The quote from Welles that begins this article is from Orson Welles and Peter Bogdanovich, *This Is Orson Welles*, ed. Jonathan Rosenbaum (New York: Harper Collins, 1992), 101. Emphasis in the original.
2. See Walter Benjamin, "The Work of Art in the Age of Mechanical Reproduction," in *Illuminations*, ed. Hannah Arendt, trans. Harry Zorn (New York: Schocken Books, 1969), 217–51.
3. John Schlesinger's *Midnight Cowboy* (1968) is one of the more memorable examples of this incorporation, but traces can also be found in films like *Bonnie and Clyde* (Arthur Penn, 1967) and the blaxploitation hit, *Superfly* (Gordon Parks Jr., 1972), as well as in Sam Peckinpah's "new westerns" such as *The Wild Bunch* (1969). The advent of the "film school" generation in the mid-seventies, especially Francis Ford Coppola and George Lucas, marked a return to more classical parameters for the cutting aesthetics and mise-en-scènes of Hollywood cinema.
4. Benjamin, "Work of Art," 228–37.
5. Ibid., 231.
6. Timothy Corrigan, "The Cinematic Essay: Genre on the Margins," *iris* 20 (Autumn 1995): 89 and 85, respectively.
7. See for example, "L'Evolution du langage cinématographique," 71–76, and "Le réalisme cinématographique et l'école italienne de la liberation," 267–73, in André Bazin, *Qu'est-ce que le cinéma?* (Paris: Septième Art, 1985); and André Bazin, *Orson Welles: A Critical View* (New York: Harper and Row, 1978).
8. Scott Bukatman, who incidentally does not advocate a wholesale postmodernist reading of *F for Fake*, does take Welles's comparison of filmmaking (including his own) to the art of deception at face value, and interprets this apparent self-reflexivity on Welles's part as a sign of a deconstructionist impulse at work in the film. He states, for example, "It is in *F for Fake* . . . that Welles's deconstructive activity reaches its fullest figuration, as questions of cultural value and legitimacy are linked to arbitrary structures of meaning production" (Bukatman, "Incompletion, Simulation, and the Refusal of the Real: The Last Films of Orson Welles," in *Persistence of Vision* 7 [Summer 1989]: Special Issue on Orson Welles, ed. William G. Simon: 85; see also 86).
9. Geoff Andrew in *The Film Handbook*, as quoted on the video box for *F for Fake*, (copyright Saci, Les Films de l'Astrophore, Janus Film und Fernsehen, 1975).
10. In Jonathan Rosenbaum, *Placing Movies:*

The Practice of Film Criticism (Berkeley and Los Angeles: University of California Press, 1995), 171–83.
11. See Michael Anderegg, *Orson Welles, Shakespeare, and Popular Culture* (New York: Columbia University Press, 1999).
12. For the distinction between "traditional" (i.e., pre-eighteenth-century) and modern magic, which began to flourish in Euro-America during the latter half of the nineteenth century, see James W. Cook, *The Arts of Deception: Playing with Fraud in the Age of Barnum* (Cambridge, Mass.: Harvard University Press, 2001), 164–71. Welles sums up this distinction by quoting the nineteenth-century master prestidigitator Robert-Houdin to the effect that "all magicians are nothing but actors"; the original statement was that modern magicians were "actors, merely playing the part of a magician," a status Welles would have been most comfortable with (from Robert-Houdin, *Comment on Devient Sorcier: Les Secrets de la Prestidigitation et de la Magie* [1878; rpt. Paris: Ressources, 1980], 29, as translated from the French and quoted in Cook, *Arts of Deception*, 169).
13. Loosely adapted from John Collier's short story "Youth from Vienna," "The Fountain of Youth" was a twenty-five-minute television pilot program produced for Desilu Studios and aired (but never developed into a series) on NBC's *The Colgate Palmolive Theatre*, September 16, 1958. See Chuck Berg and Tom Erskine, *The Encyclopedia of Orson Welles, From "The Hearts of Age" to "F for Fake"* (New York: Checkmark Books, 2003), 117–18. As its title suggests, the pilot involves an attempt by a scientist to trick his lover and her newfound, attractive, and athletic fiancé into believing that he has actually given them as a wedding gift one vial of a serum that will prevent one—and only one—of them from aging.
14. The shorts are available in a compilation on videotape under the title *Scene of the Crime*, distributed by Universal Studios/MCA.
15. The *First Person Singular* series was aired on CBS from July 11 to September 5, 1938. *War of the Worlds* was broadcast on October 30 as part of the *Mercury Theatre on the Air* series, featured on CBS radio between September 11 and December 4, 1938. See "Orson Welles's Radio Career," in "Orson Welles: A Catalogue of Works," in *Persistence of Vision* 7 (Summer 1989): Special Issue on Orson Welles, ed. William G. Simon: 164.
16. See Bill Nichols, *Representing Reality:*

Issues and Concepts in Documentary (Bloomington: University of Indiana Press, 1991), 3.

17. See Welles's commentary on this in Welles and Bogdanovich, *This Is Orson Welles*, 74.

18. See Gregg Toland, "Realism for Citizen Kane," *American Cinematographer* (February 1941), reprinted in *American Cinematographer* 72, no. 8 (August 1991): 37, 39.

19. For more on the troubled release of *Citizen Kane*, see Robert L. Carringer, *The Making of Citizen Kane*, rev. ed. (Berkeley and Los Angeles: University of California Press, 1996), 111–17, and Welles's own summary in Welles and Bogdanovich, *This Is Orson Welles*, 46–51 and 85–88. See also Pauline Kael, "Raising Kane," in *The Citizen Kane Book* (New York: Little, Brown, 1971), 1–84. For parallels between Kane's biography and that of Hearst, see Laura Mulvey, *Citizen Kane* (London: British Film Institute, 1992).

20. "Orson Welles não se casou com Dolores del Rio," *Cine-Rádio Jornal* (Rio de Janeiro), February 11, 1942, 7. For Welles's statement to the press regarding Kane's character, see Frank Brady, *Citizen Welles: A Biography of Orson Welles* (New York: Charles Scribner's Sons, 1989), 283–85.

21. Corey Creekmur, "Buffalo Bill (Himself) History and Memory in the Western biopic," in *Westerns: Films through History*, ed. Janet Walker, AFI Film Readers Series (London: Routledge, 2001), 143. Welles attributed the title to RKO president George Schaefer; see Welles and Bogdanovich, *This Is Orson Welles*, 82. For the version of the script titled "American," see Carringer, *The Making of Citizen Kane*, 18–29.

22. Tom Gunning, *D. W. Griffith and the Origins of American Narrative Film: The Early Years at Biograph* (Urbana: University of Illinois Press, 1991), 93.

23. For a comprehensive list of Welles's "essay films," which Rosenbaum traces back to the trailer for *Citizen Kane*, see Rosenbaum, "Orson Welles's Essay Films and Documentary Fictions," in *Placing Movies*, 172.

24. See Leon Pompa, *Vico: A Study of the New Science*, 2d ed. (Cambridge: Cambridge University Press, 1990), 72–73.

25. For a discussion of the possible parallels between pornography and documentary, see Christian Hansen, Catherine Needham, and Bill Nichols, "Pornography, Ethnography, and the Discourses of Power," in Nichols, *Representing Reality*, 201–28.

26. See Anderegg, *Orson Welles, Shakespeare, and Popular Culture*, 127.

27. Bukatman, 88.

28. For an insightful discussion on the philosophical and ideological differences between nostalgia and melancholy as modes of historical remembrance, see Celeste Olalquiaga, *The Artificial Kingdom* (New York: Pantheon Books, 1998), 68–76 and passim.

29. Welles and Bogdanovich, *This Is Orson Welles*, 82.

30. For an excellent example of both paths of interpretation, as well as other instances of frustrated identification for the spectator in *Citizen Kane*, see Mulvey, *Citizen Kane*.

31. Ismail Xavier, *Allegories of Underdevelopment: Aesthetics and Politics in Modern Brazilian Cinema* (Minneapolis: University of Minnesota Press, 1997), 16.

32. Timothy Corrigan, "The Cinematic Essay: Genre on the Margins," 90. See also Xavier, *Allegories*, 87.

33. Joseph McBride, *Orson Welles*, rev. ed. (New York: Da Capo Press, 1996), 196.

34. For a cogent exposition on this last topic, see Anderegg, 1–18. See also the *I Love Lucy* television episode "Lucy Meets Orson Welles," October 15, 1956, which skillfully combines Lucy's (Lucille Ball) ambitions to play opposite Welles in Shakespeare's *Romeo and Juliet* with a magical act orchestrated by Welles in her husband Ricky's (Desi Arnaz) New York nightclub for comic effect.

35. Bukatman, "Refusal of the Real," 83.

CRAIG HIGHT
JANE ROSCOE

[11] Forgotten Silver: *A New Zealand Television Hoax and Its Audience*

Although documentary texts have traditionally enjoyed a privileged position in relation to fictional media as assumed bearers of truth and knowledge about the social world, it becomes increasingly difficult for them to maintain that status. Some of the more interesting recent research within the realm of documentary theory has centered on the long tradition of documentary hybrids, from drama-documentary[1] and nature documentary[2] to the more recent explosion of reality TV, docu-soap, and reality game-show formats.[3] For both filmmakers and audiences, these hybrid forms have often profound implications for the continued stability of documentary as a recognizable form within audiovisual media. John Corner's use of the term "post-documentary"[4] in these discussions is evidence of a recognition of the different set of relationships that these hybrids entail with their audiences. At the heart of debates over fact/fiction hybrids is a tension over the continued viability of the term "documentary" and of the form that the term has traditionally meant to identify.

This article considers the implications of the emergence of more sophisticated examples of mock-documentaries, a form of hybrid that, in its potential if not always in practice,[5] challenges the continued validity of the documentary project. In common with other documentary hybrids, mock-documentaries draw on and play with audiences' acceptance of the wider cultural discourses that couch and partly articulate documentary. Mock-documentaries can be distinguished from other hybrids especially in their insistence upon taking the form of documentary as a given; they are capable of offering a direct commentary on the status of documentary rather than of serving as an exercise in its transformation through hybridity.

Although it is debatable whether documentary texts can be seen collectively as a genre, Bill Nichols suggests that they can.[6] The key to Nichols' argument is that documentary has a privileged status dependent upon the complex relationships it enacts among filmmaker, text, and audience. This article considers *Forgotten Silver* (1995), a New Zealand mock-documentary directed by Peter Jackson and Costa Botes. As a documentary hybrid, mock-documentary opens up the spaces within these relationships, and allows for the potential for reflexivity toward the genre as a whole. This program illustrates how tenuous are the relations that maintain the sense of a privileged status for documentary, and how easily there can be slippage, particularly between the agenda of filmmakers and the expectations of their audience. Taking our cue from Nichols, the analysis presented here examines *Forgotten Silver* at three levels; first, the immediate context of its production; second, its use of documentary codes and conventions to demythologize the form; and, third, the program's public reception within New Zealand.

▶ ──

Contextualizing *Forgotten Silver*

Much about the immediate context in which *Forgotten Silver* was produced effectively served to reinforce the text's documentary credentials with its audience. First, the program was screened (by Television New Zealand on Sunday, October 29, 1995) in the "quality drama" *Montana Sunday Theatre* slot. In previous weeks, this slot had screened a series of original New Zealand dramas, and finishing that series with a documentary about an apparently forgotten New Zealand filmmaker seemed appropriate, if somewhat unusual. A wider cultural context also served to further legitimate, justify, and authenticate the program and its subject matter. New Zealand was celebrating one hundred years of cinema, with the Film Commission spending much time, effort, and resources in promoting an awareness and celebration of this milestone both nationally and locally.

One such activity organized through the Film Archive has particular relevance here. Over the previous couple of years, the Film Archive had been conducting a nationwide film search, encouraging the public to hand over old films that had, in most cases, been left to disintegrate in garages and attics. Peter Jackson makes specific reference to this search at the start of *Forgotten Silver,* when explaining how he first encountered the work of Colin McKenzie. Although most of the material collected by the Archive was home movies and similar short excerpts of film, it was certainly the hope (if not the reality) that the search would uncover material of historical importance. *Forgotten Silver* claimed to be presenting a film "find" that matched, and even exceeded, the dreams of the Archive and of the many people who had contributed to the search. Given this context, it seemed reasonable to accord the announcement of the discovery and a presentation of McKenzie's work in a slot known for its promotion of high quality and original material. The fact that the Film Commission and New Zealand On Air[7] had supported the project financially only served to reinforce the legitimacy and significance of the program. It was, then, with some excitement and curiosity that an estimated audience of four hundred thousand viewers tuned into TV1[8] that Sunday night to learn more about a pioneering New Zealand filmmaker.

This first screening was preceded by a significant amount of publicity focusing on the importance of its find. *Forgotten Silver* was brought to the attention of the New Zealand audience in an article in the New Zealand *Listener*[9] that "broke" the story, claiming to herald a "sensational find" with the discovery of a hoard of long-lost films by a previously unknown New Zealand filmmaker, Colin McKenzie. The article placed Peter Jackson and Costa Botes in the role of discoverers and celebrants of McKenzie's assumed legacy. In hindsight, the article contains a number of cues as to the real nature of *Forgotten Silver,*[10] and in fact is written in the same tones as the discourse of *Forgotten Silver* itself: excitement at the importance and relevance of the work of McKenzie and of the implications that this discovery seemed to hold for both New Zealand and world cinema history.

The first public screening of *Forgotten Silver* was not unprecedented in New Zealand television broadcasting. The program could in fact be seen as part of a well-established tradition of mock New Zealand television reports. Perhaps the most well-known examples have been the numerous mock reports of agricultural developments or inventions featured on *Country Calendar.*[11] The two main nightly news programs also typically produce mock news items immediately before the conclusion of their April 1 broadcasts.[12] What was perhaps unique was the level of secrecy that went into maintaining the pretense that the program was a legitimate documentary, and the publicity surrounding this first screening. Here, *Forgotten Silver* went beyond the tradition of spoof news items to enlist the complicity of a national print publication (the *Listener*) that generally enjoys a reputation for responsible journalism.

▶ _____

Documenting Colin McKenzie

Forgotten Silver successfully convinced its audience of its claim for documentary status, probably in large part through the complexity and sophistication of its use of the language, practices, and conventions that define documentary. In a very accomplished way, Jackson and Botes utilized all the codes and conventions of documentary to turn a *fiction* into a representation that the audience could easily accept as having a basis in reality. The key to the program's success lay in the tension that the text generated between the absurdity of some of its fictional content and the sophisticated simulation of the documentary form used to present that content to its audience. To engage with the program as a parodic exercise, the audience had first to engage in a documentary mode of viewing. The filmmakers clearly intended that viewers approach the program in its first screening *as though it were a documentary,* drawing on certain well-established expectations concerning what documentaries in general can offer, and in particular how documentary texts represent the historical world. As viewers, an audience expects the people, places, and issues to be real and documentaries to treat these subjects with seriousness and authority. These expectations effectively frame the manner in which one approaches and engages with these programs.

Forgotten Silver utilizes the expositional mode of documentary, the form that relates most closely to the traditional expositional essay. It is a mode that seeks to offer an argument about the social world, incorporating editing devices designed to reinforce the argument. This mode also commonly employs a narrator, either on screen or in voice-over (the "voice of god"), and uses expert testimonies to legitimate or develop specific parts of its argument.[13] So, *Forgotten Silver* begins with Jackson in his backyard, locating him, and the story of McKenzie, in real and identifiable surroundings. As Jackson tells of his role in the story, and of the initial discovery of the forgotten films, Polaroid snapshots of the film canisters fill the screen. Documentary has used such photographic evidence to the point of cliché—it draws upon the naturalized assumption that photography represents an indexical link to the social-historical world, that a photograph offers a physical trace of actual events and location "captured" by a camera. Interestingly, the photographs are color shots, in direct contrast to the "original" and "authentic" black-and-white photographs seen later in the program.

Before the listing of the title credits, the audience is presented with a lineup of clearly labeled interviewees: Jonathan Morris, film archivist; Costa Botes, filmmaker; Harvey Weinstein, Miramax films; and film historian Leonard Maltin. All make claims regarding the historic importance of the films and the place of McKenzie as a pioneer in the history of film. They all play the role of film experts, conveying legitimacy through their status as bearers of such expert knowledge, and as such their testimonies serve to both authenticate the find and, importantly, give credibility to *Forgotten Silver.* Throughout the film, we return to these experts, with their interviews implicitly reinforcing and legitimating the overall authority of Jackson and of the arguments he presents.

Another key player in the documentary is McKenzie's "widow," Hannah. She plays the role of eyewitness, whose testimony serves as a complement to the gravity of the other, more expert, testimonies. Her interview provides access to a more personalized narrative about her apparent relationship with McKenzie, while other interviewees support the more public narrative gradually constructed by Jackson. As the film progresses she reveals vital clues that help Jackson and viewers piece together McKenzie's story. However, true to the expositional style, the program builds tension and drama by pacing these revelations at regular intervals.

The rhetoric of science, and in particular of scientific discovery, is drawn upon throughout the film to further enhance the plausibility of Jackson's findings. The revelatory nature of scientific discovery is used as the basis for much of the narrative of the film, and, more overtly, in the manner in which forms of evidence are presented: McKenzie's early inventions, such as his experiments with the egg whites he supposedly used to make film stock, or his complex attempts to develop color film, or even the computer enhancement of the newspaper date in the Pearse flight footage. These inventions are authenticated by the "experts" who explain the chemical reactions or other technological aspects of these inventions. Without specialized access to these scientific discourses, such claims are difficult to reject outright.[14]

These events in the McKenzie story are reinforced by the use of authenticating material, such as the black-and-white photographs that show McKenzie as a young man, with his family, and with his inventions. There are also stills taken from old newspapers that chart McKenzie's progress in the filmmaking business. Taken together, these "documents" provide a seeming wealth of authenticating material to support Jackson's claims for the historical authenticity and significance of McKenzie's accomplishments.

Perhaps most convincing are the extracts from McKenzie's own films, both his fictional work *(Salome)* and his "reportage" films of Gallipoli[15] and of the Spanish Civil war. The latter films are of particular importance to the argument of *Forgotten Silver* because they ground its rhetoric in the social-historical world. These references to historical events, and McKenzie's footage, reinforce each other. The program offers McKenzie's films as further documentation of historical events, which in turn helps to establish McKenzie's presence at these points in history.

Forgotten Silver also features Jackson and Botes organizing an expedition into the West Coast bush in an attempt to find the location of the filming for McKenzie's masterpiece, *Salome*. Here history is almost treated as an accessible realm, in the sense that it has left tangible remnants that can be used in its reconstruction. The journey of Jackson and Botes into the New Zealand landscape deliberately mirrors that of McKenzie and of historical documentary.[16]

It is important to reiterate that filmmakers Jackson and Botes, while succeeding in utilizing the codes and conventions of the genre and in inviting viewers to join in a documentary mode of engagement, apparently also intended that their audience would realize the joke while viewing the program. Both expressed surprise that there was a group of viewers who seemed unable, or unwilling, to move from a documentary mode of viewing to an appreciation of the filmmakers' overall parodic frame for the program: "We never seriously thought that people would believe it because we kept putting in more and more outrageous gags—custard pies in the Prime Minister's face, making film out of eggs, and the Tahitian color film. We wanted the audience to start out believing it and although by the time it was finished they no longer believed it they would still have had a good time."[17] In responding to critics, Botes in particular was insistent that they had wider intentions than simply a sophisticated in-joke: "This was fiction, but it was a full-blown celebration of Kiwi ingenuity, asking people to wake up and see what's in their backyard. Picasso said, 'We all know that art is not truth. Art is a lie that makes us realize truth.'[18] If *Forgotten Silver* causes people never to take anything from the media at face value, so much the better. Our film was better researched and, on the whole, more 'true' than most products of the 'infotainment' industry."[19]

▶ ──────────────────────────────

The Appeal to National Myths

One of the more interesting aspects of *Forgotten Silver* is its relationship to myth, and to New Zealand myths in particular. The program convincingly demonstrated the rhetorical power of couching the specific narratives constructed around the fictional McKenzie within wider established historical narratives. A crucial part of the effectiveness of the program for New Zealand audiences was based on the subtlety and variety of ways in which its filmmakers exploited cultural stereotypes and accepted notions concerning the nature of New Zealand history and society. In this way, Jackson and Botes were apparently able to generate a high degree of emotional resonance between local viewers and the character that McKenzie appeared to represent.

In terms of myth, it is critical that Jackson, as a reporter, performs the roles of both detective and tourist for the audience.[20] He operates as a

CRAIG HIGHT AND JANE ROSCOE

detective, in the sense that he presents a number of mysteries to the audience that are then solved by Jackson and Botes throughout the course of the program. The mystery of why Colin McKenzie remained unknown until discovered by the filmmakers serves as perhaps the dominant narrative device of *Forgotten Silver*. Much of the narrative structure of the program serves to unfold the story of McKenzie's life, presenting a biography with references to a number of already known historical events (such as the two world wars). How McKenzie died is one of a number of smaller puzzles solved as this story unfolds.

To solve the overarching mystery of why McKenzie remained undiscovered, Jackson and his colleagues search for a huge set supposedly built by the filmmaker in the West Coast bush for his masterpiece, *Salome*. This search, which forms the second major part of *Forgotten Silver*'s narrative (regularly and expertly intercut with McKenzie's biography), allows Jackson to perform the role of reporter as tourist as well. In the sense of myth, here the filmmakers act as representatives of the audience on a journey into the unknown, in terms of both space (into the "jungles" of the New Zealand bush landscape) and time (into the past, to establish the authenticity of McKenzie's achievements and hence his legacy to cinema history).[21] They perform an investigative role, seeking the evidence that will legitimate the narrative of McKenzie, and also in some sense the more fundamental narratives about the country that he appears to epitomize. Our trust in their suitability for this role rests partly in our belief in the professionalism of the journalist-filmmaker, but also in the manner in which cameras seem to document each step of their journey. The footage appears to capture not only the process of their discovery but the actual moment of discovery itself, images that are persuasive because they appear spontaneous and unmediated rather than crafted for presentation to an audience.

This journey into the New Zealand bush is one of the more important ways in which *Forgotten Silver* draws specifically on New Zealand myths to make its narrative so compelling. In New Zealand popular culture, the native bush and its associated landscape plays something of a similar function to the Western frontier in American folklore. The bush served as a frontier for early European colonialists, the place where the more admired aspects of a New Zealand character were forged. The resilience, independence, and persistence of McKenzie in the face of the natural obstacles provided by the West Coast bush appeal to such well-established stereotypes in New Zealand culture.

Other aspects of McKenzie's character also draw upon stereotypes established by the colonial period of New Zealand history. He is one of the legendary backyard inventors at the heart of New Zealand's mythic development, and both he and his brother Brooke serve as soldiers in the various conflicts claimed to have forged the beginnings of the nation. It is Brooke, with a camera built by his brother, who provides the first footage from the very cradle of the nation: Gallipoli. *Forgotten Silver* succeeds here by not just appealing to an important myth of the origin of the birth of the nation, but reinforcing the accepted narrative promoted by the myth, through providing the first documentary—and hence "real" and concrete—evidence of the hardships suffered by New Zealand soldiers. (For its initial New Zealand audience, this perhaps represented evidence of a slightly higher order from that constructed simply for the fictionalized narrative of McKenzie's filmmaking genius. It succeeded in tapping into quite fundamental aspects of nationalism, as did the sequence apparently proving the significance of the aviator Pearse, as discussed below.)

Above all, the character of McKenzie is the epitome of the dogged inventor-genius who perseveres despite a wealth of natural, personal, financial, and political hardships. Although McKenzie's endeavors were in vain in terms of recognition for himself during his lifetime, they could serve as a kind of historical lesson for the audience of the way things *should* have happened. In doing so, the narrative of *Forgotten Silver* both draws on and subverts some of the more basic value systems inherent to New Zealand mythology.

▶

The Public Response

The hoax was revealed in national newspapers the day following the screening, and received consistent coverage and commentary from newspapers other than the *Listener.*[22] It is worth noting that the hoax was only newsworthy because it was believed by wide sections of the New Zealand audience. Even local journalists were apparently fooled, with some not realizing it was a spoof until they phoned TVNZ to contact the filmmakers for follow-up stories.[23]

From a cursory survey of responses reported in the media, the New Zealand audience reacted to *Forgotten Silver* in varying and interesting ways. The written responses to the *Listener,* which featured the original article publicizing *Forgotten Silver,* demonstrate a range of these audience reactions. The magazine states that of "the writers of the 24 letters the *Listener* has received on the *Forgotten Silver* hoax, 16 express disapproval, five approve, and three still believe."[24] This public response could be divided roughly into the three categories explored below; these are by no means exhaustive, nor mutually exclusive, but they do serve as a useful starting point for any discussion over the willingness of the New Zealand audience to appreciate, in particular, the program's parodic approach toward many of the basic assumptions exploited by documentaries and news services in general.

1. *Uncertain:* Some viewers felt confusion over whether or not Colin McKenzie could be considered a New Zealand historical figure, or whether *Forgotten Silver* was in fact a documentary.[25] One viewer was inspired to conduct background research into Maybelle, the heroine of the film, and examined adoption records for Dunedin, coming to the conclusion that she had located a young woman almost certainly the daughter of either Brooke or Colin McKenzie.[26] These kinds of audience responses to *Forgotten Silver* testify to the effectiveness of Jackson and Botes in perpetrating their hoax and to the quality of the craft in the program.

The confusion of some viewers was perhaps also due to an expectation that there is a clearly demarcated line between reality-based television and fictional programs, that there should be something either preceding or during the program that makes this division obvious to the viewers. *Forgotten Silver* does have a deliberate degree of reflexivity—as noted above, it does feature a number of clues about the nature of its subject—but this reflexivity, these clues, were often subtle and perhaps overwhelmed by the effectiveness of the program's other devices. These viewers were also perhaps unaccustomed to being asked to judge the validity of an entire program.

2. *Positive:* A portion of *Forgotten Silver*'s audience, initially a minority, expressed some appreciation of the degree of directorial ability that went into the making of the program, and to some extent supported the idea that there were some national myths which New Zealanders should be able to laugh at:

> Congratulations to the perpetrators—it was the best New Zealand entertainment in ten years![27]

> The producers have done us all a service by showing how easy it is to hoodwink a viewing public that has been conditioned to believe that anything labeled "documentary" is necessarily the truth. Viewers should bear this experience in mind, and keep a pinch of salt handy when watching supposedly more serious documentaries or "infodocs" on current issues, especially controversial ones.[28]

In a follow-up article in the *Listener,* Botes offered the following response as his favorite: "One Network News admitted that last night's *Montana Sunday Theatre* was a hoax. Well, all credibility has gone down the tubes— I won't be believing in TVNZ's news anymore."[29] In some sense, these viewers could perhaps be termed "televisually sophisticated" in that they did not automatically assume that information structured within a documentary discourse conformed to the assumptions of objectivity, accuracy, and balance associated with the form. They at some point disengaged from a documentary mode of reading, recognized the fictional nature of the program, and eventually developed a sense of appreciation for the craft involved in its construction and the wider implications of its success as a hoax.

3. *Negative/hostile:* The most interesting responses to the program were those that expressed anger at having been taken in by the hoax, and especially at the willingness of the filmmakers to play with some more central aspects of the discourses of objectivity, balance, and accuracy that serve as the wider frames of reference for television documentary and news texts.

> I do not wish to reveal my score on a gullibility rating of 0 to 100 percent. Suffice to say, I was not entirely surprised to discover it was a hoax, but was also profoundly disturbed by the discovery that I had been duped. If on this, then on what else? God, the Pope, the integrity of Fair Go, Richard Long, Judy Bailey, the last shreds of Paul Holmes; all disappearing down a gurgling plug-hole of lost credibility.[30]

> I can't express my disappointment at having lost a genius and gained another "clever" filmmaker. A wise filmmaker of yesteryear (when standards were more stodgy) warned against tricking or insulting your audience. Whatever its motive, this film could not be said to be in sympathy with its audience. I doubt if I'll ever look at the work of Peter Jackson (or the *Listener*) in quite the same light again.[31]

> Because of the damage to true documentary and the misuse of that honored term, I for one, after a lifetime of interest in film, have resigned my membership of the Film Society.[32]

> Peter Jackson and his *Silver Screen* conspirators should be shot.[33]

These types of responses are representative of viewers who viewed the program with a number of basic assumptions. In immediate terms, these viewers seemed unable or unwilling to accept that documentary techniques are themselves conventional forms of representation, rather than tools capable of revealing some preexisting reality. These viewers' outraged reactions to the program's screening serve as an indication of how naturalized are the discourses associated with documentary and other nonfiction audiovisual texts.

The implicit acceptance of these naturalized discourses led many to express a feeling of betrayal that *Forgotten Silver* had not been labeled as fiction, and that there had been a flippant abandonment of the privileged space accorded to the documentary genre. These viewers expressed a real sense of outrage at the "violation" of the trust that they placed both in filmmakers' adopting the documentary form and in the broadcaster's responsibility in screening the program, a trust they expected to be reciprocated through a respect accorded to themselves as viewers. In more specific terms, they saw this as a violation of an assumed relationship between themselves and Television New Zealand as an institution, an expectation itself a legacy of TVNZ's history as a BBC-styled public broadcasting service.[34] A third and closely related aspect of the negative reaction to the program could be a degree of anti-intellectualism—the idea that this was a hoax that was just too clever, that it could not have been unraveled except by the most visually sophisticated viewers.

Finally, there is the issue of whether the local audience reactions to *Forgotten Silver* were complicated by a degree of uncertainty and "immaturity" in New Zealand culture over the basic character of national identity. Here the anger seems directed at filmmakers who would play with some of the more treasured popular New Zealand legends, such as the alleged pre-Wright brothers flight of Richard Pearse, in ways that appeared (to these viewers) largely for the filmmakers' own amusement. This part of the New Zealand audience is perhaps representative of social groups unable to cope with challenges to the country's more "sacred" national myths and symbols of national identity. At this stage in New Zealand history (the mid-1990s), such myths and symbols were perhaps still too vulnerable to face such an exercise in deconstruction.[35]

▶──

Discussion

Jackson and Botes's assertion that they intended *Forgotten Silver*'s audience to move from a documentary mode of reading to a recognition of the program's fictionality during viewing is founded on an understanding of a fact/fiction dichotomy, one that serves to reinforce the idea that documentary and drama are two separate entities. Such a fact/fiction dichotomy not only informs documentary as a cultural product, but also provides the framework through which viewers can judge and evaluate such texts. Documentary's privileged position within society is based on certain preconceptions, which Derek Paget argues derive from a "modern faith in facts."[36] This belief in factuality, and documentary's associated cultural status, are grounded in the metanarratives of positivistic science and the project of the Enlightenment. It is these very discourses and metanarratives that have been problematized and questioned by those working within poststructuralist frameworks.[37] Rather than conceptualizing fact and fiction as distinct entities, poststructuralism points instead to a continuum on which fact and fiction leak into each other.

Of course, documentary texts have always struggled to maintain their status as factual records. As Nichols notes, "the distinction between fact and fiction blurs when claims about reality get cast as narratives."[38] Jackson and Botes challenge, in perpetrating the hoax of *Forgotten Silver*'s documentary status, not just the acceptance of a form of representation, but a climate of believed assumptions concerning the truthfulness of documentary and other "nonfiction" texts. As audience members, we do not turn away from a documentary and say, "It's just a film." Such texts require a viewer to draw upon an assumed fact/fiction dichotomy to make sense of their representations.

Thus, the most significant legacy of *Forgotten Silver* is not its status as a hoax. As with some mock-documentaries, the program succeeds in engaging us in a documentary mode of viewing that causes us to reflect upon how these modes draw upon wider cultural discourses concerning the nature of knowledge and concerning conceptions of truth. As some viewers commented, if Jackson and Botes can make us believe in a fiction, then what are the implications for other filmmakers, and other texts, that attempt to do this on a day-to-day basis? Viewers learn that a documentary text can be partial or subjective yet nevertheless a representation of some truth.

Documentary has continued to retain something of a sacred place within contemporary society, despite widespread acceptance of the notion that experience, and its representations, is extremely, and inherently, relative. *Forgotten Silver* exposes how filmmakers gather together pieces of evidence to present a persuasive argument. As Jackson claimed in his own defense—in a television news story on *Forgotten Silver,* the day after its first screening—he is "in the business of creating illusions," a raison d'être that he effectively assumed of the very form that his film attempted to demythologize.

Forgotten Silver utilizes and relies on the fact/fiction dichotomy assumed by its audience, but also explicitly plays with and subverts the hierarchy that this dichotomy implies, while in the process opening up a space for the questioning and challenging of documentary's authority. The mock-documentary offers the potential to blur fact and fiction to the point where it is not possible for viewers to either trace the film's referents in the sociohistorical world or to clearly identify the narrative within the realm of the imaginary. Perhaps this aspect of *Forgotten Silver* most upset some of its initial viewers, and here similarities can be made between the reception of mock-documentary and another documentary hybrid, the drama-documentary. Drama-documentary has also been severely criticized for its merging and blurring of fact and fiction.[39] In particular, fears have been expressed concerning the impact of such texts on confused (and vulnerable) viewers.[40] Certainly, it would seem that some viewers do get upset by the deliberate violation of the boundaries between fact and fiction.[41]

It is not only the mock documentary that has destabilized those relationships. Similar issues have been raised in relation to what Nichols terms the "reflexive"[42] and "performative"[43] modes of documentary. Both modes challenge the primacy of the historical world as referent, and instead move toward the *viewer* as primary referent.[44]

Mock-documentaries can be located within the same terrain, but, unlike reflexive and performative documentaries, they are designed to operate at some location outside of the genre; they are ultimately intended to be recognized and valued as entertainment texts. The concern of some New Zealand viewers over *Forgotten Silver* was that its skillful parody of the codes and conventions of documentary served to undermine the genre's authority and to potentially lead to a displacing of central cultural discourses. As fact and fiction are collapsed into each other, questions concerning truth and reality became relativized, with the onus placed on each viewer to deconstruct and reconstruct meaning from such texts.

Inevitably, a challenge to the privileged status of documentary texts presents viewers with the emergence of a new era of representations. At one level, changes in the broadcasting context have meant that documentarians are now more likely to be within a commercial environment than a public service context, and are having to compete for ever decreasing funds.[45] The role of the audience has become crucial to the continued development of the whole range of nonfiction-related texts, including the variety of fact/fiction hybrids. Brian Winston has argued that a grounding of documentary in *reception* rather than in representation is the only way to preserve its validity.[46] The challenge is then for viewers to become responsible for judgments concerning the relative truth of such texts, by recognizing that their own subjective experience and subjectivity must ultimately be the basis for such judgments. The problem with such an approach is that it could ultimately lead to a collapsing of all commonly accepted truth claims.

In some sense, documentary's instability can be read as a promising development. Documentary is attempting to escape not only from the constraints of realism, but also from the Griersonian legacy of documentary as vehicle for social enlightenment and progress. Documentary has always had to "re-imagine"[47] itself in response to the development of new technologies and practices, and to some extent in response to changes in wider sociopolitical discourses. Perhaps the central question raised by *Forgotten Silver* is the extent to which mock-documentaries can offer viewers alternative platforms for the evaluation of common knowledge. Ironically, the program serves to fulfill the consciousness-raising potential claimed by documentary's early practitioners. It encourages the audience to recognize the constructed nature of documentary representations yet still to engage with them as artifacts of the social world. Some viewers may be frustrated by the lack of common terms for fact and fiction, terms still grounded in the discourses of realism and naturalism. Others will not be willing to recognize the generic implications of their own collusion with a mock-documentary text. Without reducing the reception of such texts to issues of competency, mock-documentaries do indeed require a certain level of visual sophistication and intertextual expertise. Yet mock-documentaries are an increasingly popular form within mainstream television and feature film, and consequently viewers are developing experience in engaging with such texts.

The challenge for those working within the documentary is to continue the dual task of both deconstructing the remnants of Griersonian pretensions and reconstructing spectatorship as an adventure in postmodernist narratives. Ultimately, however, the undermining of a special status for documentary forms of representation is not a matter for debate between practitioners (or academics). Documentary texts attempt to offer us a series of insights and revelations concerning the nature of the historical world and the forces that shape this world. The knowledge they impart, however relative, necessarily serves as some basis for how we make decisions, individually and collectively, about our social, economic, and political engagements. An abandonment of that special function for documentary was perhaps a fear of some of the audience members who reacted so negatively to the first screening of *Forgotten Silver*. One of the more interesting public responses to the program was the following: "The connection with Richard Pearse was tasteless and left many in South Canterbury disappointed and angry. It also may have the effect of discounting any claim that he might have of being the first to fly, for many may now dismiss his life as part of the hoax that the film has perpetuated."[48]

In a discussion of the Spielberg film *Schindler's List* (1993),[49] G. Weissman argued that in choosing not to represent on film certain events of the Holocaust, Spielberg was in effect allowing those events to "disappear from history." In a similar way, the letter referring to Pearse above suggests that the truthful elements contained within *Forgotten Silver* will now be considered tainted with the label of fiction and, as such, removed from history. However, this argument could be turned on its head to produce a very different conclusion. The fact that the life and work of Colin McKenzie has been immortalized on film (whether authentic or not), allows it to enter into the realm of history. In effect, he now has an existence within a historical reality external to the film; for better or worse, Colin McKenzie is now located within the public consciousness of New Zealand.

NOTES

1. Derek Paget, *No Other Way to Tell It: Drama-doc/Docudrama on Television* (Manchester, England: Manchester University Press, 1998), and Steven N. Lipkin, *Real Emotional Logic: Film and Television Docudrama as Persuasive Practice* (Carbondale: Southern Illinois University Press, 2002).
2. Derek Bousé, *Wildlife Films* (Philadelphia: University of Pennsylvania Press, 2000).
3. Among the many recent publications on these hybrids are John Corner, "Performing the Real: Documentary Diversions," *Television and New Media* 3, no. 3 (2002): 255–69; Jon Dovey, *Freakshow: First-Person Media and Factual Television* (London: Pluto Press, 2000); Gareth Palmer, *Discipline and Liberty: Television and Governance* (Manchester, England: Manchester University Press, 2003); and Richard Kilborn, *Staging the Real: Factual TV Programming in the Age of "Big Brother"* (Manchester, England: Manchester University Press, 2003).
4. John Corner, "Documentary in a Post-Documentary Culture? A Note on Forms and Their Functions," European Science Foundation "Changing Media—Changing Europe" program, Team One (Citizenship and Consumerism) Working Paper no. 1 (2001). Corner invariably uses the term with a question mark, to reflect his use of the term both to generate commentary and to recognize how much research still needs to be done on the significance of hybrid forms: are they responding to deep and fundamental cultural changes?
5. See Jane Roscoe and Craig Hight, *Faking It: Mock-Documentary and the Subversion of Factuality* (Manchester: Manchester University Press, 2001), for a detailed discussion of different "degrees" of mock-documentary, defined in relation to their reflexivity.
6. Bill Nichols, *Representing Reality* (Bloomington: Indiana University Press, 1991).
7. New Zealand on Air (NZOR) is a public body that has a brief to "foster New Zealand culture and identity" through funding local broadcasting. It represents the last institutional remnant of New Zealand's public service broadcasting system.
8. TV1 is one of two channels provided by the publicly owned (former public service) television broadcaster Television New Zealand (TVNZ), and four hundred thousand viewers represents a sizable audience for a nation of (in 1995) just over three million people.
9. D. Welch, "Heavenly Features," *New Zealand Listener*, October 28, 1995, 31–32.
10. In the article, Jackson is quoted as stating that there "was some pressure on us at first to possibly dramatise some aspects of Colin's life, but frankly, even though it's a documentary, the events of his life were so dramatic that the word drama is not inappropriate," and Botes apparently offers the claim that "It's as gripping as any fictional story." Among other clues, the article also specifically highlights the fact that *Forgotten Silver* was to be featured within a program slot reserved for dramatic productions.
11. *Country Calendar* is a long-running agricultural information program screened by TVNZ. Mock items have surfaced occasionally during the long run of the series, and have included "reports" on a remote-controlled sheepdog and on a farmer using his fence as a musical instrument, and an episode featuring the lifestyle of farmer Fred Dagg (comedian John Clarke).
12. These are not labeled as such, but are nevertheless clearly flagged by news front persons, and effectively these items are separated from the remainder of the news content.
13. John Corner, *Television and Public Address* (London: Edward Arnold, 1995).
14. Although, as noted, the filmmakers also intended that the sheer absurdity of these discoveries was meant to be recognized by viewers.
15. Gallipoli was the site of a minor battle on the Turkish coast during the First World War in which New Zealand (and other Allied) forces suffered heavy casualties.

Within both New Zealand and Australia, it has achieved a mythic status as one of the places where nations have been forged.

16. Philip Rosen, "Document and Documentary: On the Persistence of Historical Concepts," in *Theorizing Documentary*, ed. Michael Renov (London: Routledge, 1993).

17. Interview with Peter Jackson, *Midwest Art Magazine*, no. 10 (1996): 23. Other cues include the tenuousness of the "scientific" basis to the egg and plant chemistry experiments from which McKenzie supposedly developed film stock, an interview with an Alexandra Nevsky at the Russian embassy, the numerous references to Taurus (bull) symbols, and so on. The program starts with Jackson literally leading viewers down a garden path, while the final image has McKenzie grinning while filming himself in a mirror, with credits for the writing and direction of Jackson and Botes superimposed.

18. Costa Botes, quoted in *Listener*, November 25, 1995.

19. Botes, letter to the editor (written in response to negative letters), *Evening Post*, November 16, 1995.

20. R. Campbell, "Securing the Middle Ground: Reporter Formulas in *60 Minutes*," in *Critical Perspectives on Media and Society*, ed. R. A. Avery, and D. Eason (New York: Guilford Press, 1991) offers a breakdown of the narrative formulas commonly offered by (American) programs centered around reporters. These are of the reporter as detective, analyst, and tourist.

21. Ibid., 280–87.

22. The full text of the materials discussed in this section, together with other letters to the editor, the newspaper commentaries, and the *Listener* articles associated with the program, are available online at http://www.waikato.ac.nz/film/mock-doc.shtml.

23. *Hollywood Reporter*, October 31, 1995.

24. Letters to the editor, *Listener*, November 25, 1995: 12.

25. The film and television studies department at the University of Waikato, for example, received calls from viewers anxious to know whether or not the program was actually a hoax, and where they could view a copy of McKenzie's *Salome*.

26. Letter to *Listener*, November 18, 1995, from Ann Else, Northland, Wellington.

27. J. Chadwick (of Orewa), letter to the editor, *Listener*, November 25, 1995, 12.

28. K. C. Durrant (of Upper Hutt), letter to the editor, ibid.

29. G. Chapple, "Gone, Not Forgotten," *Listener*, November 25, 1995, 26.

30. I. McKissak (of Hamilton), letter to the editor, *Listener*, November 25, 1995, 12.

31. G. A. De Forest (of Te Atatu Peninsula), letter to the editor, ibid.

32. W. J. Gaudin (of Christchurch), letter to the editor, ibid.

33. S. Anderson (of Herne Bay, Auckland), letter to the editor, ibid.

34. It is interesting to speculate whether TV3, the much younger rival to TVNZ, would have received the same degree of vilification from members of its audience had it been the channel to broadcast *Forgotten Silver*.

35. Not surprisingly, the reaction of audiences to the program in other countries has not carried the same sense of nationalistic emotion. Foreign audiences are generally positive to *Forgotten Silver's* agenda (it has been released in various film festivals in North America, Europe, and Asia). It is invariably introduced as part of the early work of the director of the high-profile *Lord of the Rings* trilogy, and typically recognized as a piece of clever filmmaking. A common response is to immediately compare it to Orson Welles's (in)famous 1938 radio broadcast of *War of the Worlds*.

36. Derek Paget, *True Stories: Documentary Drama on Radio, Screen, and Stage* (Manchester: Manchester University Press, 1990), 8.

37. See Steven Seidman, *Contested Knowledge: Social Theory in the Postmodern Era* (Malden, Mass.: Blackwell, 1994), 94–233, for a concise overview of this debate.

38. Bill Nichols, *Blurred Boundaries* (Bloomington: Indiana University Press, 1994), ix.

39. Richard Kilborn, "'Drama over Lockerbie': A New Look at Television Drama-Documentaries," *Historical Journal of Film, Radio, and Television* 14, no. 1 (1994).

40. M. Wober, "Effects on Perceptions from Seeing a Drama-Documentary: The Case of Who Bombed Birmingham?" IBA research paper (1990).

41. For a discussion of audience negotiations of this issue, see Jane Roscoe, "Contesting the Term 'Terrorism': Audience Interpretations of the Drama-documentary *Shoot to Kill*," paper presented to the Discourse and Cultural Practice Conference, Adelaide, 1996.

42. Nichols, *Representing Reality*.

43. Ibid., *Blurred Boundaries*.

44. Ibid., 94.

45. New Zealand, for example, has undergone an era of almost total deregulation.

46. Brian Winston, *Claiming the Real: The Documentary Film Revisited* (London: British Film Institute, 1995), 253.

47. John Corner, *Television and Public Address*, 181.

48. Gaudin, letter to the editor.

49. G. Weissman, "A Fantasy of Witnessing," *Media, Culture, and Society* 17 (1995): 293–307.

MITCHELL W. BLOCK

[12] *The Truth about* No Lies *(If You Can Believe It)*

It's July 2002 and I am observing a photo shoot for a new "reality" program that will air on TNT in 2003 called (working title) *The Residents*. R. J. Cutler, producer of *The War Room* (1993) and the Emmy Award–winning series (FOX and PBS) *American High* (2000), is the show's executive producer, and his company, Actual Reality Pictures, has been making this work for the past year. *The Residents* follows a year in the life of surgical and family practice residents at the University of California, Los Angeles (UCLA)'s medical centers in that city. The residents allowed a film crew to shoot them at home and in the hospital. In most cases, they even recorded themselves on a portable video "diary" camera—"private" moments that, if selected, will be included in the television show possibly seen by millions of people. This is a publicity photo shoot of the "real" doctors who participated in sharing their real-life adventures with Cutler's two (sometimes three) crews. Gathered around a real hospital gurney, with the green leatherette pad, are nine doctors. Some are wearing scrubs and others are in nice office clothes. They have all been to the makeup and hair stylists working in an adjoining room. The PR staffers from TNT, coordinating with their photographer (who is shooting large-format still shots of the doctors on a large photo stage), carefully approve the look of each of the doctors, nodding as they are made up and their hair is styled. What is striking to this observer is that this multicultural group of attractive men and women could be actors playing doctors but they are actually made-up doctors playing themselves. They are real!

Cutler and his team of vérité crews are making reality television. A team of transcribers, story editors, producers, and editors supports the crews. They use terms such as "story arc," "beats," "the 'A,' 'B,' and 'C' story lines," to refer to the real scenes as if these were scripted, as they try to piece the events together into minidramas that will become the acts of a television hour. Shoot first, then script. Sometimes instructions come to the crews from the story editors to shoot an ending to a dramatic arc. The crews oblige. The economic advantage of using real people is clear to program executives. One does not have to pay residuals (or actors) for what will be a season's series. Real-life dramas from real-life people present a solid economic model to network programming executives. This also can be first-rate programming. But what are the responsibilities of the film-makers to the subjects? To the audience?

I have shared this experience with the reader because R. J. Cutler's work is taking place thirty years after I made *No Lies*. Cutler follows the pioneer work of Alan and Susan Raymond, who shot, and Craig Gilbert, who was executive producer of, the 1972–1973 PBS series *An American Family*, and moves stylistically from the earlier show's pacing and form toward what might be called an MTV look. I do not intend to imply one style is better than another, but rather to suggest that the pacing is a whole lot faster in recent reality programs. Many of *The Residents* crew and cast were not even born when *An American Family* aired. (*The Residents* flows from the success of R. J. Cutler's earlier work, *American High*. Many of the key crew worked on both projects.) *An American Family* also had press photos shot in a studio and 8 mm film diaries (home video was not yet usable on-air), and the crew developed relationships with the subjects; on first look, almost everything is the same. The new work is not being made in an intellectual or cultural vacuum. *The Residents*' filmmakers in many cases went to film school and have a solid grounding in film history; a number of the filmmakers involved with this program were my students at University of Southern California (USC). Despite the thirty years that have passed, there is almost no separation between Cutler and the filmmakers of the 1970s. Joan Churchill, one of the cinematographers on *An American Family*, is one of the two principle cinematographers for Cutler.

I share this with the reader because I made my work, *No Lies*, in response to *An American Family* as it was in production/postproduction thirty years ago. *No Lies* is a film about filmmaking (and filmmakers making films). *An American Family* was the catalyst. Eleanor Hamerow, one of my teachers at the New York University (NYU) graduate film program, was one of the original editors for the series. She is credited with editing its first hour. I understand she left *An American Family* because she was so concerned with the many ethical questions raised by the production process. How was the filmmaking process affecting the people who were sharing their lives with the filmmakers? How would showing the film to the public affect their lives? *No Lies* is a simple story with a simple narrative arc that explores these questions, as well as the relation-

Shelby Leverington and cameraman Alec Hirschfield during the shooting of *No Lies* (Mitchell W. Block, 1973)

ships between filmmakers and their subjects. The big difference from the "reality" programs is that my work was scripted or story-edited before it was shot. It is a drama that is fictional rather than a drama that is real. No real people were exposing their inner lives to the camera or the public, since no real people were used. The idea for the work developed, in part, because of the tensions I observed between Hamerow and Craig Gilbert, the series producer. I did not see *An American Family* until many years later, in part because of the anger Hamerow felt toward the work that was going to expose this family to public scrutiny on national television (as well as my lack of access to television, and the work not being available on film or video). I wondered, "Is it possible to film reality without changing it?" or "Could one create reality fictionally and not worry about how filming it would affect the subjects, since in my work the subjects do not exist—they are actors?"

Three years earlier, in the fall of 1968, I had the experience of seeing *David Holzman's Diary* at New York University. Jim McBride, L. M. Kit Carson and Michael Wadleigh's *David Holzman's Diary* is in many respects the staged documentary that started a movement. The screening was not part of a class but rather a thrown-together evening, a student-initiated event. Jim had been a graduate student at NYU. This screening forever changed my relationship with film. Without *David Holzman's Diary,* there would be no *No Lies.* I believed the film; I loved it. I was taken in by Carson's Holzman character. I wanted to be Holzman. Indeed, what young aspiring filmmaker in 1968 would not want to be the waspy Holzman character? His life was falling apart before our eyes but we loved this character. In the end, David's Éclair camera and Nagra are stolen, leaving him without a way to work—so the film ends over black as Holzman tells us what has happened, and this was something we all could relate to; after all, our cinematography teacher Fred (Beta) Badka kept his 35 mm cameras in a bank vault. To reiterate, Carson/Holzman (the fictional character) loses everything in the process of making this work; the hero's downward spiral, so personally and painfully documented in the film, makes it so one can't help loving his character. The film, like the French New Wave works we were seeing, is so (I can say it) cool. (*Sex, Lies and Videotape* [Steven Soderbergh, 1989] some years later has a similar feel.)

McBride, Wadleigh, and Scorsese were all classmates in NYU's pre–School of the Arts graduate film school in 1966. Around that time, John Cassavetes' *Faces* (1968) premiered. Cassavetes influenced their work with his fictional reality. *Faces* was a gutsy "real-life" drama with a tour de force, in-your-face performance by its stars. A few years later, these works, combined with the relentless screenings and analysis of *Battle of Algiers* (Gillo Pontecorvo, 1965), in the fall of 1973 in the graduate film program (where I made *No Lies* as my MFA thesis), created the intellectual atmosphere where one felt safe to challenge the conventional form of cinema. It made complete sense. We were studying with revolutionaries. Leo Hurwitz was the directing teacher in the program—our filmmaker in residence. His professional credentials were impeccable and distinctly left-wing. A one-time member of the Film and Photo League, Hurwitz had collaborated on pictures such as *Native Land* (1942), and we had the good fortune to have him as the chair and one of the master teachers in the program. Leo provided a remarkable standard for the program. Artistically, he was a powerful force; no one could doubt his ethics or integrity as an artist. He was deeply respected by all of the students even if they did not always agree with him. His take on filmmaking deeply affected me.

Finally, there was my experience working as the New York line producer of Martin Scorsese's *Mean Streets* in the fall semester of 1972. This made *No Lies* inevitable, since I needed to do a thesis work and had only limited time to write, shoot, and edit it starting in January 1973, since I was the sole graduate student in a prototype one-year MFA program: if I did not direct a film, I would not graduate.

I knew as a producer that I should do a work that would be "easy" to make. Limited locations, interior practical locations, a short shoot, few actors, low shooting ratio, no period costumes, no score, etc. Keep it really simple. The work was based on an unpublished video called *The*

Rape Tape, in which a number of women who were raped talked about their experiences. This early video diary was produced, with three other women, one of whom was Jenny Goldberg, the sound person on *No Lies.* This work was never published and was only screened privately. The women in it insisted on their privacy. *The Rape Tape* was one of the first works to personally deal with the effects of rape and was a deeply moving work that provided much of the material for the actress Shelby Leverington, who plays the woman in *No Lies.* We used a Sony Porta Pack. The location selected was Muffy Meyer's apartment. Meyer was editing documentaries (*Gray Gardens,* Albert and David Maysles, 1975) with Ellen Hovde (who became her film business partner) at the Maysles'. They were close friends of Charlotte Zwerin (who was the original editor of *An American Family,* also resigned from the project, and was a resident filmmaker at the Maysles'). Although I did not know the Raymonds (or Gilbert) at this time, I was responding to their work (without seeing it): people who had a very strong emotional reaction to the ethics of this film surrounded me. The work was the talk at many a dinner. My concern about the nature of the documentary was ongoing because of my relationship with these filmmakers. This concern cut across a range of films and the expediencies of my required thesis forced me to think continually about *David Holzman's Diary* and another fiction film from the period, *A Safe Place* (Henry Jaglom, 1971).

My fascination with this form is directly connected to my interest in the relationships between: (1) the filmmaker (Block) and the subjects—the

No Lies (Mitchell W. Block, 1973)

"camera person" and "the subject"; (2) the filmmaker (Block) and the audience; (3) the audience/viewer and the film (from the point of view of the audience). This tripartite relation is clear to see in *No Lies*, I (1) abuse the subject with an insensitive filmmaker, (2) undermine the audience's relationship with the filmmaker by making the latter unlikable and unethical, and (3) abuse the spectator by pretending to present the truth but lying. In this case (unlike that of a real documentary), I am not in the film but am manipulating it by using a nonfictional form to tell a fictional story. The filmmaker/camera person who is very much a part of the *No Lies* story is actually a character playing the filmmaker. In the traditional "real" work the filmmaker is—well, the filmmaker. While we are used to talking about the filmmaker and the subject (1), and the audience and the film (3), *No Lies* is really about the filmmaker manipulating the audience (2).

All filmmakers, in both dramatic and nonfiction forms, do this. However, in the nonfiction form, the filmmaker has an assumed responsibility to the subject. By manipulating the film, the filmmaker is manipulating reality. In a nonfiction work, the subject is a real person and not an actor. But real life is not "dramatic" within the convention of film time. It needs to be structured and edited into film form; the lack of action in real life needs to be accelerated. The structure of film allows for this manipulation of time through editing. Although picture logic allows us to see events as they really happen, this is usually not acceptable to audiences because reality is seen as slow and not usually dramatic, and filmmakers are almost never filmmaking at the "right" moment. Filmmakers therefore need to use the device of telling us what happened rather than showing us what happened. The nonfiction film is formed in the editing room to tell the story in a dramatic fashion from the mundane material shot. The editor pushes the narrative elements of the footage to make it flow in a cinematic way—faster. Editors depend on the filmmakers to be there at the key moments to film the story as it happens. If they miss filming the story, the filmmakers have to reenact the story, have the subjects tell us about what happened (voice-over or interview), provide a card, or perhaps tell us in their own words what happened. Since, most of the time, filmmakers miss these key moments, the documentary film is always rushing to catch up with the story.

The paradigm shift between Gilbert and Raymonds's *An American Family* and Cutler's *American High* and *The Residents* is that contemporary filmmakers use story producers and story editors and generally no on-site director. They radically break up their footage and there is no attempt made to show it as a whole. The sequences are diced and split by the editors into fragments that are intercut with other fragments so that the hour has a more intense pacing caused by the fragmentation of the stories. As soon as the action (or story) slows, the filmmakers cut to another story, and later cut back to the previous story. The multiple filmmaking crews become part of an industrial process—making a collective story rather than allowing the filmmakers to create a story simply of what they shoot. There is no director but only producers, directors of photography, editors, story editors, and other supervisors.

The Raymonds are credited as the filmmakers of *An American Family* but the authorship is difficult to pin down. There is no "director" credit given. *An American Family* runs the shot sequences far longer than the newer films, stays with the action/characters, and allows the pacing to be far less frenetic. Its frame is also smaller, focused on one family, not on a dozen or so high school students. Both works are character driven: *American High* focuses on the students and their interrelations; *An American Family* focuses on the lives of the family members. *No Lies* is a sequence that could be in any of these films—except the filmmakers would not be part of the action. The "fly-on-the-wall" film crew, in reality interacting with the subjects, is the hidden secret of both the *American High* and *American Family* series. The subjects tell the crew when something is going to happen and the crew apparently happens to be there to film it, or, if they miss it, they either stage it or interview the subjects about what they missed. The crew is alerted to the coming drama; the results are covered. They know what is going to happen before it happens, and sometimes nothing happens until the crew is present.

No Lies follows the strategy or style of *An American Family* for two reasons: this style gives the work the appearance of being a reality, and the story line is very simple. (My 1974 work, *Speeding*, predates the fragmentation style of *American High*, since it is an intercut story of real people and of actors playing real people.) The audience does not want to observe the two edits that cut together the three shots in *No Lies*. Like the work of Cutler, *No Lies* was actually shot on video, at least through the rehearsal stage, using now-primitive Sony Porta Pack video equipment; the *No Lies* rehearsal tapes are included in the Direct Cinema Ltd. (www.directcinemalimited.com) DVD version. The use of film for production was mandated by the unavailability of high-quality handheld video equipment. The sense of reality is captured by the conceit of the work: the whole work is presented as a single-take truth (or a nonedited work) and hence *could* not be a lie. Audiences believe single continuous shots. Meanwhile, the docu-series is always presented as the truth despite its fictional—highly edited—style. Reality uncut for fifteen straight minutes is apparently not interesting for today's MTV-style (or VH1, etc.) documentaries.

(Are there any interesting fifteen minutes without cuts in any film in our canon?) We require fragmentation to heighten the drama of the moment, fragmentation so that the work presents multiple plots to intercut. Since I was trying to make a point about making films about real people, *No Lies* suggested it is possible to craft reality without hurting anyone. This is the point of the film. One can be "personal" without begin hurtful. In my current network series, we have to deal with the choice of allowing a sailor to reveal his or her sexual preference. If the sailor does this in our series, his or her Navy career ends. A huge responsibility and choice for the filmmakers—real can have dramatic consequences. I am not comfortable ending a career for show, even if I have a release.

I love what Cutler and company are doing to the nonfiction form, and share Cutler's work to show that the form is continuing to evolve. His work, for me, is still ethically provocative. In the last thirty years, one would think, given the dominant media, real-world subjects have become more accustomed to the media intruding on their lives. They allow their trials, their arrests, and their lives to be captured. With Winona Ryder's real-life adventures captured on store video surveillance cameras, alleged criminals caught in the act on shows like *Cops*, and a host of programs like *Survivors*, we see hundreds of hours of "reality" programs. In addition, the genre is being expanded in works like *Frontier House* where real people play roles. Unlike Michael Moore's fake nonfiction works, my work has the camera person/filmmaker allowing the character to be truthful (within the context of the fiction), and, as is not the case in his works, we are intentionally betraying the audiences' trust. We are, after all, fiction, and, although we are pretending to be nonfiction, we are not nonfiction. The other extreme of this can be seen in Michael Moore's films, where a fiction is created using real people but distorting who they are and what they say. Moore is using the technique of *No Lies,* but is telling the spectator (and the subjects) that he is being truthful. If *Roger and Me* (1989) were a fiction, with actors instead of real people, it would be fine. Alas, Moore is a documentary liar; his work holds up its subjects for ridicule and scorn. We laugh at these real people who, in some cases, are being presented in a false light by Moore. Compare this to the respect with which the subjects are treated by Cutler or the Raymonds and Gilbert.

What then is "fake"? *Roger and Me* has a number of "fake" scenes and/or depictions of characters, but the filmmaker tells us that this is a documentary. My work rings true but is a fiction. It is a fake carefully built as truth (but is labeled as fiction in its credits). Although the actual rape is a fiction, and the two characters are a fiction, the emotions and feelings the woman shows in her interview, even though acted, read as truth to the spectators and to experts. Even the New York City police, when using the work in training in the 1980s, asked me for the "name of the officer who interviewed the woman in the film." Clearly, there is (or was) a training problem in police departments with the officers who interview rape victims; this came out repeatedly in researching the film. Thus, the New York Police training group wanted to interview the officer(s) on video who interviewed the actress in *No Lies* and use the interviews with the film for training purposes. (I would love to have a copy of that interview tape.)

For the past six months, I have been working on my third work in this genre. What is interesting to me is to continue to play on the relationship among the filmmaker, the subject, and the audience. I want the camera-person to again cross the line and hone in on the subject who clearly does not want to expose her feelings. He, like the television newspeople and Mr. Moore, wants to get his "Roger" on film regardless of how "Roger" feels about being on film at any moment of vulnerability. I want that moment I experienced once in a UCLA film class after a screening of the *No Lies* sequel *Speeding?* when a student asked, "How do you happen to film movie stars getting speeding tickets?" It is the moment of "aha!" in the audience, wanting to believe that the actor is the real person getting caught on film, rather than the actor playing a character who is in a fictional work.

What is critical is that spectators become more sophisticated reading the film text being presented. They need to understand how easy it is to manipulate the form so that it appears to be the truth when it is not. *No Lies* should have been called *All Lies*. We all believed the fiction of the dot-com boom or the MCI/Worldcom or Enron reports. We wanted to believe that the auditors, the government officials, the bankers, the brokers, and the analysts were telling the truth. Trillions of dollars have disappeared. The investors, like the spectators, want to believe what they are told. Everything has changed since I made *No Lies*, but I feel that everything is still the same.

EVE OISHI

[**13**] *Screen Memories: Fakeness in Asian American Media Practice*

> You know, they straightened out the Mississippi River in places,
> to make room for houses and livable acreage. Occasionally
> the river floods these places. "Floods" is the word they use,
> but in fact it is not flooding; it is remembering. Remembering
> where it used to be. All water has a perfect memory and is
> forever trying to get back to where it was. Writers are like that:
> remembering where we were, what valley we ran through,
> what the banks were like, the light that was there and the
> route back to our original place. It is emotional memory—what
> the nerves and the skin remember as well as how it appeared.
> And a rush of imagination is our "flooding."
> :: Toni Morrison, "The Site of Memory"

With this metaphor, Morrison eloquently expresses the power and the
potential of memory within historical and literary narrative.[1] Like the Mis-
sissippi River that has been "straightened," its curves and broader banks
buried under sand and mud, official history is recorded and passed down in
partial and deceptively straightforward stories, due either to the limitations
of the expressive form or to the demands of political interests. Memory,
with its nonlinear nature, its emotional power, its ambiguities, gaps, and fissures, can function as a powerful challenge to official record, much like the
river that "floods" the original places it is remembering. Because memory
is unstable, because we remember in fragments, because remembering is so
often the province of childhood, it can serve as a troubling presence, a force
that disrupts the linear flow of storytelling, of truth and authenticity. What
is most significant about Morrison's allegory, however, is that she places the
power to disrupt dominant history into the hands of the artist. It is a "rush
of imagination" that holds the potential to recover the buried and forgotten

past because only fiction, itself a flooding, an excess of the truth, can accurately give shape to what no longer exists.

Following this logic, one can argue that the most radical and revealing practice within the documentary tradition is its embrace of fiction. Or, seen another way, a most radical challenge to the documentary genre has come from artistic reimagination of the form: the fake documentary. If documentaries function as the visual record of a story or event, then fake documentaries serve as the memory, the flood of things not seen, not captured on film, or erased from the tape. Fake documentaries not only call into question the reliability of all images, but they borrow the structures and techniques of this method of truth telling to tell another story. What the fake documentary is about, then, is not so much the subject directly in front of the camera, but rather the ways in which an understanding of the subject is formed through visual and cultural codes.

Although the fictional documentary is by no means a new strategy, as is evidenced by this collection, it does have a power and relevance for Asian American artists because of the particular ways Asian American historical records have been marked by inaccuracies, omissions, mistranslations, and caricatures. Examples of lost or erroneous evidence of the past are myriad: the documents of early Asian immigrants that were fraught with untruths and misinformation from deliberate lies or careless translation; the stereotypes of Asians on film and television played by white actors in yellowface; or simply the guarded silence within families, as one generation holds on to its knowledge and secrets about the past. In response, the work of many Asian American artists has been concerned with the struggle to represent the history that remains, in excess of existing records and representation, and for this these artists have often turned to fiction. In this unstable relationship to history, Asian Americans are no different from other groups, regardless of those groups' relationships to the mainstream. As evidenced by my reliance on the writing of Toni Morrison in this essay, African American artists have also found creative ways to address issues of inaccessibility of historical truth through fiction, and the long history of fake documentaries recorded in this volume speaks to the power of these questions among filmmakers of all ethnicities. Every individual's or community's access to the past will always remain partial and mediated by political and historical circumstances.

But while the general question may be universal, the particulars are not. This essay takes three media texts by Asian Americans as examples of some ways that artists have engaged with the particular historical forces (the Japanese American internment, the refugee experience resulting from U.S. intervention in Southeast Asia, the invisibility of Asian Americans within popular culture movements and texts, the power of sexuality and identification) that contribute to the instability between fact and fiction within Asian American history and representation.

The three films and videos I examine here all deal with different aspects of the Asian American experience, and all three stand in varying relation to the standard definition of a "fake documentary." Ruth Ozeki Lounsbury's *Halving the Bones* (1995) blends fictional elements into an autobiographical documentary about the filmmaker's Japanese family, directly challenging the distinction between real and fake artifacts of history. Nguyen Tan Hoang's *Pirated!* (2000) is also an autobiographical account, dealing with the filmmaker's childhood voyage from Vietnam to the United States. Through its experimental and unconventional techniques, *Pirated!* appears to diverge most dramatically from a traditional documentary, fake or otherwise, but examining the video as a fake documentary reveals the troubling presence of fiction within all historical and visual evidence as well as the role of memory and its counterpart, desire, as both a constitutive and disruptive element within cinematic and documentary representation. Ernesto Foronda's *Cherrybomb!!!* (2000) seems to follow most closely the conventions of the fake documentary, and, as it is ostensibly about the largely white, punk girl music scene, it addresses the identity of the filmmaker only in oblique ways. Although *Cherrybomb!!!* presents itself as a Riot Grrrl *Spinal Tap*, the repressed subject of racial and ethnic difference erupts and disrupts the narrative at key moments, flooding the borders of the form and highlighting the conspicuous absence of race in both traditional "rockumentary" and "mockumentary" films.

Despite their differences, all three works converge in their strategic use of the unstable yet formative power of memory. Each truth that is remembered is soon countered with one or more contradicting memories or images, yet it is out of the flood of accumulated and clashing memories that a (variable) truth is gleaned.[2] In his book *Time Passages: Collective Memory and American Popular Culture*, George Lipsitz summarizes the effect that electronic mass media has had on our understanding of time, history, and memory:

> Instead of relating to the past through a shared sense of place or ancestry, consumers of electronic mass media can experience a common heritage with people they have never seen; they can acquire memories of a past to which they have no geographic or biological connection. This capacity of electronic mass communication to transcend time and space creates instability by disconnecting people from past traditions, but it also liberates people by making the past less determinate of experiences in the present.[3]

Halving the Bones (Ruth Ozeki Lounsbury, 1995)

In the texts that I examine, the instability referred to by Lipsitz proves the key to evoking the complexity of Asian American history, just as it is the ambiguous and unreliable cinematic medium that can best signify how a cultural common heritage is produced and disseminated, and at whose expense. The experiences of Asian Americans and other minoritarian subjects have often stood at odds with totalizing narratives of culture and citizenship, particularly ones created and enforced through electronic mass media. Insofar as these new media carry the ability to "transcend time and space," this process has often meant obscuring and distorting the history and experiences of the culturally and politically disempowered. If the technology of mechanical reproduction has been employed to blur the lines between fact and fiction in dominant culture, it follows that Asian American artists should find the same technology rich and articulate for presenting the paradoxes of the modern Asian American experience, an experience defined by distorted popular representations and multiple and contradictory notions of allegiance and home. The title of my essay, "Screen Memories," is meant not only to evoke the Freudian concept of a false memory that serves to shield the patient from remembering a traumatic event, but also to stress the tangible connection between memory and the critical and imaginative possibilities of the cinema.[4] In all of the works discussed here, and for many other Asian American screen texts, the process and the metaphor of memory are central in constructing a new picture of history and of the self.

Another image from Toni Morrison is useful here, as it emphasizes the particular power of cinematic texts as memory. In Morrison's novel *Beloved*, the former slave Sethe explains to her daughter Denver her concept of "rememory." It is the concept that everything that happens or is experienced by someone remains in the world as a physical or sensory trace, independent of the person who first experienced it. She tells Denver:

> Someday you be walking down the road and you hear something or see something going on. So clear. And you think it's you thinking it up. A thought picture. But no. It's when you bump into a rememory that belongs to somebody else. Where I was before I came here, that place is real. It's never going away. Even if the whole farm—every tree and grass blade of it dies. The picture is still there and what's more, if you go there—you who never was there—if you go there and stand in the place where it was, it will happen again; it will be there for you, waiting for you.[5]

The most powerful and disturbing rememory in the novel is Sethe's daughter, Beloved, who returns from the dead as a living, breathing reminder of her mother's brutal act of infanticide and of the horrors of slavery that precipitated her murder. The concept has salience for this discussion in that, although both real and fake documentary images of history may mimic memory's ghostly and flickering uncertainty, representation possesses a material existence that outlives its creators. Once a cinematic image has been produced, it is free to be received, interpreted, reshaped, and co-opted in innumerable ways. The power of these figments of imagination is tangible, and the makers of fake documentaries are deeply aware of this. The acknowledgment of the formative power of images remains central to their projects; they are responding to the longevity and influence of media images, and, with their own work, they have created oppositional narratives that live on in material, reproducible form.

Marita Sturken, who writes about several Asian American video texts in her article "The Politics of Video Memory: Electronic Erasures and Inscriptions," counters the pronouncement by Fredric Jameson that television and the immediacy of the electronic image have proven to be the final death of memory. Although film, for Jameson, still holds the possibility of a haunting afterimage or memory, video, with its "pure and random play of signifiers,"[6] is characterized by its "structural exclusion of memory . . . and of critical distance."[7] In response, Sturken writes:

> I would argue that the stakes in memory and history are ever present in electronic media (and postmodernism)—that despite its paradoxical relationship to the preservation of memory, television-video is a primary site of history and cultural memory, where memories, both individual and collective, are produced and claimed. It is a matter of understanding that memory is unstable, intangible, and often misread as forgetting. Video may indeed be the quintessential medium of postmodern memory.[8]

Sturken accords power specifically to video because of the spontaneity of its imagery and the ephemeral nature of its material. She writes that, even though "most independent video tapes aspire to be seen in contexts that separate them from the ongoing information flow of television, . . . the video image is implicated in the relentless electronic flow of the television image."[9] Although the texts that I examine contain a blend of film and video, and although the filmmakers I discuss address the question of the different nature and implications of film and video throughout their pieces, I do not distinguish between the two media in my contention that mass-produced imagery claims to offer a faithful and unmediated reproduction of reality even as it forever carries the possibility of forgery, multiple reception, and insufficiency in the gap between object and image. As the works discussed here show, the forms of film and video, as well as still photography, often collaborate with one another or create a new context of signification, such as (in the case of *Pirated!*) Hollywood films and porn videos watched together on a home television set.

Similarly, the aesthetic and narrative strategies, as well as the subject matter of the films, constitute additional expressive elements that are sometimes in line and sometimes at odds with the form. Rather than being defined through "the structural exclusion of memory," as Jameson theorizes, these texts use the productive play among the medium, the style

of narration, and the content, as well as a critical mixing of media, to mobilize the unsettling, evocative power of memory. In their clashes and col-
laborations, film and video together may well be seen, in Sturken's terms,
as "the quintessential medium of postmodern memory," but in their mimicking of the structures and disruptive potential of memory, they also constitute the quintessential medium of Asian American history.

In all of the films and videos discussed here, the artifacts of official
history—photos, newsreel footage, diaries, newspaper accounts—are accorded the same status as fiction and memory, posing the question: which
is more or less accurate? The changeable, partisan story created by dominant sources of history is instrumental in shaping our view of the past,
even as our memories can contest the veracity of official images. All of
these works employ multiple layers of signification. They use official and
unofficial images, some created by the filmmakers and some appropriated
from other sources like the television news, music video, or Hollywood
films. Written text is often superimposed over the visual image, and similar strategies are employed with sound: the films use a mix of original
music, pirated music, and voice-overs. Some speak in the intimate first
person, while others carry the "voice of God" authority of the traditional
documentary, although often that authority is undermined by a variety of
strategies or by the sheer volume of differing, contesting voices. No one
voice or image is ever given precedence. As a result, the body in these films
remains, like memory, unstable, contingent, and unreliable.

On the surface, Ruth Ozeki Lounsbury's 1995 feature-length film
Halving the Bones belongs to the familiar genre of autobiographical documentaries, told in a first-person voice-over, about the filmmaker's search for
her own history through the stories of her mother and grandmother. But the
film's subtitle—"making a family album?"—offers an early clue that the film
is going to raise questions more than provide answers. The film begins with
Hawaiian music played over colorful photographs of beaches and palm trees.
There is a shot of the filmmaker in her apartment, and a woman's voice informs us in Japanese, "Kanajo wa Rusu. Haffu desu." The voice then repeats
its message in English, with a heavy Japanese accent, "This is Ruth. She is
half. That means half Japanese and half American." The accented voice then
goes on to explain that, after her grandmother died five years ago, Ruth's
relatives cremated the body and took out some of the remaining bone fragments in a ceremony known as "*hone wake*, the dividing of the bones." The
relatives gave a few of the fragments to Ruth to give to her mother, who was
unable to attend the funeral in Japan, but five years later Ruth still has the
bones with her in an old tea canister. The voice explains that "the idea of her
grandmother, fragmented and ignored, has begun to bother her."

Next we hear the same voice—it is the filmmaker's—announce in un-accented American English, "My Name is Ruth, but I don't like it. It's not a good name for a young person." She says that she does not understand why her mother chose this name for her, since "there is not a person in Japan who can say my name right." In addition, her name, in the mouth of a Japanese person, is "Rusu," which means "not at home." So that when you say "Rusu wa Rusu desu," it can mean "Ruth is Ruth" or "Ruth is absent."

In the first ten minutes of the film, Lounsbury has undermined all of the expected conventions of an autobiographical documentary, in which the filmmaker introduces herself and states the purpose of her cinematic quest.[10] The title itself contains a pun, which serves as a warning that for the following seventy-two minutes nothing revealed will carry only one meaning. The pun in the title, "*Halving* the Bones," splits the visual and the aural reception of the title; it means different things if one is reading it or hearing it. This split between "halve" (to divide), and "have" (to own) echoes Ruth's own dilemma with what to do with the bones, but the trou-bling duality of the word also serves as the inaugural problem and force of her film. She says, "It was like having [halving?] the bones was a catalyst, and suddenly I found myself thinking more and more about Mom, and I started to remember all these stories about her family."

Already the narrator, our guide to the meaning of the film, has been undermined and split into three: the initial Japanese voice, which later speaks in the first person for Ruth's grandmother; the Japanese-accented English translation; and the American English voice. Lounsbury casts a shadow of doubt and uncertainty on all of the subsequent narratives we are to hear, forcing us to question our comfortable faith in the authority of a first-person narrator and the belief that English spoken with an ac-cent denotes a more authentic translation of a Japanese voice than does an American accent.

In fact, the entire film is composed of a series of translations and mistranslations. No text or image is ever presented as pure, including the opening photographs of Hawaii, which are black-and-white photos that have been tinted, a process that Lounsbury's grandmother learned while working for her photographer husband in Hilo. After introducing herself in various languages and voices, and offering several definitions and ques-tions about her own name, the narrator introduces her mother by saying that Americans have a certain picture of Japanese women as "delicate flowers, or reeds bending in the wind, or clinging vines," a stereotype that fails to capture her "strong and pragmatic" mother who is "never shy about bodily functions." Once again, we are presented with two interpre-tations that fail to match up. Indeed the central structuring device of the film is that of substitution, translation, approximation, and metaphor, with each side of the equation failing to cleanly match its pair. In this way, the project becomes a commentary on the limits and possibilities of film itself, which is, in this case, the ultimate substitution of image for reality. In this sense, the splitting ("halving") of meaning performed by the film, and implied by the very medium of representation, becomes the key to understanding ("having"), even in a contingent way, Lounsbury's elusive family and their stories.[11]

The first story we are given in depth is of her grandmother, Matsuye, who traveled to the island of Hilo, Hawaii, as a picture bride. Her story is told in first person, again in accented English, by the narrator, who explains that she is reading from a memoir that her grandmother wrote. As this grandmother, she introduces herself with these words: "My name is Matsuye Yokoyama. I am trained as a photographer's assistant, and I have spent my life putting color into my husband's photographs."

Reading from her grandmother's memoir and speaking in her grandmother's voice, the narrator tells how Matsuye traveled to Hilo as a picture bride to marry Ruth's grandfather, a "student of the botanical sciences" who photographed plant life on the island and owned a small photography business. She says that, when she reached the island, "It was love at first sight." At this point, Ruth takes over the narrative in her "own" voice to refute this story, saying that relatives have told her that this was a lie and that her grandmother was at first extremely unhappy in Hawaii. She describes her grandfather, a photographer, poet, filmmaker, and amateur botanist who "catalogued exotica and was drawn by twisted forms in nature." She states that "people say I'm like him," and she then shows us examples of some of the home movies that he made in Hilo. Introduced by handwritten French titles like "Matsuyé dans la Forêt des Palmes" and "Matsuyé sur la Plage," the films show a woman in a loose-fitting white dress wandering through the lush landscape and along the beach. She is elusive, appearing always at a distance, often running away. We soon see that she is pregnant. The camera lingers in close-up on a butterfly, a spider spinning a shimmering web, the gnarled roots of trees and vines, recalling the narrator's earlier metaphor of the (false) stereotype of Japanese women as "delicate flowers or reeds bending in the wind or clinging vines." As the camera follows a particularly long and tangled snarl of branch or root, the narrator draws a metaphoric connection to human physiology. She says, "Bones are tissue. They grow and change and die with the body. She was old when she died. The bones I have are hers, but they're not the same ones she has here." This statement draws a direct, physical connection between granddaughter and grandmother—their shared roots—even as it overturns the biological essentialism of such a link. "The bones I have" refers both to the bones she is holding in a tea canister and the bones in her own body, whose racial hybridity can be likened to the "twisted forms in nature" that so appealed to her grandfather.

Although questioning its accuracy, the narrator continues to read from her grandmother's memoir. After the birth of a son, Matsuye suddenly becomes ill with a cancerous tumor in her stomach, and she returns to Tokyo for an operation. She writes, "I board the ship bound for Japan with tears in my eyes. When would I see my husband and my beloved Hawaii again? I felt my heart to be breaking." Immediately, the narrator's American voice interrupts her "Japanese" one to say that "here again she appears to stray from the truth." The narrator then continues by revealing that, once on board the ship, her grandmother discovered that she did not have a tumor after all; she was four months pregnant with her daughter Masako, who "started life misdiagnosed as a cancer." This section follows the now familiar pattern established early in the documentary. A story is told, a fact is stated, and this statement is followed by several renunciations or counterstatements. In this case, the narrator states that she suspects that her grandmother had invented the whole tumor story in order to get out of Hawaii. In the next statement, however, she "suspect[s] she went reluctantly . . . Perhaps her memories weren't altogether accurate." Whether it is the conflicting speculations of the granddaughter or the grandmother's own unreliable memory or veracity, no one version of the story is ever allowed to stand. Nevertheless, Lounsbury concludes this section with the statement "These are the facts. But the problem remains: what are you supposed to do with a can of bones?" When facts are nothing more (or less) than an accumulation of approximations and erratic claims, the journey of the documentary becomes no longer how to reach a certain and consistent truth about the past, but rather what "to do with" the ever growing collection of alternate possibilities and coexisting realities.

After presenting "the facts" of her family's history, Lounsbury introduces another layer of uncertainty. The films presented as her grandfather's are revealed to be fake, created by Lounsbury herself. Although her grandfather did make films, his camera was confiscated after Pearl Harbor when he was taken to an internment camp for the duration of the war, and none of his work survived. Similarly, there are no letters from her grandfather to either his wife or daughter, as they were both classified enemy aliens, and he was not allowed to write to them. The grandmother's autobiography is also admitted to be a fake. The narrator confesses, "I made it up from the real family stories and from things that relatives had told me." By inventing her grandfather's films and her grandmother's memoir, Lounsbury has put words and pictures into the silences of the past. By giving substance, shape, voice, and color to the invisible, she also makes visible the historical circumstances that prevented the evidence from being made or from surviving in the first place. In addition, she underscores both the insufficiency and the excessive truth of the evidence that remains. As her mother tells her, "I don't think you can talk about accuracy in memory because I think you may want to, without even realizing it, you want to color it, make it more interesting or make it somehow to your advantage."[12]

Over black-and-white images of a Japanese woman awkwardly stuffing a turkey and diapering a baby, Lounsbury confesses that "on some level I really did think of [my mother] as a cancer, a deeply rooted conflation of sickness and race: the yellow peril, the malignant Japanese that had to be excised, the inscrutable Japanese that couldn't be trusted." A melange of media artifacts is now folded in, mostly newsreel footage and 1940s cartoons that stress the villainy of the Japanese. The narrator adds, "Her genes in my body had prevailed. So you see, it was this Eurocentric and primitive understanding of history and genetics that left me susceptible to a metaphoric confusion about my mother's origins. She'd started life as a tumor, and, cancerous, she'd spread. I was her offspring and hardly benign."[13]

Halving the Bones presents history and meaning not as a single, available truth but as a series of metaphoric substitutions: mother for tumor, Japanese for disease, baby for turkey, bride for photograph. This endless slippage of signification is due partly to the slipperiness of memory, partly to the erratic nature of the cinematic image, and partly to a "Eurocentric and primitive understanding of history and genetics." The instability of meaning—linguistic, cinematic, and cultural—ensures that no single story emerges as the truth. Instead, it is in the excess, the flood of too many possibilities, that we can glimpse the complicated, transnational, multilingual roots of a biracial daughter, granddaughter, and filmmaker.

Ruth finally presents the bones to her mother, whose response is enigmatic. Masako exclaims over the beauty of the tea canister as well as the exquisite coloration of the bones themselves: "It's as if they were painted!" Immediately, we are reminded of Matsuye's profession of coloring photographs, as well as her tendency to color her (fictional) autobiography. If Ruth is uncertain about so many of the facts of the origins of the bones, how can she know what to do with them now? Earlier she has told us about a "memory" that she has of visiting her grandmother in her nursing home in Japan before she dies. She thinks that her grandmother has asked her to take her ashes back to Hawaii after her death and to throw them into the ocean. "But," she adds, "my Japanese wasn't very good at the time, and I might have been completely mistaken about what she'd said."

Ruth tells this story to her mother and asks her what she wants done with the bones. In a section of the film called "Mom's wishes (a projection)," her mother tells her that she wants to keep the bones with her in Connecticut. Then she tells Ruth that, after she dies, she would like to be cremated, to have her ashes or bones mixed with her mother's, and she would like Ruth to take them both to Hilo and throw them into the ocean. As her mother talks, Lounsbury intercuts her mother's interview with footage—alternating color and black-and-white—of herself in Hawaii. After her mother finishes speaking, the scene shifts to a lushly colored shot of Ruth, standing on a cliff, throwing ashes into the ocean. Her mother's wish has been projected immediately onto the screen, but the shift from black-and-white to color triggers the memory of her grandmother's tinted photos, and the scene is suspect. Is this merely a fantasy? A projection of her mother's wish? Or has her mother died? Are we watching an interview with a living woman, or with a ghost who lives only on celluloid?

As if to answer these questions by way of further complication, Ruth's grandmother's voice now takes over. She tells how Ruth came to visit her in the nursing home before her death. She says, "I have no idea if she understands me at all. I wonder, will she remember me after I'm gone?" As the grandmother speaks, a new film is put together, assembled from scraps of the grandfather's films and footage of Ruth in Hawaii, walking through a field, standing at the same beach as her grandmother. It is clear now that Ruth was the stand-in for her grandmother in the grandfather's movies, and she continues the scene, now in her own body, in the current moment. The physical substitution serves to suture the various pieces of film together, the "historical" and the contemporary, and to create a continuity between grandmother and granddaughter, even as the narrative reminds us that we will never know Matsuye's real wishes and whether or not Ruth translated them correctly.

The status of visual evidence is continuously called into question, even as both still and moving photography are offered as the media that bridge the gap across time and across cultures. As evidenced by the experience of picture brides, the photographic medium is both a very real and a very unreliable connection between people. Creating fictional stories and images offers a link with her grandmother, who went to Hawaii to meet a "husband she'd married through a photograph," and her grandfather, whose own films were confiscated and destroyed. In the process, Lounsbury is able to make visible, in the most contingent and unreliable ways, the significance of the inconsistencies in her history and their formative power over her own life. The power of the war and anti-Japanese sentiment, the cause of the destruction of her grandfather's films, in turn affects the way that she fastens on to a perhaps apocryphal story about her grandmother's tumor and its connection to her sense of racial identity.

The delicate and carefully assembled fiction of the film continues to unravel through the credits, in which actors are revealed to have stood in for her family in various home movie scenes from Ruth's childhood, and in which her parents are revealed to be "alive and well and living in Connecticut." The scene of Ruth throwing the ashes is thus exposed as a fake, but no more and no less than any of the previous evidence that has been found, borrowed, or created. As the title suggests, the endless "halving" and separating of the meat of myth from the bone of truth becomes a way of owning it, of creating a connection between people and the past. This process reveals and articulates the reasons why those connections are both irretrievably lost and always being imagined anew.

While the question of desire is ever present in *Halving the Bones* in the form of family members' will for connection, Nguyen Tan Hoang's 2000 video *Pirated!* takes the question of queer desire as a central flooding device between truth and fiction. The video centers around two powerful but absent locations: the filmmaker's homeland of Vietnam, and the boat that brought him to the United States. The experiences of the two sites are articulated as both the object and the origin of desire, as examples of both the ineffable and the palpable presence of the past.

In his genre-bending autobiography, *The Motion of Light in Water,* science fiction writer Samuel Delany describes his earliest attempts at memoir. He narrated his life in two columns; the first, written in a notebook from front to back, contained his acceptable thoughts and experiences, while the second, written in the same notebook from back to front, detailed everything forbidden, sexual, queer. This split autobiography becomes, for Delany, a metaphor for subjectivity and language. He writes: "If it *is* the split—the space between the two columns (one resplendent and lucid with the writings of legitimacy, the other dark and hollow with the voices of the illegitimate)—that constitutes the subject, it is only after the Romantic inflation of the private into the subjective that such a split can even be located. That locus, that margin, that split itself first allows, then demands the appropriation of language—now spoken, now written—in both directions, over the gap."[14]

It is in the difference between what is allowed to be spoken and what is repressed, that Delany locates desire and language, which move, like light expanding and rippling through water, across the gap. Like Delany's notebook, Nguyen's *Pirated!* is formed out of the meeting between two kinds of history: the official and the unofficial, the acknowledged and the forbidden, memory and fantasy.

In a short eleven minutes, *Pirated!* tells the complex but elusive story of Nguyen's trip from Vietnam to the United States in 1978 at the age of seven. The video begins with a shot of the ocean and a woman's voice singing a Vietnamese song with English lyrics that tell of a painful parting: "When tomorrow comes/And you will say goodbye/The sea and I will cry/The trees will sway and sigh." Text appears over the image telling the following story: "1978. The year after the Fall of Saigon. Fleeing from the Communists, my family and I escaped from Vietnam by boat. I was seasick for most of the time and do not remember much about the perilous voyage. I was 7 years old." The reliability of his story is called into question from the beginning, as Nguyen reveals the insufficiency of his memory due to illness and, presumably, youth.

The narration then moves from written to spoken, as a voice continues the story by saying, "As the ship's rolling took me away from Saigon, I remember an eerie silence. I recall thinking about my home, my family, my friends, and the unknown future in America. I pray that one day I will be able to return to Vietnam." The images in this section continue to shift from footage of a crowded refugee ship to murky and distorted shots of bodies swimming through the water. The pictures are constantly manipulated, multiplied, and split using various video effects, underscoring the

Pirated! (Nguyen Tan Hoang, 2000)

pliable nature of visual evidence. The trustworthiness of the narrative is further undermined with the textual declaration that "what you are about to see is based on many true stories."

The same song heard in the beginning is now repeated, only this time with Vietnamese lyrics, emphasizing the numerous paths that an emotion or an experience can take in its expression. Written text gives further detail about the past: "At sea for 7 days on a boat of 500. Attacked by Thai pirates. Rescued by a West German ship." One of the central events of the video—an event so horrifying and violent that it remains outside the possibility of mimetic representation—is slipped into a crowded and noisy field of discourse, moving it farther away from the audience's access. The attack is placed in contrast to another slippery and inaccessible memory, the return to Vietnam. A man's voice narrates a romantic account of his journey home, an account that will be retold and challenged several times in the course of the video. "As I stood in the land of my ancestors, I was overcome with joy and a sense of belonging. There, among the fields of rice paddies, the groves of bamboos, and the fields of sugar cane, I found myself. I knew this was where I belonged."

Text now appears to mediate between these two journeys, the traumatic escape from Vietnam and the nostalgic return home. Words on the screen declare, "At long last/ I too found myself/Not among the rice paddies of my ancestors/But on the High Seas: In the arms of Pirates and under the bodies of Sailors." For Nguyen, the space of belonging and identity is not the original homeland of Vietnam but the space of fantasy and invention. Neither "origin" can be regained; the boat journey has been forgotten as a result of its traumatic nature and its location in childhood, and Vietnam will continue to signify different things for different subjects at various points in their lives. Instead, Nguyen represents these two spaces as a flooding, a fluid and ever-changing stream of images and words that signify, not through their connection to a unitary signified, but through their excess of signification.

The flooding is achieved through numerous, clashing images and effects that make up the video: news footage of Vietnamese boat people, Vietnamese music videos, Hollywood movies, and Nguyen's own staged encounters between sailors and pirates on a beach in Los Angeles. In a flagrant appropriation of mainstream images, Nguyen intercuts Hollywood film footage of Burt Lancaster, Christopher Atkins, and Brad Davis— bare-chested hunks playing sailors and pirates—with his own scenes of white and Asian men dressed as pirates and sailors, kissing, beating, undressing, and having sex with each other. The status of these images as inadequate, or excessive, signifiers of a concrete past, as outlaw representation, is given ironic commentary in the video as Burt Lancaster's voice exhorts the audience, over swelling movie music: "Remember, in a pirate ship in pirate waters in a pirate world, ask no questions. Believe only what you see . . . No, believe half of what you see."

The real pirates, who terrorized thousands of refugees at sea, haunt the historical accounts of this period as a spectral presence never completely acknowledged by documentary and political recording.[15] When they erupt into the text, it is in a flooding, a larger-than-life fiction of Hollywood imagination and the traces of its formative mark on the sadomasochistic fantasies of the queer adult artist.[16] Like Lounsbury, Nguyen gives shape and substance to the gaps and absences of the past, only this time the product has been filtered through the lens of queer desire.

Like the gap between Delany's two columns of narrative, Nguyen's video mediates between several paradoxical versions of history, desire, and identity, which include the "straight" historical account and the transgressive queer fantasy, the terrorizing pirates and the liberating sailors, the idealized fantasy of an unchanged homeland and the disappointing reality of return. His account moves like water across and between these two columns, unsettling the foundations that construct them as binary. The theoretical and aesthetic space "in between" is reimagined as an erotic, physical space, "In the arms of Pirates and under the bodies of Sailors."

Pirated! is ostensibly about a two-way journey—the filmmaker's violent and formative sea voyage to the United States, and his attempt to return to the Vietnam of his youth through memory. However, as the events of the original journey remain outside the realm of realistic representation, the return to Vietnam is similarly undermined by an excess of contradictory accounts. Over a collage of varying visual evidence, we hear the voice-over accounts of several Vietnamese Americans who have returned to the country of their birth, each offering a conflicting story. One voice describes arriving in Vietnam and discovering the fertile green landscape and welcoming people that had waited, unchanged, in his imagination for his return. Another tells of the shock and horror she experienced at finding so much desolation and poverty left over from the war. Although this strategy creates a critical statement about the difficulty of preserving and returning to a unified and stable past, this section also serves to blur the lines between the individual and the collective story, examining the ways collective history and narrative penetrate and are shaped by intimate and personal experience.

One of Nguyen's interests, evident in his other work, is the role of this nostalgia among the Vietnamese immigrant community in the United

States. The pop music that he uses plays an important role in this process. As he explains in another video:

> The majority of Vietnamese music is made up of a small repertory of songs long familiar with Vietnamese everywhere . . . The limited repertory of Vietnamese songs continues to be covered and re-covered by old and new singers alike . . . This classic case of the compulsion to repeat reflects the desire of overseas Vietnamese to preserve the memory of home, that is to say, the uncorrupted pre-Communist Vietnam that they love, cherish, and left behind.[17]

These songs serve as a nostalgic bridge to the Vietnam of the past, a Vietnam that in fact no longer exists except in the memory of the immigrants. The title of Nguyen's video *Pirated!* refers in part to the fact that this music, like his footage, is being used without permission. Although the most obvious meaning of his title refers to the role of the pirates in the creation of his fantasy, Nguyen pirates the cultural vessels of history, memory, and nostalgia for his own purposes. The video pirates not only the familiar straight beefcake images of Hollywood but also multilayered narratives of Vietnam, by both the U.S. and the Vietnamese American media, and brings them together into a celebration of queer Asian American desire and identity as well as a critical exploration of the relationships among memory, history, and desire.

Like the other texts discussed, *Pirated!* uses the medium of memory as an aesthetic practice that comments on the provisional, unsteady nature of representation. Indeed, Freud's discussion of the screen memory is predicated on the understanding that all memories are screens of some kind between the present and the past. He writes:

> It may indeed be questioned whether we have any memories at all *from* our childhood: memories *relating to* our childhood may be all that we possess. Our childhood memories show us our earliest years not as they were but as they appeared at the later periods when the memories were aroused. In these periods of arousal, the childhood memories did not, as people are accustomed to say, *emerge*; they were *formed* at that time. And a number of motives, with no concern for historical accuracy, had a part in forming them, as well as in the selection of the memories themselves.[18]

If the "real" memory of Nguyen's video is of his journey from Vietnam, then the screen memory is the appropriated and invented footage that stands in for these lost images. However, insofar as his past journey is formative of his present desire, and insofar as we can only have access to the past through the approximative images of the present, all the images can be said to exist in refracted relation to the past, with none existing as more real or original than any other. The artistic process mimics the psychoanalytic function of the screen memory in which memories do not "emerge" but are "formed at the time" of remembering. In fact, the editing together of these disparate images creates an aesthetic bridge between past and present, and between reality and desire. As a Hollywood pirate looks through his telescope, a reverse shot reveals that he is looking at the film-maker, dressed as a sailor, being whipped by a pretend pirate. Nguyen's video "queers" memory in two senses of the term; he unearths the trans-gressive erotic potential of representing a lost past, even as he reveals that past to be nothing more (or less) than desire.

In this sense, queerness provides one more destabilizing layer, another element of excess of signification within the text. In both of the queer videos discussed in this essay, the confluence of queer identity and ethnic identity is neither an accidental occurrence nor simply the accretion of separate but unrelated identity categories within one story. The instability of meaning triggered by queer desire in these two texts serves as a formal disruption within the treatment of Asian American identity and history, and vice versa. Although the three texts discussed here were chosen as rep-resentatives of an Asian American media practice, the last two in particu-lar make clear that neither ethnic identity nor sexuality can determine the entirety of a text's meaning. These elements, along with the myriad other factors that shape identity, are both insufficient and overdetermining in their explanatory power.

Ernesto Foronda's 2000 short video *Cherrybomb!!!* makes similar use of a queer aesthetic practice to mediate between individual and col-lective identities and histories; in *Cherrybomb!!!,* however, unlike in the previous two pieces, which present themselves as more directly auto-biographical documents, the connection between the filmmaker—a gay Asian American man—and the subject—the largely white riot grrrl music scene—is not immediately apparent. Nevertheless, I argue that Foronda's use of the mock rockumentary, which blends many stories, both real and fake, serves as a vehicle for expressing the impact of the music and culture on the filmmaker himself. At the same time, however, the video draws on the unreliability of the documentary form to critique the ways in which rockumentaries often fail to incorporate a real analysis of race.

Cherrybomb!!! is the most "conventional" fake documentary of the group, purporting to be an investigation into the breakup of *Cherrybomb,* a fictional punk girl band that served as the inspiration for countless girl rockers and their fans. The band and video take their name from the 1976 song by the Runaways, the influential female rock band fronted by Joan Jett, which has been covered over the years by numerous female bands in-cluding the Japanese duo Shonen Knife.

The twenty-five-minute video features interviews with dozens of real (The Need, The Butchies, The Third Sex, Kathleen Hanna) and fake (Cherrybomb, Bad Boys) bands and their fans who tell a pastiche of real and fake stories about Cherrybomb's demise. These include, of course, stories about sex, drugs, and the inevitable disillusionment and pettiness that breed within the claustrophobic world of the rock band. The video is shot in black-and-white, ironically referencing both the gritty, low-budget aesthetic of punk rock, and the familiar media cliché in which black-and-white signifies the historical and the real. Through its messy collection of real and fake stories (one is never told which is which), the video becomes an unauthorized account of an unauthorized culture.[19] Insofar as punk translates the rejection of convention and tradition into style, this video performs a similar overturning of the conventions of veracity and journalistic responsibility.

The video relies on some of the signifying systems of indie music and dyke culture: gossip, legend, and myth. Interviewees relate stories from their own experiences or those overheard in a club, ranging from the fabulous to the mundane. As is always the case with rumor, however, the more unbelievable stories are frequently the true ones, while the commonplace ones are often invented for the camera. As soon as one fan relates that the cause of the breakup was drugs, a member of the band proclaims the group to be "straight edge." As soon as the drummer claims that the guitarist is transitioning from female to male, the guitarist tells us that she is straight, while another female fan says that she slept with her. In between these contesting versions of reality, we also get stories by young women about the powerful influence the band has had on their sense of self-worth, their place in a community, their sexuality, and their politics. As one character, who met her girlfriend at a Cherrybomb concert, says, "If I didn't go see Cherrybomb . . . I'd probably be just some lame straight girl."

While the band Cherrybomb never existed, these stories, taken together, tell a larger story about the importance of an alternative music scene for girls, with its possibilities for self-expression, power, rage, and the exploration of consciousness and identity. Unlike the previous two pieces, *Cherrybomb!!!* avoids specific references to geographic locations. The grainy black-and-white imagery flattens out distinctions between location and identity, taking the color out of every scene, in a reversal of the process by which Lounsbury and her grandfather put color in.

The queer Filipino American male filmmaker finds in riot grrrl culture, with its gender-crossing appropriation of musical and political forms of self-expression, a vivid expression of his own personal and aesthetic identification. While Foronda never appears in the video, the filmmaker's presence is felt as a foundational queerness that is embodied in the paradox of the term "riot grrrl," a term that deliberately contrasts the anarchist implications of "riot" with the word "girl," its implications of youthful and delicate femininity, twisted into an unruly growl.[20] Foronda's use of the fake documentary form to tell this particular story—a personal and a communal story fashioned in unstable, refracted relation to each other—draws on the creative possibilities inherent in the queering of history and documentary practice. Just as the riot grrrl movement hijacked the symbols and angry expressive power of a male-dominated rock world, so have the narratives about real bands been hijacked and conscripted into the service of constructing and relaying the history of Cherrybomb.

Despite being both a spoof and a genuine homage to Riot Grrrl culture and aesthetic, the video enacts a subtle yet unmistakable critique of the limited perspective of the punk girl music scene around race and sexuality. The only person of color in Cherrybomb, the guitarist Mikki, played by Chinese Ecuadoran filmmaker Lala Endara, catalogs the multiple ways in which she was oppressed by her bandmates, particularly through their inability to understand the complexity of her cultural heritage. When we first meet Mikki, she is in the Asian studies section of a bookstore reading a book entitled *After Exile: Writing the Latin American Diaspora*. But, as her interviews quickly reveal, her bandmates and other members of the music scene are not able or willing to comprehend the complexities of Asian (North) American culture and identity, let alone the Latin American Asian diaspora.

As Mikki describes people's exoticizing and orientalist responses to her accent and her cultural background, the format of the video changes from fast-moving sound bites to a protracted and unrestrained rant.

Mikki in *Cherrybomb!!!* (Ernesto Forondo, 2000)

It was very hard, you know. It was very hard, like, to feel like not only was I oppressed because I was, like, a woman, but I was oppressed because I was a person of color. And there were, like, nobody else like me around, you know, and I would feel really alienated 'cause, like, nobody else would talk with an accent, you know, and, like, people would be like, "Hey, where's that accent from? It's kinda cute, whatever, whatever." And I'd be like, "What accent? What are you talking about? Like, I'm just trying to speak English. Like, you try speaking Spanish, you know." Like nobody puts themselves, like, in your place, like, goes, "Shit, like, maybe we shouldn't say stuff like that because that's *oppressive!*"

Although all of the band members are discussed and interviewed, it is Mikki who remains the source of the most controversy and contestation—over her sexuality, her gender status, her love affairs, etc. Some claim that she is a transitioning FTM; others swear that she is the biggest dyke of them all and has slept with all of her bandmates and fans. Mikki herself claims to be straight, with a boyfriend, attributing all of the rumors to jealousy. The illegibility of her race to her white peers makes her untranslatable, or vulnerable to mistranslation, at every level. At one point during the rant, her voice goes inexplicably out of synch with her mouth, opening up yet another gap between her physical image and her spoken words.

The political and musical cultures being referenced in *Cherrybomb!!!* (as well as in other documentaries, both real and fake, about punk and rock music) have never been able to adequately deal with issues of racial difference. Mikki's chaotic spewing of vitriol in the video represents the repressed subject of race that resurfaces to disrupt and explode the form. While *Cherrybomb!!!* may be seen in many ways as a celebration of the largely white riot grrrl movement, it is in the character of Mikki that tensions between the filmmaker's identity and the subject matter erupt onto the surface of the text, as Foronda speaks through Mikki's disjointed and rambling voice. *Cherrybomb!!!* follows a strain in some of Foronda's previous work in which he examines his many forms of cross-ethnic and cross-gender desire and identification. *Straight Boy Blues* (1997), for example, interrogates his desire for straight, white men, while *The Games People Play* (2002) considers the question of why all of his friends are women, either straight or lesbians.[21] In a sense, *Cherrybomb!!!* could be seen as an articulation of Foronda's own refractory relation to white girl culture, a relationship whose "queerness" can only be represented through a separation of images from their "true" referents. It is fitting that part of Mikki's illegibility to her fellow riot grrrls comes as a result not only of her Asian identity but of her diasporic identity. In Mikki, Foronda could easily be referencing the complex cultural hybridity of his own Filipino identity.

The fake documentary, which is already a critical statement on the unreliability of all visual evidence, is the perfect medium for Foronda's racial critique of both the rockumentary and mock-rockumentary tradition, for the fake documentary's critical power lies in what it (and all documentary in general) *cannot* represent rather than in what it can. The impossibility of complete and truthful representation is expressed, by all of these filmmakers, through a creative overload of signification, a surfeit of images and possibilities that most accurately captures the inadequacy, the instability, and the endless productivity of all cinematic representation.

A review of the extensive history of independent film and video by Asian American artists reveals that these three texts are by no means unique in their concerns or strategies.[22] Peter X. Feng has written that "Asian American identity is defined not by history, but by gaps in history."[23] Asian American filmmakers, such as the ones discussed here, transform these historical gaps into sites of expression, aligning them formally and theoretically with the gaps inherent in the cinematic medium and transforming them into a boundless archive of what has not and cannot be shown. Through creative flooding of fact, supplemented by fiction, propelled by desire and loss, these filmmakers produce eternally vital and flexible expressions of how meaning and history are made and unmade.

NOTES

This essay was workshopped in the Los Angeles Women's Group for the Collaborative Study of Race and Gender in Culture. The group, whose members include Gabrielle Foreman, Alexandra Juhasz, Laura Hyun Yi Kang, Rachel Lee, Cynthia Young, and myself, theorizes, writes, and produces new scholarship within a collective, progressive feminist framework. I would like to express my thanks to the members of the group as well as to Ruth Ozeki, Nguyen Tan Hoang, and Ernesto Foronda for their generosity and creativity.

1. Toni Morrison, "The Site of Memory," in *Inventing the Truth: The Art and Craft of Memoir*, ed. William Zinsser (Boston: Houghton Mifflin, 1995), 98–99.
2. Science fiction writer Samuel Delany (to whom I will be referring later in this essay) offers an illuminating model that reverses the usual relationship between history and memory, in which history is aligned with certainty and clarity while memory is aligned with instability and fleetingness. As he theorizes in his autobiography, the two terms are mutually created, with history being formed out of an (always failed) attempt to straighten out and complete the "discontinuities" of memory. He writes, "For 'History' is what we create by the scratching, the annoyance, the irritation of writing, with its aspirations to logic and order, on memory's uneasy and uncertain discontinuities . . . While 'story' is what we can create, what we can recount, what we can recall, 'History' (as one evokes it in biography, in autobiography) is what most of us do *not* remember, what most of us *cannot* speak of." Samuel Delany, *The Motion of Light in Water: Sex and Science Fiction Writing in the East Village* (Minneapolis: University of Minnesota Press, 1993), 253; emphasis in the original.
3. George Lipsitz, *Time Passages: Collective Memory and American Popular Culture* (Minneapolis: University of Minnesota Press, 1990), 5. Central to Lipsitz's argument is that history and commercialized leisure, while appearing diametrically opposed, stem from similar historical and economic sources in the rise of industrial capitalism. While history emerged as a discipline that would seek to provide a continuous and

shared sense of the past in a radically changing and fractured modern world, commercialized culture promised "at least the illusion of connection with the past" as it served the interests of capitalism's need for renewable commodities and a culture of consumers. Although this new commercial culture created a sense of community and shared history, it also provided a space for expressions of loss and nostalgia for a connection to the past as well as for the articulation of local counter-memories of class, race, and ethnicity.

4. More specifically, Freud defines a screen memory as "one which owes its value as a memory not to its own content but to the relation existing between that content and some other, that has been suppressed." This concept is extremely useful to my analysis because it emphasizes the contingent significance and power of memory. According to Freud, the "content" of the memory—the original event being remembered—is less important than the "relation" of that memory to what has been forgotten. In the texts I discuss, memory is never used as a means of accessing a certain and stable past. Rather, it is the bridge between what can and cannot be remembered, imagined, and represented. Sigmund Freud, "Screen Memories" (1899), in *The Standard Edition of the Complete Psychological Works of Sigmund Freud*, vol. 3, trans. James Strachey (London: Hogarth Press and the Institute of PsychoAnalysis, 1950), 320.

5. Toni Morrison, *Beloved* (New York: Signet, 1987), 44–45.

6. Fredric Jameson, *Postmodernism, or The Cultural Logic of Late Capitalism* (Durham, N.C.: Duke University Press, 1991), 96.

7. Ibid., 71.

8. Marita Sturken, "The Politics of Video Memory: Electronic Erasures and Inscriptions," *Screening Asian Americans*, ed. Peter X. Feng (New Brunswick, N.J.: Rutgers University Press, 2002), 175.

9. Ibid.

10. In an attempt to acknowledge the multiple layers of identity being created and cited in this film, I use different terms to refer to the three different manifestations of the filmmaker in the text: "Lounsbury" refers to the filmmaker whose conscious aesthetic practice shapes the various elements of the text; "the narrator" refers to the voice who speaks for the filmmaker and also impersonates her grandmother's voice; and "Ruth" refers to the person who moves and acts within the narrative of the film. Needless to say, the overlap and slippage among these various incarnations of identity are constant (as is my usage of the three terms),

as they constitute the central aesthetic and theoretical practice of the film.

11. In "Cinematic Projections: Marking the Desirous Body," Laura Hyun Yi Kang offers a valuable analysis of constructions of "Asian/American women" that corresponds to the way in which Lounsbury disaggregates the subject from the image and from the maker of her film. Kang examines several film texts in order to "reconsider the ways in which mediated image, perceived identity, and felt subjectivity have been too readily linked and indeed collapsed together through the presumed unity and coherence of the categories of 'Asian women' and 'Asian American women.' In arguing for the necessity of examining the ways in which image, identity, and subjectivity do not and cannot line up with each other, I would accentuate Asian/American women as a troubling subject for both cinematic figuration and interpretation." Laura Hyun Yi Kang, *Compositional Subjects: Enfiguring Asian/American Women* (Durham, N.C.: Duke University Press, 2002), 75.

12. Peter X. Feng discusses the response to the gaps within historical and cinematic representation in relation to the larger tradition of Asian American film and video. "These films and videos do not attempt to plug gaps in memory and history by reconstructing what is missing, for such a strategy denies the historical process that produced those gaps: these films and videos create imagery that fills the gap while constantly speaking its own inadequate referentiality. Similarly, by implicitly or explicitly thematizing their location in relation to mainstream cinema, these movies call attention to the forces that marginalize Asian American makers; by signifying on cinematic conventions, Asian American makers call attention to the ways those conventions participate in constructing a cinematic tradition that excludes Asian American voices." Peter X. Feng, *Identities in Motion: Asian American Film and Video* (Durham, N.C.: Duke University Press, 2002), 16–17.

13. This contrast between personal and cultural metaphors highlights a strategy employed by all of the films discussed in this essay, a strategy that George Lipsitz has called "counter-memory." Counter-memory "focuses on localized experiences with oppression, using them to reframe and refocus dominant narratives purporting to represent universal experience" (Lipsitz, 213).

14. Delany, *Motion of Light in Water*, 73–74; emphasis in the original.

15. Van Luu describes the experiences of refugees on rickety boats, who were "brutally attacked by the pirates in the waters joining

Vietnam's Mekong Delta, the coasts of southern Thailand, and northeast Malaysia . . . U.S. refugee officials interviewing the victims often write the initials 'RPM' in their case histories," a shorthand for the refugees' experiences of "rape, pillage, and murder." Van Luu, "The Hardships of Escape for Vietnamese Women," in *Making Waves: An Anthology of Writings by and about Asian American Women*, ed. Asian Women United of California (Boston: Beacon Press, 1989), 63. The source of much of Luu's information in this piece is cited as Bruce Grant, *The Boat People: An Age Investigation of Bruce Grant* (New York: Penguin Books, 1979).

The underreported experiences of Southeast Asian refugees at the hands of pirates are beginning to be addressed in other contemporary Asian American texts, such as Justin Lin and Quentin Lee's 1997 film *Shopping for Fangs* and Victor Vu's 2004 film *First Morning*. In each of these feature films, the experience of rape and murder by pirates on the voyage to the United States is an unspoken secret and is only revealed at the end of the film. In fact, in both cases, this experience remains the repressed secret around which the narrative circles. When the secret is eventually revealed or remembered, the mysteries of the narrative are resolved. Trac Vu's 1997 short film *Among Others* also situates the trauma of the boat voyage—in this case, a story of shipwreck and cannibalism—as both the foundational and the closing story of the film's narrative.

16. Isaac Julien employs a similar strategy in his 1993 short film, *The Attendant*, in which a black museum guard imagines a painting, inspired by F. A. Biard's *Scene on the Coast of Africa* depicting the African slave trade, to be a contemporary scene of interracial gay s-m sex. As in Nguyen's video, a traumatic facet of the historical past reemerges as a shaping force in a contemporary queer sexual imaginary. Julien writes, "My film creates a number of tableaux vivants drawn from the painting. Although the current images of 'whips' and 'chains' in the representational practice of s/m have been borrowed from this colonial iconography, the refashioning of these accoutrements (i.e., rubberisation, polished surfaces, latex, polished metal) has transformed them into sexualised, stylised fetish clothing for the queer body. The imperialist slave iconography is appropriated and repositioned." Isaac Julien, "Confessions of a Snow Queen:

Notes on the Making of *The Attendant*," *Critical Quarterly* 36, no. 1 (Spring 1994): 121–22.

17. This quote comes from Nguyen's 2000 video *Cover Girl: A Gift from God*, a fascinating and hilarious documentary about Dalena, an Anglo American singer who has achieved extraordinary success and fame within the Vietnamese American community for her ability to perfectly mimic the sounds and style of Vietnamese popular music, despite not understanding a word of what she is singing.

18. Freud, *Complete Psychological Works*, 322.

19. In his history of punk rock and the meaning of style, Dick Hebdige writes, "Subcultures represent 'noise' (as opposed to sound): interference in the orderly sequence which leads from real events and phenomena to their representation in the media. We should therefore not underestimate the signifying power of the spectacular subculture not only as a metaphor for potential anarchy 'out there' but as an actual mechanism of semantic disorder: a kind of temporary blockage in the system of representation." Dick Hebdige, *Subculture: The Meaning of Style* (London: Routledge, 1979), 90. The form of the fake documentary performs a similar "blockage in the system of [cinematic] representation" in that it disturbs the viewer's comfortable relationship to the veracity of its—and all—images.

20. Foronda's independent music label, Heartcore Records, also represents many of the bands featured in the video.

21. In the five-minute video *The Games People Play*, the filmmaker is played by Foronda's sister in yet another cross-gender identification.

22. Perhaps the best-known example of an Asian American fake documentary is Marlon Fuentes's *Bontoc Eulogy* (1995), but numerous other Asian American films and videos address the question of memory, history, and the fertile unreliability of the cinema. Some of these include Rea Tajiri's *History and Memory: For Akiko and Takashige* (1991), Janice Tanaka's *Memories from the Department of Amnesia* (1989), *Who's Going to Pay for These Donuts, Anyway?* (1992)m Yunah Hong's *Memory/all echo* (1990), Richard Fung's *Dirty Laundry* (1996), Trac Vu's *First Year* (1997), and the work of Trinh T. Minh-ha, to name only a few. See Feng, *Identities in Motion*, for a good discussion of many of these pieces. See also Fuentes's interview in this anthology.

23. Feng, *Identities in Motion*, 17.

IV   Conclusions

ALISA LEBOW

[14] *Faking What? Making a Mockery of Documentary*

This volume is predicated on a category, the fake documentary, that the editors have chosen over and above the term mockumentary, for reasons they have amply delineated. It is considered that mocking is only one possible stance that the fake documentary can take. It can also copy, mimic, gimmick, play with, scorn, ridicule, invert, reverse, repeat, ironize, satirize, affirm, subvert, pervert, convert, translate, and exceed documentary style (see Juhasz' introduction to this volume). For all of that range of "play" available to them, the editors have chosen predominantly to focus on fiction films that mimic documentary style while somehow announcing themselves as Not Doc. Although I realize this specificity can serve to contain multiple and proliferating categories, thereby positioning the films more clearly in opposition to their supposed referent—the documentary—this particular form of containment is not my aim.

To some extent, the distinctions between different kinds of "faking" are not crucial, and no amount of conscious or intentional "faking" can undo the fact that documentary is itself already a fake of sorts, insofar as its claims to capturing reality have never yet proven fully authentic, definitive, or incontestable.[1] For my present purposes, I am equally interested in films that pass effectively as documentaries, films that never announce themselves as anything in particular, neither "pure doc" nor "pure fake," those that parody the form as well as those that lovingly and faithfully abide by it. The films that attempt some formal or conceptual distinction from the venerable documentary are in some senses the least challenging of all of the mockumentary modes, in that they can efficiently serve to authorize documentary as the proper nonfictive model, from which they then depart. I am less optimistic than is Juhasz about the ideologically subversive effects of the fake documentary, though I do agree that the potential for subverting the authoritative discourses of documentary through mimesis does exist. Subversion is simply not inherent in the project of faking, as Lerner duly affirms in his introductory remarks.

One further note: I tend to prefer the term mockumentary, even while availing myself of the many valences implied in Juhasz's panoply of "attitudes" of the fake documentary. I believe the term "mockumentary" more effectively works to signal a skepticism toward documentary realism, rather than to reauthorize documentary's "truth" against the fake doc's "false." Like "fake doc," the term "mockumentary" incorporates and implicates *documentary* into its referent while still implying some distinction from it. But with mockumentary the distinction remains productively undefined, whereas, I believe, the term "fake doc" too eagerly accepts and reconfirms the binary (fake vs. real) from the outset. Fake doc needlessly concedes that documentary itself is "real" or at least authentic (the genuine article, i.e., not fake), while my hope is that *mockumentary* might more successfully attenuate, if not ultimately destabilize, the credibility of documentary by, if you will, mocking the very concept at its core.

With a title like mine, I am clearly taking a polemical position vis-à-vis documentary studies and the nascent interest in what seems to be presented of late as a spin-off discourse about the mockumentary. I offer this essay as an inoculation against overinvestment in the factual pretensions of documentary and overdependency on the stability of the categories themselves. I find problematic the assumption that underpins mockumentary: namely, that it depends and responds to the "real" or "true" original, documentary. The idea that the category of documentary supports and sustains mockumentary as its "straight" or "upright" other—that documentary in effect props mockumentary up—is troubling to me. What an unreliable pedestal upon which to construct a claim. Is there an objective or superior rendition of the actual—or better yet, the "real"—that documentary can possibly claim that would enable a mockumentary parody? Who is parodying whom, I want to know.

Couldn't it be *mockumentary* that is doing the propping, setting a stage by which documentary may finally appear as a stable and coherent category? Certainly the burgeoning field of mockumentary studies seems to incline us toward this position. This process of propping, anaclisis, has its psychoanalytic implications. A drive, which, as psychoanalytic theorists maintain, is always sexual, must have its prop, its antecedent, which is a nonsexual or presexual instinct.[2] The oral drive, for instance, is predicated on, or propped up by, the hunger instinct. This position implies that there is a presymbolic urge lurking behind the staging of fantasy, which here might be said to be the fantasy of representing reality: so with the relationship between documentary and mockumentary, where one "urge" presupposes and depends on the other.

Logically, we may assume that documentary is the urge that props up mockumentary, documentary being the drive more directly oriented toward its object. Mockumentary adds a layer of fantasy, "sexing up" documentary and detaching it from its supposedly straightforward relationship with its "natural" object. Conversely, we may deduce that mockumentary is bringing documentary back to life, as it were, at least at the level of documentary studies. If this is so, then mockumentary is working in the service of documentary's self-preservative instincts, performing an anaclitic reversal whereby the supposed derivative is actually doing the propping, taking over the life-sustaining task. Mockumentary, by making the field of documentary studies sexy, is actually revitalizing and reorienting what might otherwise be a withering subject. Again, the question of who is propping whom emerges. Clearly, with doc/mock/umentary, it is difficult to know which urge comes first.

This is a false conundrum, since both practices may be said to be propped up by a more primal urge: the urge or instinct to gaze upon the Real.[3] Documentary's quest for reality, and mockumentary's complex and often cagey reproduction of documentary realism, may both be seen as strategies to approach the ever-elusive Real. "Unmediated reality" then constitutes the limit of the sayable or the representable, i.e., the *Real* of both documentary and mockumentary. Although the real in this case is neither genre's privileged province, I do want to argue that it may be both genres' motivating "instinctive" urge.[4]

In what follows, I will loosely trace the genealogies of documentary and mockumentary, fused as they are historically and conceptually; I will discuss the problematic generic status of both, and I will attempt to devise an approach that circumvents, if not transcends, the specious fact/fiction divide (some would say continuum) that dominates so many debates on the topic. In the process, I will be searching for some useful distinctions between the two rhetorical modes that are not reducible to the unrewarding questions of objectivity or facticity. It should be noted here that I depart from conventional documentary theorists in that I will argue, using a Lacanian paradigm, that the documentary form (as seen in both documentary and mockumentary) implies and is motivated by a kind of *psychic investment* that cannot be characterized in terms of a slavish wish to faithfully represent *reality* (which in any event only accounts for some documentary practice); rather, this quest for reality (however that term is understood) constitutes the *Real* of documentary, and it is this promise or possibility of revealing the Real that drives both documentary and mockumentary practices.

In other words, I am not entering this debate to decide which form, documentary or its supposed replica, can claim the greater degree of indexicality to reality, or even which one is better situated to critique such a claim. I am more concerned with what undergirds both endeavors that is not simply, in the case of documentary, to see reality represented with the greatest fidelity, or, in the case of the fake documentary, to merely problematize the notion of fidelity, authority, and/or indexicality. I am suggesting that both forms, in different ways, train their sights from various angles in an effort to glimpse the nebulous, vertiginous, ever-elusive Real. I make this bold assertion because I strongly suspect that animating the desire to document or mockument is a drive to see "something more." Hence, the truth claims that are made in either register (and it is important to acknowledge that mockumentary makes truth claims as well) aspire beyond ideology and beyond reality to the ultimate, though also ultimately unrepresentable, truth, the "hard kernel" up against which all quests for true reality must come—i.e., the Real.

The field of documentary studies has made great strides in the last twenty years, with an accelerated development in the last ten. Theorists have done much to, at once, elucidate and problematize the practice, thus relativizing its attendant meanings. There is not one documentary critic who has not had to negotiate the problematic status of documentary as a genre, even as most try to sidestep implications of their claims. Eager to establish and consolidate a discipline, most documentary theorists, like documentary practitioners, have chosen to overlook the stubborn refusal of documentary to be properly disciplined. The category of documentary has always been an elusive one. Every definition of the term has proved partial and of limited use, whether Bill Nichol's "discourse of sobriety," Brian Winston's "scientific inscription," or Paula Rabinowitz's "instruct[ion] through evidence."

We are no closer to consensus now than we were ten years ago as to an adequate working definition of documentary.[5] Is documentary the filmic apotheosis of realism, or is it not? Does it or does it not have a special indexical relationship to reality? And if it does, as so many theorists and filmmakers claim, what is the nature of this seemingly objective reality that is reputedly available to indexical representation? Is or is not reality (let alone *the Real*) ultimately representable? Clearly the answers vary greatly, depending on which documentary theorist one asks, though none would venture to say that reality (much less the Real) is ever representable in any complete or unmediated way.

Whether documentary has a more intimate relationship to reality or history than fiction has never been sufficiently established. In fact, what would constitute such an "intimacy" in representational terms? More to the point, indexicality to something (reality) that is always already mediated through the same symbolic system as that which purports to indexically represent it (documentary), is an infinitely repeating house of mirrors—always already at a distinct, if unquantifiable, remove. It is not that documentary practices must be seen as synonymous with fiction: of course there is a difference. But that difference cannot be deciphered based on documentary's "cozier" relationship to reality—i.e., that which is always already at a distinct remove.

In brief, it seems that the reason to maintain documentary as a conceptual category has more to do with cultural capital than it does with any necessary intimacy, indexically or otherwise conceived, to reality. Documentary is a culturally sanctioned performance, wielding an authority built up through what genre critics have called "intertextual relay" (i.e., promotion and context of exhibition) that create "horizons of expectations" for the spectator.[6] These expectations play upon an almost irresistibly strong force field of the desire to know (epistephilia), or rather the desire for the illusion of mastery through knowing. Here I am only rehearsing the arguments of several prominent documentary theorists, Brian Winston, Trinh T. Minh-ha, and Elizabeth Cowie among them.[7]

The highly disputable distinction between documentary and mockumentary rests upon this fragile fulcrum of expectations and the desire to know. The much-celebrated documentary spectator's epistephilia shifts—in the case of mockumentary, but also in the case of an "educated" documentary spectator—to a different kind of knowingness. Mockumentary, in particular, fails to please precisely when this knowingness is withheld and expectations of unadulterated epistephilia have already been induced. Yet these disappointments are predicated on a prior disavowal, which the documentary enacts (and which I would not like to see documentary theory reproduce): namely, of the documentary genre's failure to produce anything more than the (normative) codes of reality, i.e., realism, not the real (thing) itself. In her article, "The Spectacle of Actuality," Cowie reminds us of the pleasures, as well as the aporias, of this disavowal, and warns that in the end it is a violent and repressive disavowal.[8] Cowie suggests that documentary is a prosthetic device, extending the spectator's perceptual abilities (through the superior optics of the camera) while simultaneously admitting the deficiencies of the human power of sight and the scopophilic drive.[9] Perhaps we can see documentary as striving for "something more" as well, desiring to bionically extend the viewer's abilities beyond that which can be seen, to the unseen. This would imply that documentary seeks and simultaneously disavows (covers over) that which it seeks but is impotent to capture: the Real. But perhaps I am getting ahead of myself.

Having outlined documentary's problematic ontological status, I want to now elaborate on the position against the legitimation of the category of mockumentary as distinct from documentary. Such a legitimation only serves to affirm the impression that documentary is a discrete and defensible category. I want to suggest that this construction of mock versus real doc relies on a fallacy (a *fake*) and that if the notion of mockumentary mocks anything at all, it is the very viability or sustainability of the documentary category. Paradoxically, this undermining mockery will only come to light once we have questioned the range of mockumentary practices and whether they are necessarily subversive.

As mentioned earlier, definitions of documentary are notoriously weak. Tellingly, theorists more often proffer inevitably flawed descriptions of what documentary film is not (not fiction, not acted, not scripted) than of what it may actually be. I say "flawed" because many, if not most, documentaries do contain scripted sequences, do employ or engage (perhaps nonprofessional) actors and acting, and partake, at the very least, in the narrative imperative (telling stories), no less than do fiction films. The positive ascriptions for documentary turn out to be no less problematic ("sober," "based on actual events," "essayistic," etc.).[10] For every definition offered, one can think of notable exceptions that, rather than prove the rule, effectively disprove the definition. On the other hand, the term mockumentary remains poorly defined as well, never having entered the lexicon as a formal description or clearly defined genre of filmmaking. For example, the authors of *Faking It: Mock-documentary and the Subversion of Factuality* have chosen to locate what they call mock-documentaries in yet another series of unstable and overly constricting categories, such as drama documentary and docudrama.[11] For them, the mock documentary is that film that is clearly demarcated as a fiction film yet utilizes documentary techniques to (usually) comic and parodic effect. This seems an unnecessarily limiting definition and, with all due respect to the authors of this groundbreaking text, their taxonomy seems based more on the desire to identify that which may be subversive in these practices, excluding or disregarding those mock-doc practices that do not conform to the hopes and expectations of subversiveness.

At the very least, mockumentary is generally assumed to take its inspiration derivatively from the documentary film. To mock can mean, of course, to mimic (usually, but not necessarily, in a parodic sense) or to ridicule (though not necessarily in an imitative vein). Mockumentaries may be said to include parodies of documentary, the humor being based in either the deception of the audience (Peter Jackson and Costa Boles's *Forgotten Silver,* 1996) or the absurdity of the premise (Nick Park's *Creature Comforts,* 1990, or Woody Allen's *Zelig,* 1983). However, I believe we should conceive of the category more broadly still, including mimetic fiction films that borrow documentary realist techniques to avail themselves of the authoritative verisimilitude that documentary films attempt to inspire so as then to subvert that authority (Mitchell Block's *No Lies,* 1975, or Michele Citron's *Daughter Rite,* 1979, being two archetypal examples). I would also include the far less recognized practice of the nonparodic mimetic mockumentary, such as Elisabeth Subrin's *Shulie* (1997) or Jill Godmillow's *What Farocki Taught* (1998), which take seriously the lessons of the scribe, painstakingly and lovingly reproducing the images, if not the sounds, of a model text in order to reaffirm its initial value in a new temporal context. This type of mockumentary is a form of translation, producing differences and excesses (or differ*a*nce) not through language or enunciation per se, nor through parody, satire, or irony, but through representation and reiteration *in* time.[12]

There are also mockumentaries, such as docudramas, that are devoid of any hint of parody or irony and may easily be received in the same epistephilic register as a straight documentary. This practice is as old and well-established as documentary itself. Yet mockumentaries (and those who study them) seem to bear the cachet of the new, raising expectations of the disruptive potential of the subversive maverick. It is important to remember, though, that, although the term may be new, the practice is not (see Jesse Lerner's discussion in the introduction to this volume). Moreover, there are no necessarily ideologically subversive implications to the endeavor. Availing oneself of the authoritative rhetorics of documentary can be an effective maneuver in the circulation of discursive power. In fact, Cowie reminds us that documentary's realist pretension, its verisimilitude, is subject to highly conservative, normative codes of reality. As Cowie states, "verisimilitude is . . . central [to] the documentary film—just as much as and perhaps more than for the fiction film. The world presented must be believable, it must be like what we expect the world to be, in order for the film to sustain our belief in its claim to reality."[13] Mockumentary, even in its parodic variations, participates in the normative coding of reality, insofar as it compels audience belief in its veracity as a documentary. As Juhasz states in the conclusion to her introductory remarks, "fakery is an inherently conservative practice, even at its most explicitly political." Mockumentary may even attempt to outdo the outmoded codes of documentary realism—as the better, more truthful, verisimilar address—much as reflexive documentary has done.

Happy Birthday, Mr. Mograbi (Avi Mograbi, 1999). Photograph courtesy of First Run/Icarus Films.

I am reminded here of a mockumentary by Israeli filmmaker Avi Mograbi, *Happy Birthday, Mr. Mograbi* (1999). In it, Mograbi plays a filmmaker obsessed with videotaping all aspects of his life, which include working on a video project for an Israeli producer about Israel's fifty-year "jubilee" celebrations, while simultaneously shooting footage inside Israel for a Palestinian production about "Al Nakba"—the fifty-year "disaster" mourned by the Palestinians. These events, which are of course two interpretations of the same event, coincidentally occur on the filmmaker's forty-second birthday. When not working on either of the two projects, Mograbi narrates a story in direct address (complete with flashback reenactments and "hidden" camera sequences) about himself and a plot of land he bought several years earlier as an investment for his retirement and his children. The video is shot in vérité style, documenting the process of building a house on the plot of land, which erroneously includes an extra, unpaid for, parcel. He sells the house to an old, irate Israeli, but the neighbors figure out that the new house has been built on property that was properly theirs. There is a conflagration, where it becomes clear that the neighbor is acting irrationally, as is the buyer. The seemingly decent, upright filmmaker/ Israeli is caught in the middle of this rapidly devolving dynamic through a mistake not entirely of his own making, yet one that he was willing to (reluctantly) capitalize on and only belatedly willing to amend.

The allegory in this modern parable becomes ominously clear: Mograbi's character represents the typical Israeli, well-intentioned but caught in a no-win situation. The buyer represents the irrational Jewish settlers who refuse to renegotiate an agreement even once they learn it was made in bad faith. The neighbor represents the justifiably angry yet inexplicably violent Palestinians, who act so "primitively," so "barbarously," that whatever sympathy one may have had for them initially is lost in the end. The identifications constructed through the first-person direct address, and the playful mockumentary style, are clearly meant to be aligned with the filmmaker's character, and thus with the poor, hapless, self-interested yet generally ethical, average Israeli—over and above the "extremists" on either side. This disingenuously naïve portrayal is insidious, refusing as it does its own complicity, and indeed instrumentality, in the mechanisms of oppression. Ironically, the sincerity of this mockumentary—its reflexivity, its humor, its intelligence—serves the author's self-exculpating position seamlessly.[14]

As this example attests, there is no necessary political or ideological subversiveness of the mockumentary mode as such. However, neither is mockumentary a more degraded practice than documentary: a poor imitation of the shining original. Whether to deceive, amuse, challenge, propagandize, or reenact, these films do much more than merely adopt documentary techniques for their own mischievous (or even conservative) purposes. Insofar as mockumentaries mimic documentary, they implicitly contaminate it at the level of its generic status, revealing the impurity of the category itself. If there can be said to be any necessarily subversive implication of mockumentary practice, it would be this: as with all effective imitations, it reveals the performative limits of the original. To adapt and loosely paraphrase the insights of such thinkers as Judith Butler and Homi Bhabha, mockumentary mimesis inevitably reveals the impossible ideal of the purported real thing (i.e., the documentary "original").

Several years ago, I wrote an article, with my friend and colleague Marcos Becquer, on an obscure video that thematized transvestism and transsexuality "borrow[ing] the wisdom" of drag and mimesis (known as "realness" in the African-American and Latino drag community) in its chosen mockumentary form. It was a documentary about drag as much as a documentary in drag. We thought then, and it may be worth reiterating now, that the model of gender mimesis had some unexpectedly compelling parallels to that of genre mimesis, specifically with reference to mimicking "the real." To adapt a quote from this prior paper, "[mockumentary] prompts us to see documentary realism, like drag and transsexuality, as an attempt to imitate and embody the codes and the ontology of the real; to construct the real through its adaptive embodiment; to see it, that is, as a form of realness . . . "[15]

Bhabha reminds us that mimesis always entails excess. No mimesis or adequation is ever complete. At least, for it to be effective, it must always produce its "slippage, its excess, its difference."[16] And those who make this discomfiting fact of incompleteness apparent (women, the colonial subject, transvestites, and, here, mockumentaries) are subject to regulatory practices meant to contain the threat (why else would the editors of this volume invoke the specter of "movie jail?"). What is threatening is not that the subaltern, in Bhabha's example, and the mockumentary here, is revealed to be an inadequate replica, a poor imitation, of the true authoritative model, but rather that the authoritative model itself is implicated in this inadequacy. There is no effective originary model that stands apart, independent and assured. Here it becomes clear that the original is already a poor, or in fact an impossible, replica of an ideal. The alleged replica, in its stipulated performativity of the very idea of originality and even authority, only serves to compromise further the integrity of its alleged original. Reality is itself implicated as a poor rendering, an unconvincing rendition of the unattainable ideal (of the Real).

Arguably, one key problem at the core of the discussion of mockumentary is precisely that of origin, i.e., which form precedes the other? Is the documentary historically prior to the mockumentary, as is commonly presumed, or is it quite the other way around? Who imitates whom, and further, who imitates whom, imitating what, we might ask. If the histories of the nonfiction film are to be believed then *all* of the most exemplary early documentary films, whether those of Flaherty, Grierson, Vertov, or even Edison's and the Lumières' actualities, are also exemplary mockumentaries. In fact, with Flaherty's "cinema of romantic preservationism,"[17] Grierson's "creative treatment of actuality," and Vertov's "higher mathematics of facts," prompted as that arithmetic was by an albeit ideologically laden conception of "truth" or "pravda," we have a veritable set piece for mockumentary *(avant la lettre)* as the foundational discourse of documentary itself.

If we analyze verisimilar representational techniques, we have little choice but to concede that some key strategies currently associated with "mockumentary" (scripting, acting, reenacting, staging, etc.) have antecedents in the earliest days of so-called actuality or documentary films (before and after 1926, when the term "documentary" was coined), and came to signify documentary practice itself for at least half a century, without any apparent contradiction. In this sense, documentary cannot be said to be historically prior to mockumentary; at the very least, their origins are coeval. I want to underscore not this temporal simultaneity, but rather a formal equivalence. Mockumentary and documentary are not merely coincident—identical twins separated at birth—they are, in their origins, if no longer in their present-day effects, one and the same.

Beyond the question of origins, precedence, or propping, even more pressing is the question of the "original"[18] object that both documentary and mockumentary aspire to represent, and that is, I contend, the "Real" itself. As laid out earlier, I refer here to the Lacanian Real, as distinct from reality—indeed, as that which constitutes reality's radical resistance to full representability, even as it is structured by this representability. The Real (as ever-elusive event), in other words, is the ostensible terrain of documentary film. In *Looking Awry*, Slavoj Žižek sets out to prove that any notion that we may have about the Real is essentially a fake. The more we grasp at the elusive Real, the more likely we are to come up empty-handed. The Real eludes or resists direct representation—faking us out, we might say, at every attempt to grab hold of it. As that which is foreclosed from incorporation into the symbolic, the Real nonetheless structures our semblance of reality. Yet it only appears as disturbances or illusions in this reality. In this Žižek is pointing to the Lacanian insight that the Real exceeds the bounds of representability and can only be the unattainable substance of our fantasy. He claims the Real is the "pulsing of the pre-symbolic substance"[19] that only attains meaning and form once we as subjects enter the symbolic through the subjective web of our desires. Clearly, once meaning is ascribed to the Real, it is no longer a thing in itself, but rather a projection to which we can have no direct access. The hard kernel of the Real cannot be penetrated by the symbolic system; it is in fact defined by its inaccessibility.

Žižek argues, following Lacan, that the Real cannot be glimpsed head on, that it defies the forthright gaze. From the straightforward view (the angle to which documentary aspires), rather than seeing the Real, clearly and without distortion, we see *indistinct confusion*.[20] I am thinking here of Benjamin's analysis of Atget's fin-de-siècle documentary photographs of deserted Parisian streets, which were said to have been photographed "like scenes of crime"—evacuated, desolate, and activating the anxiety of witnessing an unmediated yet ultimately unrepresentable event: in short, the Real. Tellingly, Benjamin notes that simultaneously "picture magazines begin to put up signposts for [the viewer]; . . . for the first time, captions have become obligatory."[21] This demand for captions precisely reflects the desire or need to submit the Real to a symbolizing procedure, to tame and contain it—not in fact, to effectively represent it. A more prosaic example may be Winston's claim that "at its best, at its most observationally pure," ethnographic film is something only an anthropologist could love—something totally indecipherable to the average spectator without the benefit of interpretation (captions).[22] To the degree that documentary narrates, i.e., symbolizes, the event, documentary renders it at once decipherable and radically removed from the possibility of ever glimpsing the Real.

This point might be best exemplified in relation to documentary's limit case: death. Death is typically invoked as the definitive arbiter of documentary's indexicality to reality. Everyone knows that when human death is recorded in a documentary, an actual person in the world has died, whereas, in a fiction film, an actor will resume breathing as soon as the director yells "Cut." Yet, think of the archetypal shot of death in documentary, where a cameraman "records" his own death in Patricio Guzmán's *The Battle of Chile* (1974). What do we see of this death? A wild shot gone out of control and then darkness as the filmmaker cuts to black. Certainly we do not "see" death. What we see is ultimately Žižek's "indistinct confusion." Even when a camera records another's death, we cannot "see" (let alone "know") that death. For example, in Mark Massi and Peter Friedman's *Silverlake Life* (1992), Tom Joslin's death can never be made apparent to us in direct visual representation. We are reminded through a number of conventionalized codes that a life has been lost, but death itself remains elusive, radically defying representation; i.e., it refuses to yield its secrets, to make itself knowable to the *direct* gaze.[23]

When American documentary filmmakers began to pursue the *direct* cinema approach, what is it they hoped to achieve, if not to "capture the 'real'" on celluloid—without bias, unmediated by interpretation (i.e., gazed at forthrightly)?[24] Even though I concede Juhasz's point, made in an article about strategic uses of direct cinema techniques, that many direct cinema practitioners were not as naïve as such an assertion would make them seem, even today rhetoric about the unmediated *real* of documentary is prominent in production circles.[25] Filmmakers and producers tend to speak unselfconsciously about documentary's unique relation to reality and also (albeit without Lacanian intentions) to the real. HBO documentary impresario Sheila Nevins extols the virtues of the new compact digital cameras and their ability to deliver "purer" documentaries. Legendary documentarian George Stoney can claim that what keeps documentaries fresh and interesting is "the combination of real footage and reenactments." Barbara Koppel exuberantly celebrates the singular advantage of documentaries over fiction films by claiming that "nonfiction films *are real*."[26]

These filmmakers and producers are, of course, talking about "reality" per se, but the recourse to discourses of purity and superiority indicate a type of transcendentalism ascribed to the documentary mode that implies a higher aspiration than merely the faithful recording of actuality (were that even possible). Documentary theorists are subject to such slippages, as well. Without any apparent need to problematize the term, Winston calls his revisionist history of documentary film *Claiming the Real*.[27] The authors of *Faking It*, theorists who, like Winston, can be expected to be familiar with relevant distinctions between the terms "reality" and "the real," make reference to documentary's pose as the only representational medium "that can construct . . . a *direct* relationship with the *real*."[28] Given these contemporary claims and postures, it is not unreasonable to assume that documentary aspires (both through the efforts of the filmmakers and through those of the spectator) to the status of an unfettered, i.e., direct, representation of the Real.

Although it is not so much Žižek's "indistinct confusion" one sees with vérité and direct cinema approaches, clearly it is also not unmediated reality, let alone the Real. When we look closely at realist documentary, we see the techniques of dissimulation at work, no less than in the seamless continuities of narrative fiction films. The wizard is working overtime behind the curtain—even, maybe most especially, in "straight" documentaries—to make us believe in the illusion of the reality represented. In this, documentary realism can be said to disavow its fantasy, and, according to Žižek, it is precisely fantasy that is necessary to achieve a glimpse of the Real. In its imaginative flights of fancy (or more precisely fantasy), mockumentary may be just different enough from documentary to achieve such a glimpse. It is here where mockumentary (in some forms) may distinguish itself most effectively, mocking documentary's continued, head-on quest to pass itself off as the forthright gaze onto the Real.

If the direct gaze can reveal nothing of the Real, then it follows that the satirical, that is to say *wry*, look of at least some mockumentaries may just create the proper context to catch a glimpse of the Real. One must look askance at mockumentary (i.e., not be fooled by it) in order to apprehend, enjoy, or see what it has to reveal. This implies a doubling irony, the knowing gaze at a satirical parody (or some other kind of mocking mimesis)—a double awry—which allows for a defamiliarization effect or an estrangement, that may in fact be the path to that which is truer than fact, to that which even subverts the very illusion of facticity, pointing the way to a miasmic, vertiginous, yet somehow exhilarating possibility. This may indeed be the more interesting and useful distinction to be made between documentary and mockumentary, if one is ultimately to be found. The double awry look produced by the mockumentary opens up the possibility of the best we can hope for: a glimpse at the elusive Real.

The combined insights of Bhabha, Butler, and Žižek might lead us to conclude that reality itself is a mockumentary, for which there is no "doc."[29] If we concede my point that the true objective of both forms lies beyond (the nonetheless impossible goal of) representing reality, to actually achieving a glimpse of the Real, there is some credibility to the assertion that documentary is a failed project—or, better yet, that mockumentary is perhaps the truer documentary form.

♦ ————————————————————————————————

NOTES

I would like to thank Alex Juhasz for encouraging me to follow through on an early conversation we had about this book and to more fully anatomize my reservations about the category of the fake documentary. I would also like to thank Marcos Becquer for his close reading of several drafts, without which this paper would be considerably poorer, and to Elizabeth Cowie and Bülent Somay for their incisive comments on an earlier draft.

1. Clearly not all documentaries claim to represent reality, or at least they don't all claim to represent it in the same way, yet there is something that can be said to link documentary practice across the board, and that is perhaps the arrogation of authenticating discourses that have aspirations to represent reality, even if there may be a knowing stance projected (in self-reflexive documentaries, for instance) of the impossibility of that claim.

2. See Jean Laplanche on anaclisis in *Life and Death in Psychoanalysis*, trans. Jeffrey Mehlman (Baltimore, Md.: Johns Hopkins University Press, 1976), 20. See also Mary Ann Doane's discussion of Laplanche's definition in her 1981 article, "Woman's Stake: Filming the Female Body," reprinted in *Feminism and Film*, ed. E. Ann Kaplan (London: Oxford University Press, 2000), 90.

3. The "Real" here is distinct from "reality" in the psychoanalytic sense, though both doc and mock forms do also partake of the fantasy of representing reality, albeit in different ways.

4. I am not trying to somehow anthropomorphize documentary here, but rather to suggest that the drive to make documentary films, as well as the drive to watch them, may be motivated by a psychic mechanism akin to a presymbolic, instinctive, urge.

5. Like all genres, documentary conventions have changed over time and differ, too, from one cultural iteration to another. However, documentary seems to be particularly resistant to adequate definition, even provisionally conceived.

6. See Steve Neale's summary of the uses of the terms "intertextual relay" and "horizons of expectation" in literary and film genre studies in *Genre and Hollywood*

(New York: Routledge, 2000), 39–40 and 42 respectively.

7. See Brian Winston, *Lies, Damn Lies and Documentary* (BFI, 2000); Trinh T. Minh-ha, "The Totalizing Quest of Documentary," in *Theorizing Documentary*, ed. Michael Renov (New York: Routledge, 1993), 90–107; and Elizabeth Cowie, "The Spectacle of Actuality," in *Visible Evidence*, ed. Jane Gaines and Michael Renov (Minneapolis: University of Minnesota Press, 1999), 19–45.

8. Cowie, "Spectacle of Actuality," 23.

9. Freud makes the link between the camera (among other modern mechanical apparati) and prosthesis in *Civilization and its Discontents* (New York: Norton, 1961 and 1989), 43–44.

10. Must a documentary be "sober"? Hopefully not. Would that make its opposite "drunk" (as Vertov claimed, calling all fiction films, "film vodka")? Aren't biopics and historical dramas also "based on actual events"? Isn't the essayistic form only one possible approach to documentary (think of lyrical or experimental documentaries, for instance)?

11. See *Faking It*, ed. Jane Roscoe and Craig Hight (Manchester, U.K.: Manchester University Press, 2001).

12. There are other possible interpretations of the conceptual project of these nonparodic, mimetic mockumentaries. Homage is clearly one, recontextualization is another, but there is also the appropriative urge, whereby the artist must put her stamp on the earlier work, make it her own. Clearly, whether in painting, photography, film, or any other reproductive art, the project of conscious mimesis is also a commentary on the nonoriginary nature of the medium.

13. Cowie, "Spectacle of Actuality," 30.

14. An alternate and more charitable reading, which actually aligns better with Mograbi's own critique of Israeli society and its well-protected sense of innocence, allows that Mograbi's character is meant to parody and thus expose the untenability of such naiveté in the face of the gravity of the political situation. However, this does not discount the fact that Mograbi plays his character so sympathetically that the critique of mainstream Israeli society is all but obscured.

15. Marcos Becquer and Alisa Lebow, "'Docudrag,' or 'Realness' as a Documentary

Strategy," in *The Ethnic Eye: Latino Media Arts*, ed. Chon Noriega and Ana Lopez (Minneapolis: University of Minnesota Press, 1996), 143–70. The video in question was Felix Rodriguez's *One Moment in Time* (1992). The term "realness" can be used to denote any kind of effective passing, usually with regard to gender, but also class, age, race, sexuality, professional status, etc.

16. Homi Bhabha, "Of Mimicry and Man," in *The Location of Culture* (New York: Routledge, 1994), 86.

17. This is Fatimah Tobing Rony's phrase. *The Third Eye: Race, Cinema, and the Ethnographic Spectacle* (Durham, N.C.: Duke University Press, 1996), 102.

18. The scare quotes around "original" here are meant to signify a difference, for this is no ordinary original, of the kind that Bhabha and others would have us question. This "original"—the Real—is merely a structural placeholder with no substance of its own. It is paradoxically a limit (Žižek's "hard kernel") and an empty signifier, available to be filled by any kind of content, which is always already an inadequate substitute. It is an ontological impossibility: simultaneously inimitable and infinitely (though always inadequately) imitable.

19. Slavoj Žižek, *Looking Awry* (Cambridge, Mass.: MIT Press, 1993), 14.

20. Ibid., 11; emphasis mine.

21. Walter Benjamin, "The Work of Art in the Age of Mechanical Reproduction," in *Illuminations* (New York: Schocken Books, 1969), 226.

22. Brian Winston, "Documentary: I Think We Are in Trouble," in *New Challenges for the Documentary*, ed. Alan Rosenthal (Berkeley and Los Angeles: University of California Press, 1988), 29.

23. This is hardly a new or novel position. In her article "Inscribing Ethical Space: Ten Propositions on Death, Representation, and Documentary," Vivian Sobchack argues this point at length. She declares that "the representation of the event of death is an indexical sign of that which is always in excess of representation, and beyond the limits of coding and culture. Death confounds all codes." *Quarterly Review of Film Studies* (Fall 1984): 287.

24. See Lerner's discussion of these early claims "for the technology's ability to provide an unmediated, objective, and truthful transcription of the real," in the introduction to this volume.

25. Alex Juhasz, "They Said We Wanted to Show Reality, All I Want to Show Is My Video: The Politics of Feminist, Realist, Documentaries," *Screen* 35, no. 2 (Summer 1994): 171–90.

26. See *The Independent,* October 2002: 51, 54–55.

27. Winston, *Claiming the Real* (BFI, 1995).

28. Roscoe and Hight, *Faking It,* 181; emphasis mine.

29. Of course I am aware that Butler and Žižek are engaged in an ongoing debate over the interpretation of the Lacanian Real and its beneficial relationship to the project of the political, but here I think it is not too far of a stretch to imagine them at least in this regard to be provisionally compatible. See *Bodies That Matter* (New York: Routledge, 1993), 187–208, for Butler's challenge to Žižek's interpretation of the Lacanian Real as delineated in his book *The Sublime Object of Ideology* (London: Verso, 1989).

ALEXANDRA JUHASZ
JESSE LERNER

[**15**] *As a Finale: Reflections on a Phantasm*

In the year 2001, we held a series of screenings in Claremont, California, about the fake documentary, F Is for Phony, that culminated in a symposium (and later, this collection). Imagine our surprise when, near the day's end, an unidentified Claremont College undergraduate arose from the audience and demanded that we "screen his film here and now," one he insisted would be of the greatest relevance to the day's lofty proceedings. Imagine our greater surprise when we found that his film did throw into crisis all that had been discussed that day, as well as most of the issues central to the discussion of fake documentary addressed in this anthology!

Watson Testifies is a documentary (though not, by Juhasz's definition, a fake documentary) about Sir Arthur Conan Doyle's interest in photography as a means of documenting the supernatural. The images used in the film are almost entirely archival stills, spiritualist photographs from Doyle's own collection.[1] Here we see, documented in the flesh, the ghosts and other-worldly beings that Doyle was set to prove inhabited this realm as well as the one that comes next. The sound track is drawn principally from three sources. First are Conan Doyle's writings on spiritualist photography, extracted from his book *The History of Spiritualism*.[2] These are read aloud, in voice-over, by our student, and the words introduce a side of Doyle far more credulous and less rigorously empirical than his famous creation Sherlock Holmes. The second element of the narration moves the film into the category of metadocumentary: not an actor's interpretation of Conan Doyle's words, but rather audio recordings, only recently discovered in St. John's Wood (and purchased on e-Bay by our student, who is, like many of our undergraduates, a young man of independent means), of Conan Doyle's own voice, made just prior to his death in 1930. In these rare recordings, Doyle revisits the question of spiritualist photography, this time carefully reconsidering the authenticity of the image and the camera's

Sir Arthur Conan Doyle with the ghost of his son in *Watson Testifies* (Anon., 2001)

value for the documentation of reality in all its many layers. Finally, a budding spiritualist in his own right, our young filmmaker brings the infamous Dr. Watson back to life by channeling him during a séance staged with his classmates (as indeed Conan Doyle was forced by popular demand to resuscitate Holmes). It is firmly established in the documentation of this wondrous event that Watson has learned enough about the rigorous search for truth, based on evidence from his former roommate, to regard Conan Doyle's credulousness with a healthy skepticism, and thus Watson subjects his creator to a scathing, nearly patricidal, dressing-down.

Throughout, *Watson Testifies* uses spiritualist photography as a sustained metaphor for the documentary image, the phantom evoked being documentary authenticity rather than the ghost of some deceased loved one. It is a film in which many of the issues that recur throughout this volume—the (mis)representations of history, the use of archival materials, falsification and hoax, the authority and originality of the documentarian—consort and conspire to unsettle any stable delineations of the fake documentary. Without giving away the many surprises in *Watson Testifies,* it should suffice to say that the film, with its heady mix of archival (real and otherwise), staged, and authentic materials, is one that most effectively subverts any of the definitions and taxonomical schema set forth thus far. Blending the corrosive subversion of Buñuel's *Tierra sin pan,* the spirit of intellectual play of Welles's *F for Fake,* and the doppelgänger effect of Elisabeth Subrin's *Shulie* and Jill Godmillow's *What Farocki Taught* with a firm belief in all-that-is-and-just-might-be-seen, this faux film fakes it in a way so compelling that we end haunted by its visions.

Regretfully, although many scholars of the documentary and the fake documentary might demand to view this film, and learn themselves from its revealing secrets, our student seems to have played a hoax of his own. All attempts to communicate with him and re-view his masterful film have failed. It turns out that he was not, and had never been, registered at the Colleges, and that he and his film seem to have vanished into thin air after its one, apocryphal premiere.

◆ ———————————————————————————

NOTES

1. These have been exhibited previously, most recently as part of the exhibition at the Metropolitan Museum in New York entitled "The Perfect Medium: Photography and the Occult."

2. Arthur Conan Doyle, *The History of Spiritualism* (New York: Doran, 1927), 345–46.

NIZAN SHAKED

Filmography

Agarrando Pueblo, Luis Ospina and Carlos Mayolo, 1978

Among Others, Trac Vu, 1997 (distributed as part of *Park City* shorts collection: Vanguard Cinema, 800/218-7888, info@vanguardcinema.com)

The Attendant, Isaac Julien, 1993 (Frameline, www.frameline.org)

The Battle of Chile, Patricio Guzmán, 1976 (First Run Icarus Films, www.frif .com)

Best in Show, Christopher Guest, 2000 (commercially available)

Blair Witch Project, Daniel Myrick and Eduardo Sanchez, 1999 (commercially available)

Bontoc Eulogy, Marlon Fuentes, 1995 (Cinema Guild, 212/685-6242, orders@ cinemaguild.com)

Cannibal Ferox (a.k.a. *Make Them Die Slowly*), Umberto Lenzi, 1981 (commercially available)

Cannibal Holocaust, Rugero Deodato, 1979 (commercially available)

Cascabel, Raúl Araiza, 1976 (commercially available)

Cherrybomb!!!, Ernesto Forondo, 2000 (HEARTCORE, 323/821-1973, heartcore73@earthlink.net)

Close Up, Abbas Kiarostami, 1990 (Facets Video, www.facets.org/asticat)

The Connection, Shirley Clarke, 1961 (films around the world, inc., 212/599-9500, www.filmsaroundtheworld.com)

The Countryman and the Cinematograph, Robert W. Paul, 1901 (as part of *The Movies Begin*: Kino Video, www .kino.com)

The Couple in the Cage, Coco Fusco and Paula Heredia, 1993 (Third World Newsreel, www.twn.org)

Cover Girl: A Gift from God, Nguyen Tan Hoang, 2000 (Video Out Distribution, 604/872-8449, videoout@telus .net)

Daughter Rite, Michelle Citron, 1979 (Women Make Movies, www.wmm .com)

David Holzman's Diary, Jim McBride, 1968 (Direct Cinema Limited, www .directcinema.com)

Davy Jones in the South Seas, Vitagraph, 1911 (Library of Congress)

Dirty Laundry, Richard Fung, 1996 (National Asian American Telecommunications Association, distribution@naatanet.org)

Far from Poland, Jill Godmillow, 1984 (Facets Video, www.facets.org/asticat)

F for Fake, Orson Welles, 1974 (Home Vision Entertainment, 800/826-3456, www.homevision.com)

First Morning, Victor Vu, 2002 (Strange Logic Entertainment, strangelogic@hotmail.com)

First Year, Trac Vu, 1997 (Frameline, www.frameline.org)

Forgotten Silver, Peter Jackson and Costa Botes, 1995 (First Run Features, www.FirstRunFeatures.com)

The Games People Play, Ernesto Foronda, 2002 (HEARTCORE, 323/821-1973, heartcore73@earthlink.net)

Grand Hotel to Big Indian, AMB, 1906 (Library of Congress)

Halving the Bones, Ruth Ozeki Lounsbury, 1995 (Women Make Movies, www.wmm.com)

Happy Birthday, Mr. Mograbi, Avi Mugrabi, 1999 (First Run Icarus Films, www.frif.com)

The Hellstom Chronicles, Lawrence Pressman and Walon Green, 1971 (commercially available)

History and Memory, Rea Tajiri, 1991 (Women Make Movies, www.wmm.com)

Holdup of the Rocky Mountain Express, AMB, 1906 (Museum of Modern Art, New York)

Honeymoon at Niagara Falls, Edison, 1906 (Museum of Modern Art, New York)

Hostage: The Bachar Tapes, Walid Raad, 2001 (Video Data Bank, www.vdb.org)

Inextinguishable Fire (Nicht Löschbares Feuer), Harun Farocki, 1969 (available on 16 mm film from Harun Farocki [www.farocki-film.de] or on video from the film circulating library of Museum of Modern Art, New York)

In Search of Ancient Astronauts, Erick van Daniken, 1975 (commercially available)

In the Haunts of Rip van Winkle, AMB, 1906 (Library of Congress)

In the Valley of the Esopus, AMB, 1906 (Library of Congress)

Ivan Istochnikov, Luis Escartín, 1997 (available online as streaming video at www.smartvideoserver.org)

Land without Bread [also known as *Tierra sin pan, Las Hurdes,* or *Unpromised Land*], Luis Buñuel, 1932 (Kino Video, www.kino.com)

L'Arroseur arrosé, Lumière, 1895 (as part of *The Movies Begin*: Kino Video, www.kino.com)

Les Carabiniers, Jean-Luc Godard, 1963 (commercially available)

The Lost Reels of Pancho Villa, Gregorio C. Rocha, 2003 (Subcine, www.subcine.com)

Man Bites Dog: It Happened in Your Neighborhood, Remy Belvaux and Benoit Poelvoorde, 1992 (Criterion, www.criterionco.com)

Memories from the Department of Amnesia, Janice Tanaka, 1989 (National Asian American Telecommunications Association, www.naatanet.org)

Memory/all echo, Yunah Hong, 1990 (Women Make Movies, www.wmm.com)

A Message from the Stone Age, John Nance, 1983 (available from the artist)

A Mighty Wind, Christopher Guest, 2003 (commercially available)

Moi, un Noir, Jean Rouch, 1957 (Cine Video Film)

No Lies, Mitchell W. Block, 1972 (Direct Cinema, www.directcinema.com)

Peep Show, J. X. Williams, 1965 (The Other Cinema, www.othercinemadvd.com)

Petomane: Fin-de-Siècle Fartiste, Igor Vamos, 2001 (Cinema Guild, www.cinemaguild.com)

Pirated! Nguyen Tan Hoang, 2000 (Video Out Distribution, 604/872-8449, videoout@telus.net)

Policeman's Tour of the World, Pathé, 1906 (Museum of Modern Art, New York)

The Positively True Adventures of the Alleged Texas Cheerleader-Murdering Mom, Michael Ritchie, 1993 (commercially available)

Roger and Me, Michael Moore, 1989 (commercially available)

Ruins, Jesse Lerner, 1999 (Subcine, www.subcine.com; Third World Newsreel, www.twn.org; Video Data Bank, www.vdb.org [as part of the *Frames of Reference* series])

Shopping for Fangs, Quentin Lee and Justin Lin, 1997 (Vanguard Cinema, www.vanguardcinema.com)

Shulie, Elizabeth Subrin, 1997 (Video Data Bank, www.vdb.org; for 16 mm prints, subrin@mindspring.com). [The filmmaker requests that *Shulie* be screened with supplemental educational materials, including director's statement and FAQ provided by the distributors.]

Silverlake Life, Mark Massi and Peter Friedman, 1993 (Docurama, www.docurama.com)

The Skyscrapers of New York, AMB, 1906 (Library of Congress)

Speeding, Mitchell Block, 1975 (Direct Cinema, www.directcinema.com)

Sporting Blood, Lubin, 1909 (Library of Congress)

The Story the Biograph Told, AMB, 1903 (Library of Congress)

Straight Boy Blues, Ernesto Foronda, 1997 (HEARTCORE, 323/821-1973, heartcore73@earthlink.net)

This Is Spinal Tap, Rob Reiner, 1984 (commercially available)

Tren de sombras (Train of Shadows), José Luis Guerín, 1997 (ArtKino Pictures)

A Trip to Berkeley, California, AMB, 1906 (Library of Congress)

The Tunnel Workers, AMB, 1906 (Library of Congress)

Un Chien Delicieux, Feingold, 1991 (Facets Video, www.facets.org [as part of the collection *The Works of Ken Feingold*])

Uncle Josh at the Moving Picture Show, Edison, 1902 (Library of Congress)

Waiting for Guffman, Christopher Guest, 1996 (commercially available)

The Watermelon Woman, Cheryl Dunye, 1995 (First Run Features, www.FirstRunFeatures.com)

What Farocki Taught, Jill Godmilow, 1998 (Video Data Bank, www.vdb.org)

Who's Going to Pay for These Donuts, Anyway? Janice Tanaka, 1992 (Women Make Movies, www.wmm.com)

Contributors

STEVE ANDERSON received a PhD in film, literature, and culture from the University of Southern California and an MFA in film and video from California Institute of the Arts. He writes about historiography, digital media, and avant-garde film.

CATHERINE L. BENAMOU teaches American culture, Latina/o studies, and film and video studies at the University of Michigan, Ann Arbor. She was associate producer and senior researcher on the documentary reconstruction *It's All True: Based on an Unfinished Film by Orson Welles* (Les Films Balenciaga), distributed by Paramount Pictures, and is currently at work on the preservation of remaining *It's All True* footage at the UCLA Film and Television Archive in Los Angeles. She is the author of *It's All True: Orson Welles in Pan-America, 1941–2003*.

MITCHELL W. BLOCK is executive director of Direct Cinema Limited (www.directcinemalimited.com), a nonprofit film and video distributor. He was executive producer of the Academy Award–winning documentary *Big Mama*. He teaches independent producing for the Peter Stark Producing Program in the School of Cinema–Television at the University of Southern California. He is currently executive producer for a ten-hour television documentary series and a two-hour feature documenting *Carrier* with Mel Gibson's Icon Productions.

LUIS BUÑUEL (1900–1983) directed more than thirty films in Europe and Mexico, only one of which, variously titled *Tierra sin pan, Las Hurdes, Unpromised Land,* or *Land without Bread,* might be called a documentary.

MARLON FUENTES is a Philippine-born filmmaker and photographer. His work as a visual artist is represented in many collections, including the National Museum of American Art at the Smithsonian Institution, the National Museum of American History, the Library of Congress, the Corcoran, the Houston Museum of Fine Arts, and the Santa Barbara Museum of Art. His films have been shown at the Museum of Modern Art in New York, the Guggenheim, and numerous international museum and festival venues.

CRAIG HIGHT is a senior lecturer with the Screen and Media Studies Department at the University of Waikato. He is coauthor (with Jane Roscoe) of *Faking It: Mock-Documentary and the Subversion of Factuality*. His recent research focuses on digital technologies, including their relationship to documentary practice, and aspects of the production, construction, and reception of documentary hybrids.

ALEXANDRA JUHASZ is professor of media studies at Pitzer College. She writes about and makes activist and alternative media; her works include the feature documentaries *Video Remains, Dear Gabe*, and *Women of Vision: Eighteen Histories in Feminist Film and Video*, as well as the feature film *The Watermelon Woman*, which she produced. She is the author of *Women of Vision: Histories in Feminist Film and Video* (Minnesota, 2000) and *AIDS TV: Identity, Community, and Alternative Video*.

CHARLIE KEIL is associate professor of history and director of the cinema studies program at the University of Toronto. He is the author of *Early American Cinema in Transition: Story, Style, and Filmmaking, 1907–1913* and coeditor (with Shelley Stamp) of *American Cinema's Transitional Era: Audiences, Institutions, Practices*. His writings on documentary include an essay in the anthology *Documenting the Documentary: Close Readings of Documentary Film and Video*.

ALISA LEBOW is senior lecturer in film studies and video production in the School of Cultural Studies at the University of the West of England, in Bristol. Her research is primarily in the areas of documentary, mockumentary, experimental, and first-person film. Her book on Jewish autobiographical film is forthcoming from the University of Minnesota Press. She is also a filmmaker, whose work includes *Setting the State for Justice: The World Tribunal on Iraq* (forthcoming), *Treyf*, and *Outlaw*.

JESSE LERNER is a documentary filmmaker. He has written on photography, architecture, and documentary for *Afterimage, Cabinet, Film History, History of Photography, Visual Anthropology Review, Wide Angle,* and *Architectural Design.* As a curator, he has organized film and video series for the Robert Flaherty Seminar and the Guggenheim Museums in New York and Bilbao. His films include *Natives, Frontierland/ Fronterilandia, Ruins, The American Egypt,* and *T.S.H.*

EVE OISHI is associate professor of cultural studies at Claremont Graduate University. She is the author of *The Memory Village: Fakeness and the Forging of Family in Asian American Literature and Film.* She is an independent curator and has curated film and video programs for numerous film festivals in New York, Los Angeles, San Francisco, and Philadelphia.

ROBERT F. REID-PHARR is professor of English at the Graduate School of the City University of New York. He is the author of *Conjugal Union: The Body, the House, and the Black American* and *Black Gay Man: Essays.*

GREGORIO C. ROCHA was born in Mexico City. Following studies at the Centro Universitario de Estudios Cinematográficos, he produced and directed more than twenty documentaries, some of which have aired nationally in Mexico. His most recent film, *The Lost Reels of Pancho Villa,* was broadcast on WNET in New York. Most of his work blends his personal quests with social history. His films have been honored by the Rockefeller and MacArthur Foundations, the Fondo Nacional para Cultura y las Artes, the Latin American Studies Association, and the Fulbright Program, and have been shown at festivals throughout the United States and Europe. He has been a visiting professor at New York University and Pitzer College, and is currently teaching documentary at the Centro de Capacitación Cinematográfica in Mexico City.

JANE ROSCOE is programming executive at SBS Television in Australia. She has taught screen studies in the United Kingdom, New Zealand, and Australia, and has published extensively on documentary, mockdocumentary, audiences, and new television hybrids. She is the author of *Documentary in New Zealand: An Immigrant Nation* and coauthor (with Craig Hight) of *Faking It: Mock-Documentary and the Subversion of Factuality.*

CATHERINE RUSSELL is professor of film studies at Concordia University in Montreal. She is the author of *Narrative Mortality: Death, Closure, and New Wave Cinemas* (Minnesota, 1995) and *Experimental Ethnography: The Work of Film in the Age of Video*. She is the editor of *Camera Obscura 60: New Women of the Silent Screen: China, Japan, Hollywood*. She has also published numerous articles on Japanese cinema and on Canadian film and video.

NIZAN SHAKED is an independent curator and visiting assistant professor of art history at the University of La Verne. Her exhibitions include *Fetish: Art/Word*, at the UCLA Fowler Museum of Cultural History; *The Politics of Memory*, at the Occidental College Art Galleries; and *Symmetry*, at the MAK Center for Art and Architecture at the Schindler House.

ELISABETH SUBRIN has exhibited and screened her award-winning trilogy of experimental biographies widely in the United States and abroad. Presented at the 2000 Whitney Biennial, *Shulie* premiered at the New York Film Festival and received the Los Angeles Film Critics Award for Best Independent/Experimental Film. Subrin participated in the Sundance Institute Writers and Directors Labs with her screenplay *Up*, currently in development with Forensic Films with support from the Rockefeller, Guggenheim, and Creative Capital foundations. She teaches filmmaking and video art, most recently in the visual and environmental studies department at Harvard University. She is currently completing *The Caretakers*, a new film commissioned for the MacDowell Colony's centennial.

Index

actuality, the, 39, 42
actuality shots, 44
aesthetic strategies, 201
African American, 197. *See also* black; identity
Agarrando pueblo, 29
allegory, 165, 230; significance of, 110; undoing of, 166
Allen, Woody, 4, 229
American Egypt (Lerner), 74
American Family, An (Raymond), 188, 191–93
American High (Cutler), 187–88, 192–93
American Historical Review, 77
Among Others (Vu, Trac), 219
analogy, 166–67
Anderegg, Michael, 149
anthropology: avante garde and, 101; and ethnographic film, 116; humanist, 114; method of, 108; politics of representation in, 103; visual, 25, 119
anti-genre, 168
anti-illusionism, 117
anti-intellectualism, 181
anti-Mexican, 55–56
anti-Semitism, 110
archival materials, 117, 119, 120, 123, 240
Arredondo, Carlos Martínez de, 74
Arthur, Paul, 79
artificially aging, 69–70
Asian American, 197–99, 215. *See also* identity
assemblage, 53, 56
Atget, Eugene, 233
Atkins, Christopher, 210
Attendant, the, (Julien) 219
audience, 192, 195. *See also* spectator
authenticity, 8, 11, 71, 74, 79, 84, 111, 117, 127–28, 143, 146, 162, 174, 196, 238, 240; in *Shulie (#2)*, 64
authenticating material, 175
authority, 74, 104, 166, 174, 203; and authenticity, 84
authorship, 57, 73, 147–48, 165
autoethnographic film, 119, 122

avant garde: and cinema, 102, 107, and anthropology, 101
awareness *(coscienza)*, 157

Badka, Fred "Beta," 190
Barthes, Roland, 108
Bataille, George S. 99, 108–9; and "The Big Toe," 108. *See also Documents*
Battle of Algiers (Pontecorvo), 190
Battle of Chile, The (Guzman), 234
Bazin, André, 148, 157
Becquer, Marcos, 231
Beloved (Morrison), 200. *See also* Morrison, Toni
Benjamin, Walter, 84, 99–100, 111–13, 145–46, 233
Best in Show (Guest), 3. *See also* Guest, Christopher
Bhabha, Homi, 231–32, 235
Biard, F. A., 219
binary, the: fake vs. real, 224
Birth of a Nation (Griffith), 56, 133
"black, the," 133. *See also* African American; Black American; blackness; identity
Black American: cinema and film criticism, 28, 46, 133
blackness, 135
Black Skin, White Masks (Fanon), 135
Blair Witch Project (Myrick and Sanchez), 10, 12
blaxploitation, 136–37
blended films, 42, 158
Block, Mitchell, 229. *See also No Lies*
blurring, 49, 66, 70, 100, 146
Bob Roberts (Robbins), 4
Bogdonovich, Peter, 163
Bonnie and Clyde, (Penn), 169
Bontoc Eulogy (Fuentes), 25–26, 87, 116–29, 219
Border Cinema, 13, 57
Botes, Costa, 172–76, 179, 181–82. *See also Forgotten Silver*
Brechtian elements, 117–19, 124
Bronson, Lisa Marie, 130. *See also The Watermelon Woman*
Brooks, Albert, 11. *See also Real Life*

Brooks, Peter, 44
Bukatman, Scott, 159–60, 168–69. See also F is
    for Fake
Buñuel, Luis, 13, 26, 99–114, 240. See also Land
    Without Bread
Butchies, the, 214
Butler, Judith, 231, 235, 237

Cahiers du Cinema, 148
Campers, Fred, 49
Carson, L. M. Kit, 189. See also David
    Holtzman's Diary
Cascabel (Araiza), 29
Cassavetes, John, 190
charlatan, 144, 156, 167
Cherrybomb!!! (Forondo), 198, 213–17
Chimes at Midnight (Welles), 154, 156, 160. See
    also Welles, Orson
Chronicle of Anna Magdelana Bach (Straub and
    Huillet), 87
Churchill, Joan, 188. See also American Family, An
cinema history. See early film
Citizen Kane (Welles), 144, 147, 150, 153–54, 156–57,
    159–60, 162, 165. See also Welles, Orson
Citron, Michelle, 9, 229. See also Daughter Rite
Claiming the Real (Winston), 235. See also Brian
    Winston
Clarke, Cheryl, 131
close-up, 29
collage, 152
collective story, 193
compilation film, 53
Connection, the (Clarke), 29
contemporary, the, 207
context, 172
Coppola, Francis Ford, 169
"Cops," 167, 194
Corner, John, 171, 185
Corrigan, Timothy, 166
Couple in the Cage, The (Fusco and Heredia),
    20, 25
Cotten, Joseph, 144, 154. See also Welles, Orson
Cover Girl: Gift from God (Nguyen), 219
Cowie, Elizabeth, 227, 229
Creekmur, Cory, 154
cultural appropriation, 85
cultural distortions, 128
culture of amnesia, 78
culture of the copy, 73
Cutler, R. J., 187–88, 192–94

Dandridge, Dorothy, 131
Daughter Rite (Citron), 9, 12, 49, 229
David Holzman's Diary (McBride), 12, 118, 189,
    191. See also McBride, Jim
Davis, Brad, 210
Davy Jones in the South Seas, (Vitagraph), 46
death, 234
deceit. See deception
deception, 77, 84, 85, 139, 165; Orson Welles as
    "master of audiovisual," 148
De Hory, Elmer, 144, 156, 165–66. See also F is
    for Fake

Delany, Samuel, 208–9, 211, 217. See also Motion
    of Light in Water
Deutelbaum, Marshall, 41
diegesis, 154–55, 164; diegetic realism, 157–58,
    165; extradiegetic, 156; heterodiegesis, 155
digital imaging technologies, 79
Dirty Laundry (Fung), 219
dishonesty. See deception
docudrama, 228, 229
documentary: authenticity, 240; codes and con-
    ventions, 174, contract of authentic reality,
    110; as culturally sanctioned performance,
    227; as disruptive force, 45; and fiction, 147,
    197; hybrids, 171, 183; meta-, 69, 238; mode
    of engagement, 176; mode of viewing, 174;
    as nostalgia, 15; post-, 171; as prosthetic
    device, 227; proto-, 101; realism, 110; semi-,
    19; similarities with forgery, 83; staged, 189;
    techniques, 180; veracity, 99. See also docu-
    mentary, types
documentary, types: autobiographical, 29, 198,
    202–3; biographical, 50, 60; cinema verite,
    29, 60, 84, 230; direct/fly-on-the-wall, 29, 59,
    149, 165, 167; essay, 147; observational, 29;
    performative, 193, 234; voice of god, 102, 202;
    voice over, 19, 60, 82, 101–2,
Documents, 99–100, 108–11. See also Bataille,
    George S.
docu-series, 193
Doublier, Francis, 19
doubt, 104
Doyle, Arthur Conan, 238–40
Dunye, Cheryl, 130–40. See also Watermelon
    Woman, The
dyke culture, 214. See also lesbian; queer

early cinema/film, 22, 39, 43, 46–47, 55, 117, 155
Edison, Thomas Alva, 232; and Honeymoon at
    Niagara Falls, 44
editing, 118, 193, 213; non-edited, work 193
Eitzen, Dirk, 8
Electronic mass media, 198, 200–201
Ellison, Ralph, 140
Endara, Lala, 215
Enlightenment, the, 181
episodic film, 54–55
epistephelia, 227
Escartin, Luis, 23
ethnographic fragment, 120–21, 122
ethnographic representation, 117
ethnography, 25, 233; anthropology and, 116,
    colonialist, 102, experimental, 103; "Objects
    of Ethnography" (Kirshenblatt-Gimblett), 120;
    and surrealism, 26, 99, 108. See also anthro-
    pology; ethnology
ethnology, 112
evidence, 62, 65–66, 77, 139, 158, 166, 174, 177;
    misleading data as, 72; visual, 103–5, 198,
    206–7, 210–11, 217
exhibition, 42; value, 113
experimental cinema, 64, 101. See also
    surrealism
expert(s), 143–44, 146, 159, testimony, 174–75